THE ETHICS OF PEACEBUILDING

EDINBURGH STUDIES IN WORLD ETHICS

Other titles in the series:

The Ethics of Peace and War
Iain Atack

The Ethics of the Global Environment
Robin Attfield

Ethics, Economics and International Relations
Second Edition
Peter G. Brown

World Ethics: The New Agenda
Second Edition
Nigel Dower

The Ethics of Development
Des Gasper

THE ETHICS OF PEACEBUILDING

Tim Murithi

EDINBURGH UNIVERSITY PRESS

For Bonnie

Tim Murithi, 2009

Edinburgh University Press Ltd
22 George Square, Edinburgh

www.euppublishing.com

Reprinted 2011

Typeset in Times by
Iolaire Typesetting, Newtonmore, and
printed and bound in Great Britain by
CPI Group (UK) Ltd, Croydon, CR0 4YY

A CIP record for this book is available
from the British Library

ISBN 978 0 7486 2447 8 (hardback)
ISBN 978 0 7486 2448 5 (paperback)

CONTENTS

ACKNOWLEDGEMENTS

I would like to acknowledge and thank colleagues, students and policy-makers who have debated the virtues of peacebuilding with me over the years. There have been many who have challenged my optimism in human nature to achieve a more peaceful future. They have also in their own way contributed to this book. Specifically, I would like to thank Nigel Dower, the editor of this series, for seeing the value of this book as a contribution to the debates on ethics and international relations and supporting its development at every stage. I would also like to thank Nicola Ramsey for her patience and enthusiasm during the completion of this book.

I would like to thank John MacMillan and Andrew Linklater, who inspired some of the research that led to the production of this book. I would also like to thank my parents and siblings Jeremiah, Esther, Sara and Victor, as well as my in-laws Joel, Anna, Herschel and Natacha for their continuing love and support.

Above all I would like to thank my loving wife Bonnie Berkowitz, who sacrificed many weekend outings so that I could complete the book and who also read some of the chapters. She is my dearest friend, companion and a true embodiment of the ethical person.

PREFACE

The first decade of the twenty-first century has proven to be as violent as previous periods of human history. Conflict and political violence have afflicted all continents and fragmented or undermined the integrity of several nation-states, including Somalia, Afghanistan, the Democratic Republic of the Congo, the Sudan, Colombia and the former Yugoslavia, to name but a few. Tremendous harm has been done to ordinary people and innocent communities. Somehow these innocent people will have to find a way to move beyond the atrocities that they have endured and rebuild their lives. This book will argue that in the years and decades to come there will be a need for effective, sustainable and ethical peacebuilding in order to heal and restore the conditions for coexistence in these fractured communities.

The process required to heal the hearts, minds and psyches of those harmed is challenging. This book proposes that the process of peacebuilding requires an open engagement with the values and virtues of victims, perpetrators and peacemakers. In other words, understanding the ethics of peacebuilding is necessary for the establishment and implementation of an effective process for building durable peace.

One might ask why peacebuilding is necessary. Is peacebuilding even possible? This book will critically review the definition of peacebuilding and describe it as a process that seeks to moves beyond the notion of negative peace – which is understood as the absence of violence. It will advance an understanding of peacebuilding as the quest for positive peace which is the presence of healing and reconciliation based on social and economic justice and equality. It will analyse the ethics of peacebuilding inherent in the actions and dispositions of peacemakers and peacemaking institutions like the League of Nations, the United Nations, the African Union, non-governmental organisations, ecumenical groups and civil society associations. These organisations have established mechanisms for promoting ethical political negotiation and for mediating in ongoing disputes around the world. This book will further examine the ethics of negotiation and mediation. These processes are increasingly being relied upon to assist parties to move beyond disputes and enter a moral space where they can begin to coexist, rebuilding and healing their lives. Specific case studies will focus on the efforts of the League of Nations, the United Nations and the Quakers.

The process of coming to terms with the harm that has been done is equally difficult and painful for victims and perpetrators alike. For forgiveness and reconciliation to succeed these actors need to draw upon their own value-systems. The perpetrator has to acknowledge the harm that he or she has done, make reparations where possible and ask for forgiveness from the victim. The victim should, but is not compelled to, grant mercy and accept the compensation or reparations made, and only then can the process of genuine forgiveness begin and lead to healing and reconciliation.

These processes are difficult for both the victim and the perpetrator because the first impulse for most victims is to seek revenge through some form of punishment for the perpetrator. In some cases this may be necessary and perhaps the only option. The first impulse of the perpetrator is to deny having done any harm, to deflect blame from him- or herself and re-assign it to an external authority or institution. Simply put, it is difficult to counter the impulse to seek revenge. The idea of vengeance might be prevalent because most people actually believe it is a right, even a duty, to seek revenge even at the cost of peace. Therefore we cannot assume that there is an intrinsic value to achieving peace at all costs. However, this book will argue that when attempting to restore the conditions for coexistence following a brutal ethnic conflict, the act of punishing perpetrators only promotes a vicious cycle of mistrust, suspicion and resentment. At a later point in time these sentiments generally resurface and manifest at a later point in time as social, economic or political exclusion. The moral exclusion experienced by this process can lead to resentment and can function as a catalyst to reignite violence. In this context, the book will argue that engaging in restorative justice rather than retributive justice is a necessary although insufficient factor for genuinely healing a nation and bringing about moral inclusion. This can only be done if both perpetrators and victims are prepared to engage in a process of ethical peacebuilding by drawing upon moral principles which this book will discuss. In particular, this book will explore the moral argument for engaging in forgiveness and reconciliation and will discuss the case studies of the Truth and Reconciliation Commissions in South Africa and Sierra Leone. Ultimately, the book will assess the issue of whether institutions such as the UN Peacebuilding Commission can indeed promote an ethical peace.

This is a timely book because understanding the ethics of peacebuilding will provide peacemakers, victims, perpetrators and peacebuilding institutions with an analysis of the moral disposition and ethical tools necessary to achieve sustainable peace in a world that has been afflicted by the scourge of violent conflict.

CHAPTER 1

INTRODUCTION

This book will assess the ethical dimension of peacebuilding. The twentieth century witnessed some of the worst war atrocities committed in the history of humanity. This included the genocide in Armenia, the Holocaust and the wanton carnage of the Second World War. The Cold War retained this pattern of destruction with proxy wars being fought along the East/West or Soviet/US ideological divide. In the aftermath of the Cold War the hope for a more stable and just international order was rapidly dissolved by the internecine conflicts that plagued all continents. These conflicts took on a pernicious form in the sense that they undermined the very fabric of the nation-state. The implosion of Somalia and Yugoslavia remain the most salient examples of this phenomenon. In February 2008, Kosovo, a former province of Yugoslavia, declared its independence, to the resentment of Serbia, which considered Kosovo a key component of its national body politic. The Kosovar independence declaration did not happen overnight, rather it was the culmination of a lengthy and drawn-out confrontation between the sub-national groups in Kosovo and the Serbian nation-state. Therefore, what we can discern is that a key feature of the majority of conflicts that we witness today is their sub-national nature. The term sub-national describes the subsidiary political, social and cultural polities that exist and function within the nation-state. Sub-national conflicts have proved to be highly resistant to the intervention of inter-governmental organisations like the United Nations (UN) and regional organisations. In effect the international system has endeavoured to resolve such conflicts with limited success. The world continues to be plagued by sub-national conflicts in places such as the Darfur region of the Sudan, the Kashmir region of India and Pakistan, Lebanon, Nepal, Sri Lanka, Tajikistan, Uganda and Western Sahara. Efforts to build peace have come under increasing scrutiny. It has also become important to question whether the appropriate moral norms are in place in order to

1

facilitate effective peacebuilding. In particular, it is useful to explore the qualitative challenges posed by sub-national conflicts in order to understand how ethical processes, procedures, institutions and mechanisms can be established to enhance peacebuilding. This book proposes to assess the ethical dimensions of negotiation, mediation, forgiveness and reconciliation in order to provide insights into some of the components of peacebuilding.

There has been a substantial body of literature that has been developed to explore the morality of war. There has also been a significant amount of literature on the ethics of peace, including two books in this series, namely Nigel Dower's *World Ethics: The New Agenda* and Iain Atack's *The Ethics of Peace and War*.[1] However, additional research is required on the ethics of peacebuilding and conflict resolution. As Bruce Barry and Robert Robinson note, there is 'a relative dearth of scholarly attention to the wider field of ethics in conflict resolution'.[2] Furthermore, they argue that it is important to 'identify the ethical dimensions of relationships among disputing parties and interveners as a common thematic element that may represent a fruitful avenue for thinking about the distinctive role of ethics in the resolution of conflict'.[3] This book seeks to contribute towards a response to these suggestions by questioning the role that ethics plays in promoting and consolidating peacebuilding.

It is worthwhile to note that there is a wide field of ethics and international relations. Specifically, these traditions can be found in cosmopolitanism and in global ethics. In particular, Dower has undertaken an extensive study into what he calls ethical cosmopolitanism, and notes that 'it provides both an ethical basis for the assessment of what individuals ought to be . . . and it provides a basis for the critical assessment of what states and other collectives do'.[4] Dower further develops an understanding of global ethics which emerges from the obligation for individuals to behave in a particular way, and proposes international ethics as pertaining to the way that states and other collectives act. Atack also reviews political realism and international idealism and contrasts their attitudes towards the role of ethics in international relations and the implications that this has for the use of force.[5] He also discusses 'what cosmopolitanism, as a theory about the role or place of ethics in international politics, has to say about the specific problems of war and armed conflict'.[6]

There is a range of traditions in international relations that this book could engage with to advance its discussion of the ethics of peacebuilding. However, it will engage exclusively with a critique of the realist and statist assumptions in international relations because this serves as an important platform from which to understand the contemporary challenges of peacebuilding.

The purpose of this book, therefore, is to contribute towards the growth of knowledge on the ethics of peacebuilding. This will indirectly contribute towards developing an understanding of the ethics of international relations. However, prior to engaging further in a discussion of the ethical dimension of peacebuilding, we first need to establish a working definition of peacebuilding.

DEFINING PEACEBUILDING: CONTESTING THE CONCEPT

In 1992, the *Agenda for Peace*, published by the then United Nations Secretary-General Boutros Boutros-Ghali, defined peacebuilding as the medium- to long-term process of rebuilding war-affected communities. It defined peacebuilding as 'action to identify and support structures which will tend to strengthen and solidify peace to avoid a relapse to conflict'.[7] Over time the definition of peacebuilding has 'gradually expanded to refer to integrated approaches to address violent conflict at different phases of the conflict cycle'.[8] Peacebuilding therefore includes the process of rebuilding the political, security, social and economic dimensions of a society emerging from conflict. At a fundamental level peacebuilding involves addressing the root causes of the conflict and enabling warring parties to continue to find solutions through negotiation and when necessary through mediation. Peacebuilding includes overseeing the process of demobilisation, disarmament and reintegration (DDR) as well as security-sector reform. Building peace requires the promotion of social and economic justice as well as the establishment or reform of political structures of governance and the rule of law. These activities are ultimately striving to bring about the healing of a war-affected community through reconciliation. Reconciliation, however is not sustainable without socio-economic reconstruction and development, neither of which can be done without the mobilisation of resources. Peacebuilding is effectively a political activity but one that seeks to unify the social and economic spheres.

A report published in December 2004 by the UN High-Level Panel on Threats, Challenges and Change, entitled *A More Secure World: Our Shared Responsibility*, highlighted the importance of peacebuilding and proposed the establishment of a UN Peacebuilding Commission.[9] In March 2005, the former UN Secretary-General Kofi Annan issued a report entitled *In Larger Freedom: Towards Development, Security and Human Rights for All*, which also endorsed and proposed the establishment of a UN Peacebuilding Commission.[10] Ultimately, the UN General Assembly *Outcome Document*, of 14 September 2005, established the Peacebuilding Commission.[11]

It goes without saying that one cannot conduct peacebuilding without including local populations in the design, planning and implementation of peacebuilding initiatives. Specifically, one cannot conduct peacebuilding only from the top down. If there is any activity that should be conducted from the bottom up it is peacebuilding. It is therefore important for local actors to take ownership of peacebuilding initiatives and to identify priorities which external actors can assist with and support.

So despite the formation of the UN Peacebuilding Commission, peacebuilding is not something that governments and inter-governmental organisations can do *to* their people. Rather, it is something that governments and their people have to do together. Peacebuilding is an ethical process that requires a close partnership, respect and dialogue among all the actors. In a very real sense, then, there is a need to emphasise the fact that peacebuilding can ultimately only succeed if it is conducted on the basis of an ethical framework. Yet this fact is often understated, if expressed at all, by both practitioners and analysts of peacebuilding. This book seeks to remedy this lack of an ethical analysis of peacebuilding.

FROM NEGATIVE PEACE TO POSITIVE PEACE

Concretely, peacebuilding involves strategies to prevent violent conflict from igniting, escalating or relapsing. Therefore, institutions and mechanisms of negotiation, mediation, forgiveness and reconciliation are central to peacebuilding processes. This book will focus on these processes and analyse some of the institutions and mechanisms that have been established to consolidate peace. Given that the ultimate objective is to develop a better understanding of how to consolidate peace, we still need to have a clearer understanding of what we are referring to when we speak of peace. The notion of peace therefore also needs to be unpacked. When we refer to peace we need to consider that there are two broadly defined ways to understand the nature of peace. For most commentators there is a distinction between a condition of negative peace and a condition of positive peace. Negative peace is the condition that most people refer to when they are discussing issues to do with peace and conflict: it is the condition in which peace is based on the absence of violence. We need to work more towards the notion of positive peace, which means a peace that promotes reconciliation and coexistence on the basis of human rights and social, economic and political justice. In this context, therefore, when we talk about peacebuilding we are referring to the process whereby the goal is to strengthen the capacity of societies to promote positive peace. Within most of the peacebuilding and development actors and agencies there is increasingly a focus on the importance of promoting positive peace. Among these actors, in the last decade we have witnessed a resurgence of the role of civil society in actively advocating for, pursuing and implementing peacebuilding strategies.

Traditional international relations practices place more of an emphasis on the notion of negative peace as the absence of violence. Increasingly, peacebuilding literature is making the case for mainstreaming the notion of positive peace. The tacit assumption that this book adopts is that there needs to be a transition towards adopting the notion of positive peace, in order to ensure that there is an ethical commitment towards promoting and consolidating genuine peacebuilding.

Given the expansive definition of peacebuilding, there is a sense that peacebuilding can include every social, political and economic activity under the sun. This would, however, render the ability of practitioners to focus exclusively on one rather complex aspect of peacebuilding. The reality on the ground is that peacebuilding requires adopting a very country- or region-specific approach to addressing a particular situation. This means that peacebuilding is context-specific and should only be undertaken following a due consideration of the political, social and economic conditions. Such an assessment would reveal the most appropriate approach to consolidating peacebuilding on the ground.

In effect, stakeholders involved in peacebuilding need to undertake an ethical assessment of the local situation and determine what aspect of peacebuilding (from a selection of reconciliation, DDR, security sector reform, governance and development processes) should be undertaken.

UNDERSTANDING MINIMAL–MAXIMAL AND NARROW–BROAD PEACEBUILDING

There is, however, no contradiction between practitioners and analysts who place an emphasis on a minimal or narrow definition of peacebuilding and those who highlight the importance of a maximal or broad definition of peacebuilding. The key lies in understanding that the notions of negative and positive peace are not mutually exclusive. One cannot proceed towards laying the foundations for positive peace without first establishing negative peace. In other words, negative peace is a necessary although insufficient condition for achieving positive peace. In effect, negative and positive peace lie on the same spectrum of peacebuilding. Ethically, a peacebuilding continuum needs to be established from negative to positive peace.

The practical implications of adopting a minimal or narrow definition of peacebuilding in guiding policy and action would only lead to the establishment of negative peace. Therefore it is ultimately necessary to adopt a maximal or broad definition of peacebuilding to guide policy and action in order to ensure the consolidation of positive peace. In this context, this book will adopt the broad and maximal definition of peacebuilding.

THE PEACEBUILDING SPECTRUM

FROM PRE-CONFLICT PEACEBUILDING TO POST-CONFLICT PEACEBUILDING

Post-conflict reconstruction and the structural and institutional prevention of conflict are in effect the same process addressed in different contexts. In fact, a useful way of thinking about peacebuilding is to acknowledge that communities are constantly in the process of peacebuilding. The notion of post-conflict peacebuilding is self-evident in the sense that there is a recognition that following a conflict processes have to be put in place and institutions and mechanisms have to be established to build confidence between erstwhile disputants, typically through negotiation and mediation. Subsequently, additional processes have to be initiated to encourage forgiveness and promote reconciliation as well as to simultaneously ensure that communities feel secure and can engage in the process of development. However, the notion that communities are building peace in situations where there is manifestly a state of peace such as in liberal democracies is more challenging to accept. Indeed, liberal democracies are at peace, and are in a state of constant peacebuilding through the constitutional and judicial provisions which manage, resolve and also prevent disputes from getting out of control in a democratic setting.

This book will focus on post-conflict peacebuilding; however, it is equally important to recognise that pre-conflict peacebuilding can provide us with additional lessons. Pre-conflict peacebuilding in this context refers to efforts to maintain harmonious societies in which norms of coexistence and political and economic accommodation are adhered to and sustained. The processes and institutions that are put in place to ensure democratic governance, the rule of law, access to social and economic justice, gender mainstreaming, environmental sustainability and reconciliation all contribute towards pre-conflict peacebuilding. A discussion of pre-conflict peacebuilding therefore needs to focus on these processes and institutions with a critical engagement with situations in which conflict was prevented through the activation or mobilisation of the processes and institutions discussed above. Such a study is beyond the scope of this book. Specifically, this book will focus on post-conflict peacebuilding in order to maintain its analytical coherence.

MACRO/MESO/MICRO PEACEBUILDING

In addition to recognising the expansiveness of peacebuilding, it is useful to acknowledge that this activity is also performed at different levels by different actors. As Tobi Dress notes, 'no single organisation, institution, sector, group, gender or UN department, regardless of its stature, can be expected to singularly shoulder the enormous burden of creating sustainable peace in any given community, let alone worldwide'.[12] Peacebuilding is an expansive, inclusive and collaborative process which takes place simultaneously at three different levels: the macro, meso and micro levels.

MACRO-LEVEL PEACEBUILDING: INTERNATIONAL PEACEBUILDING

At the international level peacebuilding proceeds through the activities of the United Nations and its agencies, as well as continental and sub-regional mechanisms. For the last sixteen years the policy framework that has outlined the broad parameters of macro-level peacebuilding is the *Agenda for Peace*. Subsequently, there have been additional reports outlining strategies for implementing peacebuilding, including the High-Level Panel report, mentioned earlier and the UN Secretary-General's report *In Larger Freedom*. Concretely, in order for peacebuilding to succeed there has to be a macro-Level policy and institutional framework to create the necessary conditions.

MESO-LEVEL PEACEBUILDING: NATIONAL AND SUB-NATIONAL PEACEBUILDING

The meso level of peacebuilding refers to the national and sub-national processes to promote and sustain peace. Governments of war-affected countries generally tend to adopt policy frameworks to enhance their efforts to consolidate peace. Meso-level national peacebuilding initiatives need to complement the macro-level frameworks and institutions in order to maximise the synergy that is directed towards peacebuilding.

MICRO-LEVEL PEACEBUILDING: LOCAL AND GRASSROOTS PEACEBUILDING

Micro-level peacebuilding refers to activities that take place at the sub-national level or at the level of local communities. Grassroots and indigenous leadership structures have an important role to play in securing and sustaining peace. In addition, non-governmental and ecumenical groups can also implement and take part in micro-level peacebuilding initiatives.

The macro-level, meso-level and micro-level frameworks can exist independently of each other, but effective peacebuilding can only be implemented when each level complements the other. At the macro level peacebuilding processes are often imbued with self-interest and often operate on the basis of ethical scepticism and political realism. There are cases in which micro-level peace processes and indigenous mechanisms can implement ethical processes.

This book argues that whereas we witness attempts at imbuing peacebuilding with a strong positive ethical foundation at the micro level, to a large extent meso-level and macro-level peacebuilding efforts need to embrace a greater degree of ethics. One conclusion that can be inferred from this multi-level analysis of peacebuilding is that there is a need for a greater degree of synergy between micro, meso and macro peacebuilding structures.

THE CHALLENGES OF GLOBAL GOVERNANCE: TRANSLATING THE MICRO-/MESO-LEVEL TO THE MACRO-LEVEL

There is, however, the challenge of translating the micro- and meso-level processes of peacebuilding to the macro-level. This is in effect a challenge of how to ensure global governance. Specifically, Dower notes that people 'working in NGOs as part of what is called "global civil society", do now in some sense participate in global governance'.[13] Therefore, by engaging in micro- and meso-level peacebuilding NGOs are already contributing towards the governance at a macro-level; thus the linkage between these levels is implied in such activity. In effect, through their localised and regionalised peacebuilding initiatives civil society is contributing towards bringing order to global public affairs. Therefore by extension they are involved in translating micro- and meso-level peacebuilding to the level of international relations. There are, of course, challenges to ensuring this transition which will be discussed further in Chapters 3 and 7 in this book. The normative framework for such a synergy also needs to be articulated. In effect, there is a 'need to develop a shared doctrine of norms and values to form the pillars for preventing the deterioration of peace and security'.[14]

THE ETHICS OF PEACEBUILDING

Having established a working definition of peacebuilding and enumerated its multi-level framework we can now begin to question the ethical processes that are likely, or not, to prevail at the different levels. Concretely, peacebuilding involves strategies to prevent violent conflict from escalating or from relapsing. This book will focus on negotiation, mediation, forgiveness and reconciliation processes. On this basis it will question how ethical peacebuilding should proceed. It will undertake an ethical inquiry into each of these processes in turn.

This book seeks to examine, discuss and make the case for the importance of recognising that there is a tacit morality implied in peacebuilding. It is not uncommon for belligerent parties to a conflict to view the peace process as a strategic opportunity to regroup and reconstitute their forces to continue perpetuating their violent campaigns. Secondary parties in conflict situations do not always adopt an ethical posture with regards to assisting the disputants to find sustainable solutions to their problems. Furthermore, external actors do not always adopt a strict moral code with regards to the exploitation of natural resources in war-affected areas. Thus the unethical behaviour of external actors in peacebuilding settings can undermine the efforts to bring about order and stability.

Negotiators and mediators in peacebuilding situations also need to adopt an ethical stance towards the parties that they are assisting. This is an aspect of peacebuilding that has not been sufficiently explored by the existing literature. The role of forgiveness and reconciliation in consolidating peacebuilding cannot be underestimated. These processes are tacitly imbued with ethical and moral considerations. This book will therefore assess the ethical dimensions of forgiveness and reconciliation.

Ultimately, this book seeks to explore the question: once the guns have fallen silent how do we morally repair the emotional and mental harm that has transpired between human beings? This book makes the argument that a fundamental understanding of the ethics of peacebuilding is necessary in order to respond to this question. Societies must resolve disputes, deal with criminality, establish shared norms and rules, and adopt strategies to promote their collective well-being. What are the ethical underpinnings of the peacebuilding process? What moral assumptions are made about peace processes in general? Are all peace processes ethical? Do some people use peace processes to achieve immoral objectives? Do people make unethical claims to be seeking a moral peace, whilst immorally undermining the very foundation of such a peace?

CONTENT AND STRUCTURE OF THE BOOK

This book will begin by discussing the importance of developing and contributing towards the growth of moral knowledge. Chapter 2 will assess the validity of moral knowledge by drawing upon the work of various philosophers and relate this to the growth of peace research. Chapter 3 will make the case for a moral approach to conflict resolution and peacebuilding. In particular, it will assess the emergence of the phenomenon of sub-national conflict and discuss how it has altered the international geopolitical terrain. This chapter will also make the case that the international system is ill-equipped and ill-designed to effectively address sub-national conflicts and consolidate peacebuilding. It will argue that it is important to recognise the morality inherent in conflict resolution and peacebuilding processes. It will also discuss the challenges of translating micro- and meso-level peacebuilding to the level of inter-national relations or the macro-level. In particular, it will discuss the promotion of peacebuilding as a challenge to global governance.

Chapter 4 will assess the processes of negotiation and mediation in order to illustrate the ethics inherent in both processes. It will assess the efforts of the League of Nations to establish an ethical framework for pacific dispute settlement. This chapter will also assess the efforts of the League to promote peace in the Åland Islands, Upper Silesia and the Saar region. It will then assess the United Nations' framework for resolving conflict and the objectives of the Mediation Support Unit within the UN Department of Political Affairs (DPA). It will go on to assess the peacebuilding efforts of the Quakers during the Biafran war in Nigeria in the late 1960s. Key lessons will be highlighted to demonstrate the importance of establishing ethical frameworks for building and consolidating peace.

Chapter 5 will assess the process of forgiveness. It will outline a philosophical basis for forgiveness by referring to the work of Jürgen Habermas on discourse ethics, and Lawrence Kohlberg on moral development. It will ultimately discuss how forgiveness proceeds on the basis of victims and perpetrators gradually undergoing a process of moral development to the point where the other is viewed as existing within common parameters of the moral community. Chapter 5 will also assess the efforts of the Moral Re-Armament civil society group to convene and implement forgiveness forums.

Chapter 6 will look at the process of reconciliation. It will examine the different ways in which reconciliation has been analysed and understood. In particular, it will enumerate the social, political and economic aspects of reconciliation. This chapter 6 will also look at the nexus between reconciliation, peacebuilding and transitional justice. It will present an innovative peace with justice matrix which outlines how peace and justice are not polar opposites, but in fact complementary processes. In order to move from a condition of negative peace to one of positive peace, a simultaneous emphasis has to be placed on moving away from a framework that emphasises retributive justice to one that promotes restorative justice. In this context, Chapter 6 will also discuss the role of the International Criminal Court (ICC) in addressing atrocities committed during war. It will also assess the key aspects of the South African and Sierra Leone Truth and Reconciliation Commissions. Chapter 6 concludes by assessing the role that indigenous approaches to peacebuilding can play in promoting healing within society. Specifically, it will examine the *ubuntu* world-view which articulates an ethical way of being, based on the traditions of the Bantu communities of South and Central Africa.

Chapter 7 will propose an agenda for promoting ethical peacebuilding. It will begin by highlighting the complex nature of sub-national conflicts. This chapter will make the point that sub-national conflicts can also be thought of as moral conflicts and therefore would ideally be resolved through establishing ethical processes and institutions to address them. Chapter 7 will also assess the role of international institutions in promoting peacebuilding. In particular, it will assess the newly established UN Peacebuilding Commission and question whether it will fulfil the objective of promoting ethical peace around the world. Chapter 7 will also assess the importance of a post-conflict democratisation process that re-defines the nature of the relationship between sub-national groups and the nation-state. In particular, the efforts to promote peace in Northern Ireland will be assessed to illustrate how a post-national polity is being established in which sovereignty over the province is effectively shared between two nation-states, the United Kingdom and Ireland.

This book makes the argument that the absence of an assessment of the ethical dimensions of peacebuilding is a contributory factor to the limited success that has been experienced in consolidating peace. The ethical dimensions of the practical peacebuilding adopted in this book will therefore make an innovative contribution to the literature.

NOTES

1. Nigel Dower, *World Ethics: A New Agenda*, 2nd edition (Edinburgh: Edinburgh University Press, 2007); Iain Atack, *The Ethics of Peace and War* (Edinburgh: Edinburgh University Press, 2005).
2. Bruce Barry and Robert Robinson, 'Ethics in Conflict Resolution: The Ties that Bind', *International Negotiation*, vol. 7, 2002, pp. 137–42.
3. Ibid., p. 137.
4. Dower, *World Ethics: A New Agenda*, p. 80.
5. Atack, *The Ethics of Peace and War*, p. 6.
6. Ibid., p. 10.
7. Boutros Boutros-Ghali, *An Agenda for Peace: Preventive Diplomacy, Peacemaking and Peacekeeping* (New York: United Nations, 1992).
8. Necla Tschirgi, *Peacebuilding as the Link between Security and Development: Is the Window of Opportunity Closing?* (New York: International Peace Academy, 2003), p. 1.
9. High-Level Panel on Threats, Challenges and Change, *A More Secure World: Our Shared Responsibility* (New York: United Nations, 2004).
10. Kofi Annan, *In Larger Freedom: Towards Development, Security and Human Rights for All*, UN document A/59/2005, 21 March 2005.
11. United Nations General Assembly, *Outcome Document*, 14 September 2005.
12. Tobi Dress, *Designing a Peacebuilding Infrastructure: Taking a Systems Approach to the Prevention of Deadly Conflict* (Geneva: United Nations Non-Governmental Liaison Service, 2005), p. 6.
13. Dower, *World Ethics: A New Agenda*, p. 79.
14. Bethuel Kiplagat, 'Foreword', in Dress, *Designing a Peacebuilding Infrastructure*, p. xii.

CHAPTER 2

MORAL KNOWLEDGE AND PEACEBUILDING

INTRODUCTION

This chapter will examine the conceptual and normative issues that arise when attempting to analyse the ethics of international relations in general and peacebuilding in particular. The chapter begins by assessing developments in the growth of knowledge. It will assess anti-foundationalist critiques of the possibility of knowledge and will adopt a moral convergence approach towards international relations knowledge. It will argue that since the ultimate objective is to promote positive peace, then achieving consensus on this point requires a degree of moral convergence at the level of practical judgement and knowledge production. Practical convergence, however, does not require common positions of beliefs and world-views to retain its validity. This chapter will go on to explore the possibility of advancing a moral epistemology of peacebuilding knowledge. The work developed by the critical school and in particular by Jürgen Habermas on discourse ethics will be assessed to reiterate this point. The argument for the importance of knowledge serving an emancipatory function is central to the critical theory school of international relations. Peace is therefore valued and is being explicitly argued for in the formulation of bodies of knowledge. This chapter seeks to set out the basis upon which the case can be made for the intrinsic value of peacebuilding research. The account of knowledge here might not be knowledge in an objective sense; nor does this chapter try to make the point that it is seeking to establish objective moral knowledge. Rather, it seeks to demonstrate the subjective nature of all knowledge and therefore make the case that there is no prima facie basis for either accepting or rejecting moral knowledge as it is presented in the chapter. This normative conclusion is necessary in light of the critiques of the possibility of knowledge from anti-foundationalism and the realist critique of the possibility of moral values infusing how we know about international relations, and how we develop this knowledge. This chapter will argue that in a very practical sense effective peacebuilding requires practitioners, parties and analysts to adopt a conceptual framework that is conducive towards promoting positive peace. Ultimately, these actors have to accept certain ethical values even though they have different moral theoretical positions.

DEVELOPMENTS IN THE GROWTH OF KNOWLEDGE

From the era of ancient scholarship through to the Enlightenment, questions about what we know and how we know have played an important role in the growth of human knowledge. Over the last decade there has been a resurgence of debates about the purpose of international relations knowledge, with these debates revolving around the possibility of value-free international relations knowledge. In the development of any body of knowledge normative assumptions and prescriptions are unavoidable. Therefore the development of any body of knowledge has to recognise this condition and establish a clear orientation for its focus. The theme and focus adopted in this book reveal a normative emphasis on studying international relations, and peacebuilding in particular, with a view to understanding the potential for reducing socio-economic and political injustice and promoting positive peace.

MORAL THEORIES AND THEIR INFLUENCE ON KNOWLEDGE

A review of moral theories will set the scene for engaging with contemporary feminist and post-structural criticisms of foundationalist epistemologies. Ethical egoism will be discussed to illustrate the ethical scepticism which underpins political realism and how this has impacted upon international relations knowledge. Adherents of the political realism school of thought have traditionally claimed to be value-free, and claimed only to offer an objective analysis of international affairs. This promulgated an orthodoxy of positivism. Any attempt to introduce normative concerns into the analysis of international politics was considered to be 'old fashioned' and 'very unacademic'.[1] In effect, this section will demonstrate that far from eschewing a moral foundation, political realism is in fact value-laden and predicated on a variant of ethical egoism which emphasises practical and theoretical self-interest.

An assessment of critics of realism will be undertaken to make the case more explicitly for grounding peacebuilding knowledge on normative moral theory.

The need for a moral epistemology of peacebuilding is beyond question. Since all knowledge is to some extent value-laden, and in effect generated out of self-interest, then this disabuses the notion that there exists a body of knowledge that can claim a monopoly of absolute truth and reality. Knowledge is always generated for someone and for some purpose and therefore moral introspection, or reflexivity, is an essential component of knowledge production. Ideally, knowledge should not be used to perpetuate dominance over others, even though this is commonplace in inter-human relations. The social scientific researcher needs to be cognisant of his or her ethical duty to strive for knowledge which is universally beneficial to humanity, or at least not harmful to certain sections of global society.

THE CASE FOR GENERATING MORAL KNOWLEDGE

Why should we concern ourselves with the moral philosophical dimensions of knowledge production? Surely in a world increasingly defined in terms of a plurality of world-views and epistemological relativism, any attempt at presenting a framework of moral knowledge which is at once universalising and prescriptive has to be misconceived? Yet we cannot escape from the fact that moral evaluation permeates the human world. Creating moral standards which we use to understand and evaluate our actions is a process which proceeds often unnoticed in our daily lives. Knowledge production is no exception to this rule. Professing scepticism about the possibility of moral inquiry into society is a normative evaluation. Advocating relativism in our moral judgements likewise is an activity imbued with ethical presuppositions. For Jenny Teichman, moral philosophy 'is important because whether we like it or not the human world is dominated by ideas about right and wrong'.[2] She goes on to note that moral philosophy is important for the further reason that 'action is important and the way people act is influenced by what they believe'.[3] This position is relevant when we look at peacebuilding as an activity. During the Cold War, international relations were constrained by superpower rivalry and this was reflected in the dominance of certain forms of knowledge when it came to understanding how to resolve conflict. In the post-Cold War world, peacebuilding should be viewed as a moral activity underpinned by moral presuppositions with definite moral implications. The moral assumptions that are held by peacebuilding practitioners will always impact upon their strategies and practical efforts on the ground, which is why this book seeks to examine the ethical dimension of peacebuilding.

FOUNDATIONALISM AND THE POSSIBILITY OF MORAL KNOWLEDGE

There is a branch of epistemology which maintains that it is possible to establish fundamental principles for guiding and evaluating our moral activity. According to Jonathan Dancy, this approach argues that there are 'highly general truths from which particular moral prescriptions can be derived'.[4] This approach, also known as foundationalism, strives to put ethical knowledge on a secure footing based on the dictates of reason. With reference to cosmopolitanism, which was discussed in Chapter 1, Nigel Dower observes in his book *World Ethics: A New Agenda* that 'according to the cosmopolitan there is a common moral framework through which to assess issues to do with war and peace'.[5] For those who adopt the cosmopolitan world-view, ethics necessarily informs how we can develop our understanding of war and peace. In addition, the cosmopolitan imbues peace with a moral value and seeks to condemn the propensity towards war. The cosmopolitan therefore works from a set of value assumptions that maintain that there is an intrinsic value to peace. The nature of research that the cosmopolitan is likely to engage in is therefore likely to be conducive towards promoting peace. Knowledge generated by the cosmopolitan would therefore instrumentally seek to promote peace through the propagation of his or her body of work. This chapter explicitly seeks to defend such a position. Iain Atack, in his book *The Ethics of War and Peace*, concludes that:

> we must also acknowledge the inadequacy of cosmopolitanism on its own to provide a clear and unambiguous response to the moral and political problems associated with war and armed conflict, without further exploring issues in both normative ethics and political theory.[6]

This chapter will therefore seek to argue that all knowledge is value-laden and therefore, as the cosmopolitan, we can choose or decline to create a body of knowledge which is imbued with value-assumptions. A detailed analysis of this approach is beyond the scope of this chapter. The next section explores the schools of thought that deny the possibility of knowledge.

ANTI-FOUNDATIONALISM, POST-STRUCTURALISM AND THE IMPOSSIBILITY OF MORAL KNOWLEDGE

According to some thinkers the claims of traditional moral knowledge are highly problematic. It is worthwhile to assess the counter-arguments raised by the moral relativists, moral sceptics and ethical egoism before engaging with feminist critiques.

Georg Wilhelm Hegel laid the groundwork for modern strands of thought which are sceptical of the possibility of generating moral knowledge independent of a subject who in effect is the generator of this knowledge.[7] The work of Martin Heidegger, Friedrich Nietzsche and Ludwig Wittgenstein further promulgated the Hegelian tradition.[8] By way of an abbreviated summary, these converging yet distinct approaches to knowledge criticised Kant and others who entertained totalising conceptions of reason and the rational organisation of moral knowledge and society. The main argument put forward by them maintained that such totalising activity was lacking a sufficiently critical view about reality and humanity's place in that reality. As far as generating moral knowledge is concerned, they questioned whether it was at all possible to view the human self as a subject divorced from his or her environs, and thus endowed with the ability to correctly represent objects in the external world. This would be to assume that a subject/object duality was possible. For these thinkers foundationalism holds on to presuppositions with which it seeks to establish an ideal of certainty which in reality cannot be attained.

Hegel, for example, argued that the subject/object duality was fundamentally misleading. Therefore, establishing moral epistemology on such a foundation would only yield 'objective' moral knowledge, in the traditionally accepted, or socially constructed, understanding of the term. Writing much later, Heidegger was also critical of the tendency to totalise and universalise the foundations of moral knowledge. He believed that we should treat moral epistemology 'as part of technology, the Western tendency to treat reality as a world view on hand for our inspection and use'.[9] Nietzsche developed a more radicalised understanding of this condition when he suggested that objective moral knowledge was not possible. He believed that 'we simply lack any organ for knowledge, for "truth": we know or believe or imagine just as much as may be useful in the interests of the human herd, the species'. Nietzsche argued that even what we may refer to as 'utility' is 'ultimately also a mere belief, something imaginary'.[10] For Nietzsche, there was no conception of the world which could not be tainted by a human interpretation. An interpretation is, in the final analysis, entirely subjective.

The 'truth' of specific moral approaches can only be determined with reference to 'facts specified internally by those approaches them-selves'.[11] Wittgenstein takes this position further when he argues that 'ethics so far as it springs from the desire to say something about the ultimate meaning of life, the absolute good, the absolute valuable, can be no science. What it says does not add to our knowledge in any sense'.[12] He argues that moral beliefs are part of a 'language game' which proceed along the lines of internal rules. Moral beliefs do not have any validity independent of their progenitors and thus they cannot be objectified or universalised. In this sense moral knowledge is relative and localised.[13]

POST-STRUCTURALISM AND MORAL KNOWLEDGE

Variants of these themes are also evident in the work of Jacques Derrida and Michel Foucault, to name two thinkers whose views have received substantial analysis elsewhere and will only be addressed briefly here. Derrida and Foucault seek to challenge what they see as the excessive ambitions of traditional Western philosophy, particularly epistemology. The basis for their suspicions is derived from their scepticism 'about the referential function of language, the capacity of language to say objec-tively true things about the world'.[14] In Derrida's case, he developed a style of questioning which is based on rejecting the traditional philo-sophical distinction between what is conventionally known as philoso-phy and other fields of human thought. Derrida argued that traditional philosophy has gone astray, in that it has become too *logocentric*.[15] He suggested that Western moral philosophy had proceeded predominantly on the basis of an Aristotelian logic of identity and non-contradiction, hence logocentrism. Raymond Morrow notes that logocentrism reflects a 'metaphysics of presence' in which 'the metaphysical assumption is that language refers directly to something present and outside of itself in an unproblematic way'.[16] In this way the referential function of lan-guage is taken for granted. Logocentrism does not adequately reflect on the historical origins, operation and deployment of rational or scientific language. It therefore equates and transforms scientific language into a formal language, which is then deployed by positivists to explain the world. Positivism in this sense is guilty of logocentrism. In criticising logocentrism Derrida put forward the view that 'reality is to be under-stood both in terms of difference, rather than self-identity, and in terms of perpetual deferment, rather than eternal presence'.[17] Therefore, moral epistemology and any claims to objectively valid reason have to be subjected to fundamental questioning. This can only lead to an anti-foundationalist stance which no longer tries to achieve mastery over things, and a relegation of moral epistemology to the status of being only one vocabulary of knowledge amongst many others. As one vocabulary among many others, moral epistemology does not possess any de facto objective validity.

Foucault approached the problem of the 'referential function' of language and its capacity to objectively determine reality from a slightly different angle. He argued that the truth-conditions of our statements, or the conditions under which the things that we say are true or false, are necessarily relative to our particular 'discursive practices'.[18] For Foucault a discursive practice entailed 'a body of anonymous historical rules, always determined in the time and space that have defined a given period, and for a given social, economic, geographical, or linguistic area, the conditions of operation of the enunciative function'.[19] This assessment of the historically contingent referential function of language clearly has implications for moral epistemology. Through his 'genealogical' method Foucault sought to 'unearth, not just the unconscious rules which lead members of a community to accept some statements as true and reject others as false, but also the subtle historical and social conditions which bring about the institutions in which those rules are accepted'.[20] In the formulation of an epistemology Foucault would seek to uncover its discursive practices and problematise the rules inherent in the 'enunciative function' and thus challenge its view of reality and knowledge acquisition. With reference to the practices that gained currency during the Enlightenment period, Foucault articulated an emphasis on self-examination, but unlike the foundationalist project which seeks to demarcate what reason is capable of, the genealogical method would 'not deduce from the form of what we are, what it is impossible for us to do and to know'.[21] Given that the attributions of truth and falsity are, in Foucault's view, relative to the various discursive practices then it is necessary to remain sceptical towards any tendencies proclaiming an objective truth. One can therefore detect in this position traces of the influence of Hegel's work which problematised the subject/object duality claimed by foundationalists. These views raise important questions for the field of moral epistemology. However, they are also problematic because by denying the possibility of objective moral knowledge, such views purport to produce a body of knowledge which claims to be 'true' and 'right', as will be discussed in the next section.

THE PERFORMATIVE CONTRADICTION:
A CRITIQUE OF ANTI-FOUNDATIONALISM

A major criticism raised with regards to this sceptical tradition is its own tendency towards a totalising normativity or a universalising position. Anti-foundationalism rejects any Archimedean points of reference against which critical moral judgements can be made about its own system of critique. Thomas McCarthy observes that anti-foundationalist 'accounts of rationality invariably fall into the self-referential or "performative contradiction of having *implicitly to presuppose what they want explicitly to deny*"'.[22] McCarthy argues that 'the politics of otherness and difference makes sense only on the assumption of the very universalist values – freedom, justice, equality, respect, tolerance, dignity – that they seek to deconstruct'.[23]

Habermas refers to the *crypto-normativity* of anti-foundationalist positions in general and with reference to Foucault's position in particular. He argues that the wholesale critique of rational humanism is itself paradoxical and that these criticisms of rationality are hinged upon a self-referential paradox in the sense that they base their critique of reason on *normative standards that either implicate reason or prescind from it*.[24] Habermas suggests that methods that emphasise the primacy of subjectivity and relativity in knowledge production are incapable of providing a 'coherent' account of their own 'objectivity'. In effect, the 'truth' of their statements is in essence a function of their own 'groundless formation rules'.[25] In other words, for the various degrees of relativism that find sanctuary in these sceptical positions, it is worthwhile to note that 'relativism is incoherent because, if it is *right*, the very notion of *rightness* is *undermined*, in which case relativism itself cannot be *right*'.[26] As Seigel notes, 'the assertion and defence of relativism requires one to presuppose neutral standards in accordance with which contentious claims and doctrines can be assessed; but relativism denies the possibility of evaluation in accordance with such neutral standards'.[27] He goes on to conclude that 'the doctrine of relativism [in its various formulations] cannot be coherently defended – it can be defended only by being given up'. By denying the possibility of an Archimedean point of reference against which critical moral judgements can be assessed, these sceptical and anti-foundationalist traditions are vulnerable to a form of crypto-normativism in which they deny 'the existence of founding norms whilst nevertheless having to appeal to them'.[28] This has led Bernstein to suggest that a hidden form of universality does in fact underpin anti-foundationalist and post-structural thought evident in their defence of tolerance and respect for difference and alterity. Critical theoretical perspectives, drawn loosely from the Frankfurt School tradition, make explicit their foundationalist and universalist positions with regards to rationality, but they seek to safeguard against succumbing to the dogmatism of their own 'discursive practices'.[29] McCarthy notes that:

> if the end of foundationalism means anything, it means at least the permanent openness of any proposed universal frame to deconstructive and reconstructive impulses . . . it is folly to suppose that social and cultural studies can get along without general conceptions of reason and rationalisation.[30]

He maintains that 'the interpretive and evaluative frameworks that invariably, albeit often tacitly, inform the ways in which socio-cultural phenomena are selected, described, ordered, analysed, appraised, and explained, typically include categories and assumptions tailored to grasping the "rationalisation" of modern society'.[31] Critical theory being on one level a critique of epistemology and on another a critique of society explicitly implicates itself in foundationalism. Yet this foundationalism has traditionally been developed without much regard for its inherently gendered history and bias. This glaringly problematic feature of foundationalist knowledge must be addressed.

GENDERED (RE)VISIONS OF MORAL KNOWLEDGE

Moral knowledge production has not until recently expressed its views on the issue of gender and knowledge. The various traditions of feminist epistemology bring a revisionist programme to the practice of moral knowledge production.[32] Feminist epistemologies have engaged with positivism and its claims to value-neutrality, and have developed a critique that questions for whom and for what knowledge is generated. Emerging from the feminist movement of the 1960s, feminist epistemology questions the disparity between women's diverse experiences and the theoretical frameworks which purported to know and explain these experiences. Virginia Held has argued that historically 'ethics has been constructed from male points of view, and has been built on assumptions and concepts that are by no means gender-neutral'.[33] She further observes that this situation has resulted in the privileging of reason, which is assumed to be a male trait, over emotion, which in turn is ascribed to the feminine aspect. Genevieve Lloyd also concurs that 'rationality has been conceived as transcendence of the feminine'.[34] This suggests that moral knowledge production has to become more conscious of the associations made between reason, maleness and knowledge. So, according to Held we 'should certainly now be alert to the ways in which reason has been associated with male endeavour, emotion with female weakness'.[35] She further believes that we need to determine:

> how the associations, between reason, form, knowledge, and maleness have persisted in various guises, and have permeated what has been thought to be moral knowledge as well as what has been thought to be scientific knowledge, and what has been thought to be the practice of morality.[36]

Thus, by unravelling the 'exclusionary assumptions that have enabled the epistemologies of the mainstream to establish their authority, feminists are effecting shifts in the perceived tasks of epistemology'.[37]

Feminist epistemology is not unified in any sense; rather it is a collectivity of various schools of thought.[38] Kimberly Hutchings observes that 'any feminist theory is "critical" in the general sense that it is premised on challenging the oppression and marginalisation of women in both theory and practice'.[39] Feminist critical theory, drawn from the Frankfurt School tradition, like other approaches problematises gender but also simultaneously seeks to engender a moral vision. Feminist post-structuralism, drawn from the deconstructivist perspective, on the other hand rejects the possibility of any meta-narrative, particularly one that proposes a universal moral value.[40] Feminist critical theory endorses the approach of critical theory which is to ensure reflective self-comprehension, but its added value is in also developing an understanding of how gender can and does play a role in the construction of normative and moral knowledge. The pitfalls of adopting a feminist post-structuralist perspective is that by rejecting all meta-narratives, so narratives that perpetuate the logic of self-interested power can also flourish. It is necessary to also advocate for a progressive moral vision of human and international relations. The assumption that all ethical theory is always advocating different forms of progressive ways of being in the world is erroneous. There is a branch of ethics which advocates self-interest and provides a foundation for international relations schools of thought such as political realism.

ETHICAL EGOISM AND KNOWLEDGE CREATION

The moral approaches discussed so far are challenged by the pervasiveness of ethical egoism. As Sterba observes, 'the ethical egoist, by denying the priority of morality over self-interest, presents the most serious challenge to a moral-approach to practical problems'.[41] He further notes that the basic principles of ethical egoism state that 'everyone ought to do what is his or her overall self-interest'.[42] As such, some theorists have questioned whether this school of thought can be described as 'ethical' in the strict sense of the word. The ethical egoist would argue that right action should be based on self-interest and such a person would be willing to see his or her claim universalised. However, Teichman notes that 'egoism can be defined either as practical or theoretical. Practical egoism consists of behaviour characterised by systematic selfishness, theoretical egoism is a theory which bases morality on self-interest'.[43] Egoism bases its ideas on a theory of human nature which holds that human beings are always motivated by selfishness, even to the extent that actions which seem to be unselfish as they manifest are really selfish actions in disguise. There are research approaches within social sciences such as certain branches of game theory and economics which predicate their conceptual frameworks on the assumption that self-centred action is more rational than altruistic behaviour.[44] Yet Teichman remains sceptical of this claim and argues that 'we cannot prove that benefiting oneself is more rational than not without assuming the point to be proved', namely, that egoism is more rational than altruism. The opposite premise is equally valid, such that 'the egoist is rational according to his own axiom, and the altruist is rational according to his'.[45] Clearly, such a framework would have major implications for the construction of knowledge. The knowledge generated would only hold utility for the person, or persons, who generated it, creating a condition in which knowledge is in effect self-centred.

INTERNATIONAL RELATIONS, POSITIVISM AND PEACE RESEARCH

The discipline of international relations was born of a historic concern with the possibility of understanding the realities of peace and war.[46] In its formative years the field of international relations was dominated by the idealist school of thought which adopted an explicitly normative and prescriptive approach. This normative approach advocated a research agenda that held as its core tenets the consideration of norms, values, morality and an ideology of reform.[47] In subsequent decades the realist school of thought became more dominant and brought with it a paradigm shift towards positivism and an embrace of the scientific method based on value-free analysis.[48] During the Cold War positivism permeated peace research, so it is worthwhile to explore some of its dimensions to see whether it can inform our inquiry into the ethics of peacebuilding.

EARLY AND CONTEMPORARY POSITIVISM

The developments in positivism were defined by its transition from a critique of theological, metaphysical dogmatism in the nineteenth century to an emphasis on the importance of logic and mathematics in the twentieth century. At its core is the belief that 'positive knowledge – in contrast to "metaphysical" or "moral" knowledge – is reliable because it corresponds directly to the observable, empirical realm'.[49] Even though there are multiple formulations of positivism,[50] the early brand of positivism formulated by Auguste Comte in the nineteenth century sought to introduce positivism as a 'science of society'. He proclaimed positive science as the sole vehicle for intellectual progress and its advance constituted an improvement on speculative approaches to knowledge. For Comte sociology referred to the 'positive study of all the fundamental laws pertaining to social phenomena'.[51] He attempted to define its method, doctrine and objectives by contrasting it to the 'theologicial-metaphysical state', which he viewed as 'ideal in its procedure, absolute in its conception and arbitrary in its application'. Thus, for Comte the true positive spirit in the quest for knowledge consists above all 'in seeing for the sake of forseeing; in studying what *is*, in order to infer what *will be*, in accordance with the general dogma that natural laws are invariable'.[52]

This theme, which persists today and remains a dominant force in epistemology, was further developed by the logical positivists who convened in Vienna, Austria, in the 1920s and early 1930s. The logical positivists felt that Comte's rendition of positivism 'suffered from a number of impressions and even internal contradictions'.[53] Logical positivism had many followers who adhered to different scientific traditions. They generically held the view that positivism was defined by its adherence to the doctrine that science is the only form of knowledge and that there is nothing in the universe beyond what can in principle be scientifically known. Furthermore, they believed that it was 'logical' because of its independence from developments in logic and mathematics, which could 'reveal how a priori knowledge of necessary truths is compatible with a thorough-going empiricism'.[54] For the logical positivists the scientific world-view was exclusive and everything beyond the reach of science, like morality, was cognitively meaningless. It was meaningless in the sense that one could not determine its truth or falsity and so it could not be a meaningful object of cognition. To underpin this argument positivists constructed a criterion for meaningfulness which they found in the idea of empirical verification, expressed through the view that a 'sentence is said to be cognitively meaningful if and only if it can be verified and falsified in experience'.[55] Barry Stroud expands on the view held by the logical positivists when he observes that in reference to this criterion of meaningfulness 'moral and aesthetic and other "evaluative" sentences are held to be neither confirmable nor disconfirmable on empirical grounds, and so are cognitively meaningless'. Stroud further points out that 'they are at best expressions of feeling or preference which are neither true nor false. Whatever is congnitively meaningful and therefore factual is value-free'.[56] For logical positivists, as for Comte, 'metaphysical' knowledge was not legitimate knowledge, scientifically speaking. They held the view that metaphysical questions, or questions about being and morality, lacked any cognitive meaning because they could not say anything that could be verified or falsified in experience. In this way, sense experience became the purveyor of all knowledge. Stroud exposes the all-encompassing and monopolising tendencies implicit in the positivists' epistemology when he observes that 'since science is regarded as the repository of all genuine human knowledge, this [knowledge] assumes the task of exhibiting the structure, or as it was called, the "logic" of science. The theory of knowledge [or epistemology] thus becomes the philosophy of science'.[57]

POSITIVISM'S INFLUENCE ON PEACE RESEARCH

The significance of the preceding discussion is that these ideas have had a significant impact on the growth of peace research. As with other social sciences, the field of international relations, which gave expression to the sub-field of peace research, was seduced by positivist assumptions. Michael Banks describes this influence on international relations when he notes that:

> in the years between World War I and World War II, there was a brief period in which the liberals, or utopians as they were often (wrongly) called at the time, dominated thinking as a result of the reaction to the disaster of World War I.[58]

He argues that the first war challenged the established mechanisms of international politics, including the use of alliances, arms races, secret treaties and diplomacy. In effect the two wars 'destroyed faith in all the liberal analyses and prescriptions'.[59] The prevalence of positivist epistemology is the legacy of the attitudes towards the knowledge which held currency in the 1940s and 1950s when political realism emerged as a dominant school of thought. There was a widespread belief in 'the intellectual capacity of realism to explain the world, to predict it and to provide prescriptions that would enable decision makers to control it and to deal with problems'.[60] One of the pioneering founders of realism, Hans Morgenthau, proclaimed that:

> it is the task of theory to detect in the welter of the *unique facts of experience* that which is uniform, similar, and typical. It is its task to reduce the *facts of experience* to mere specific instances of general propositions, to detect behind them the *general laws* to which they owe their existence and which determine their development.[61]

Here then we can perceive the arguments of Comtean and logical positivism, notably in the primacy of 'sense experience' and the quest for universal and timeless 'general laws'. In his pioneering work on political realism, entitled *Politics Among Nations*, Morgenthau laid down the foundations for the tradition by proclaiming that a theory of international politics 'must meet a dual test, an *empirical and logical* one: do the *facts as they actually are* lend themselves to the interpretation the theory has put upon them, and do the conclusions at which the theory arrives follow with *logical* necessity from its premises?'.[62]

The hallmarks of an attempt to create a positivist theory of international relations knowledge are evident. In particular, there is a belief in the objectivity of the laws of international politics derived empirically from the realm of phenomena. Positivist theory derided the propensity towards drawing from the metaethical-metaphysical realm to determine the laws of international politics. Adherents to this school of thought believe in the 'truth' function of laws derived empirically, precisely because they are not judged by some preconceived abstract principle or by a concept unrelated to reality. Ultimately, there is also an inherent belief that the logical and scientific basis of such a theory is realised only if, according to Morgenthau, the 'conclusions' which are derived from the theory 'follow with logical necessity from its premises'. This is in line with the tenets of logical positivism.

Steve Smith observes that 'in good Weberian fashion, International Relations analysts tried to keep values and analysis apart'.[63] Armed with such epistemological tools realists were able to perpetuate their quest for a scientific analysis of international relations. Building upon the foundation laid by realism, behaviouralism was able to filter into the international relations field in the 1960s and early 1970s. Behaviouralism sought

> law like generalisations, that is, statements about patterns and regularities about international phenomena presumed to hold across time and place . . . they tried to

replace subjective belief with verifiable knowledge, to supplant impressionism and intuition with testable evidence, and to substitute data and reproducible information for mere opinion.[64]

Again the legacy of Comte and the logical positivists is evident. The dichotomy between metaphysical knowledge, in the form of 'subjective belief', 'impressionism and intuition' and positive knowledge in the form of 'verifiable knowledge', 'testable evidence' and 'data and reproducible information', provides additional evidence. The prevailing attitude, as Stanley Hoffman observed, was a belief that 'all problems can be resolved, and that the way to resolve them is to apply the scientific method . . . and to combine empirical investigation, hypothesis formation and testing, and that resort to science will yield practical applications that will bring progress'.[65] The dominant form of knowledge which was generated during the Cold War is reflected in this realist-positivist orthodoxy which became intertwined with superpower ideology. As Banks observes 'much of the work in international relations was a vested interest of those who advised the foreign policy establishments of the great powers, particularly in the United States'.[66] He further points out that in due course 'many scholars began to see their job as to give advice to government on how to maximise the *values* that represented American interests in world politics: international order and stability, alliance cohesion, counter-insurgency, and the effective use of military force'.[67] What is interesting is that in a crude sort of way a commitment to objective knowledge was underpinned by 'values'. Banks notes that 'these became major concerns in the discipline, but *they are not explanatory theories of how the world as a whole works*; they are merely the perceived policy needs of one status quo actor in a dynamic and complicated system'.[68] Under the pretext of operating on a positivist epistemology seeking, in the words of Morgenthau, 'to bring order and meaning to a mass of phenomena' and thus draw 'conclusions' from the 'empirical realm', realism as described by Banks did not explain how 'the world as a whole' worked. Smith uncovers what in essence is the fundamental paradox of the attempt to create a science of international relations when he suggests that 'lying at the heart of value-neutrality was a very powerful normative project, one every bit as "political" or "biased" as those approaches marginalised and delegitimised in the name of science'.[69] Ethical knowledge was in fact being generated by the political realists. The moral referents were the superpowers themselves and the meta-ethical presuppositions of this knowledge were based on variants of ethical egoism, with its emphasis on the imperatives of self-interest.[70]

The sub-field of peace research and conflict resolution theory were subsumed into this positivistic epistemological matrix. The 1950s saw the emergence of the belief in a 'science of peace'.[71] This school of thought emerged from an anti-metaphysical and anti-idealist stance. Peter Lawler observes that:

> its antecedents can be found in numerous, often obscure, works which celebrated the possibility of a 'science of peace' and the application of mathematical and social scientific techniques to the study of social conflict. The establishment of conflict research in the fifties saw an exponential growth in quantitative, empirical research into war.[72]

This fostered the emergence of a host of 'peace science' methodologies, many of which prevail today. The debate within peace research became 'concerned with methods, with proof, testing, with the structure of theories, and with the quality of explanations that could be regarded as satisfactory in international relations'.[73] Though peace science possessed normative and value-laden presuppositions it tended not to concern itself with understanding the ethical dimensions of its research activities; rather it focused on what could be quantified to the satisfaction of dominant schools of thought in international relations.

Peace research was caught up in this sphere of influence generated by the realist-positivist dominance of international relations, which as stated earlier was intertwined with superpower ideology.[74] In the context of the Cold War rivalry between the USA and USSR and their client states, paradoxically, mechanisms of conflict resolution and the building of peace, such as institutions of the UN, were often employed as strategic foreign policy instruments.[75] The institutions of the UN and regional organisations like the European Community and the Organization of African Unity operated within a power-political framework. A significant number of conflict resolution initiatives were effectuated within a realist framework of international politics.[76] Nation-states were considered to be rational actors pursuing their own self-interests. Zartman and Touval observed that in a Hobbesian international system, third parties or mediators often initiated conflict resolution and peace processes because of their self-interest in securing a particular outcome, thus perpetuating a logic of ethical egoism in peace processes.[77] This provided the mediator with bargaining power and the ability to coerce the parties involved into an agreement. This clearly would not have been in the interests of the parties to the dispute, yet this approach to international conflict resolution was repeatedly utilised during the Cold War and continues to be practised in the post-Cold War world.

What emerges is that there was a dynamic interplay between theory and practice. The central tenets of the positivist doctrine, with their presumption towards the rejection of normative knowledge, permeated the field of international relations and have subsequently influenced peace research. We must question whether this process has contributed to the stagnation and retardation of international relations theory in general and to the moral knowledge of peacebuilding in particular. Under the guise of value-free knowledge the realist-positivist approach asserted epistemological superiority. In contributing towards the development of peacebuilding meta-theory it is important to question the extent to which realism-positivism was aware of its own moral edicts. This exposes realism-positivism as being insufficiently self-reflexive.

NORMATIVE KNOWLEDGE AND NON-COERCIVE APPROACHES TO CONFLICT RESOLUTION AND PEACEBUILDING

The influence of positivism on political realism in turn has exerted an influence on the study of international relations. Michael Banks notes that:

> if we look back at those Cold War decades and examine the way international relations was studied then, especially in Britain and in the United States, three particularly distressing features of it stand out; it was a period of realist dominance, without any liberal balance, and without the refreshment of radical thinking.

In the 1970s, disaffected with this realist dominance and its state-centric assumptions, several scholars in the field began to draw attention to how the actions of actors other than governments influenced international relations. They also began to assess how international relations could be influenced by other motivations besides self-interest and the pursuit of power. They emphasised the role played by transnational processes and liberation movements, and how ethnicity and ideology featured in the global sphere. There was clearly the need for a more expansive theoretical framework predicated on a 'multi-actor analytical scheme'.[78] In the sub-field of peace research and conflict resolution it was possible to discern a normative stance, even though there was no explicit reference to ethics.[79]

BURTONIAN NORMATIVITY IN CONFLICT RESOLUTION APPROACHES

Among the leading critics of realism's epistemological dominance was a group of scholar-practitioners including Adam Curle, Ronald Fisher, Herbert Kelman and John Burton. They adopted different normative foundations to realism and were committed to seeking to understand conflict through an examination of the multiple actors within global society and the possibility for those actors to act as agents of evolutionary transformation.[80] Implicitly they did not accept the view that the status quo was a timeless given and they believed that there was a role for values in informing international relations knowledge and practice.

Burton argued, for example, that it was necessary to establish a theory of international relations based on the vision of a world society in which there were links between the sub-national, national and transnational realms. This in effect questioned the privileged status of states within the international system. The realist approach to resolving conflict placed an emphasis on the state as the key actor. It also assumed that conflicts could only be resolved through the strategic manipulation of parties and the application of threats, and driven by the self-interest of the intervening third party.[81] Burton pointed out that if 'all human relationships could be regulated and controlled by an authoritative third party, then with sufficient courts and alternative means of settlement, and with sufficient means of enforcement, we could be assured of harmonious relationships domestically and internationally'.[82] He argued that 'history shows that this is not the case: *there are situations, both domestic and international, that are not subject to authoritative or coercive settlements*'.[83] Burton went so far as to argue that conflict resolution should be viewed as a political philosophy which rejects value-freedom and emphasises the reduction of injustice and inequality as a means to achieving peace. As far as conflict resolution was concerned, for Burton the element of coercion, advocated by realists, had to be replaced with cooperation. Burton suggested that most conflicts were related to the needs of the parties in dispute. Thus, it was necessary to understand that 'there are such conflicts at all societal levels, that is, situations in which ontological needs of identity and recognition, and associated human development needs, are frustrated'.[84] These conflicts could not be 'contained, controlled, or suppressed' but could only be resolved and prevented by the satisfaction of the parties' needs. Burton believed in a more accommodative approach to conflict resolution. This approach relied on 'altering the attitudes and perceptions' of parties to a conflict so that 'on the basis of this reduced hostility and tension they may be able to come together for serious and productive negotiations'.[85] This position establishes conflict resolution as a normative political philosophy which proceeds on the premise that 'parties can change their goals, and that the importance of one value in terms of other actual or potential values is always, at least theoretically, subject to reassessment'.[86] In such a framework the third party involved in making peace recognises that the parties and their relative coercive capability is not the most important thing; rather it is their ability to reframe their dispute in a way that can mutually satisfy all their needs. Burton's normativity is therefore predicated on challenging the 'predetermined and fixed set of laws' that realists insist define the world we live in.

Burton is unequivocal in his criticism of realism and maintains that his approach is more suited to resolving and sustaining conflict in the long term. Political realism and its coercive approach to resolving disputes has a short-term superficial utility. Burton can be viewed as a contemporary progenitor of a moral and critical theory of conflict resolution. He sees an emancipatory objective in the acquisition of conflict resolution knowledge. As far as a moral epistemology of peace is concerned, there is scope for radicalising and extending the presuppositions which we find in Burton's approach. In particular, there is the possibility of generating further knowledge which has an emancipatory function to reduce injustice and inequality, rather than trying to explain the world as it supposedly is.

CRITICAL THEORY AND REFLEXIVE MORAL INTROSPECTION

The notion of metaethical self-reflection is highly pertinent to a field like peacebuilding, where a healthy dynamic should be encouraged between moral theory and practice. As we saw earlier in this chapter, we can trace the 'culture' of the critique of the growth of knowledge from feminist theoreticians, post-modern and post-structuralist perspectives. The early and late Frankfurt School of critical theory instituted a project that retained the initial concerns of Kant.[87] The term 'critical theory' (*Kritischtheorie*) was used in 1937 by the social philosopher Max Horkheimer in an article he wrote for the journal produced by the Institute for Social Research, originally set up in Frankfurt, Germany in 1923.[88] Critical theory sought to question reason's claim to validity and challenge its assumptions. It strived to do this through the critical and moral reconstruction of the Enlightenment objectives, which critical theory considers to be an unfinished but perpetual project. Thomas

McCarthy observes that critical theory 'called for a continuation-through transformation of the critique of reason, a materialist account of its nature, conditions and limits'.[89] Critical theory perceived a moral function in keeping in check any move towards a dogmatism that takes as given the ideas and practices which society instils in its members. It acknowledges that 'causal reasoning itself is blind to its conditioning, and as a consequence all the more subjective, lacking as it does a *reflexive self-comprehension*'.[90]

CRITICAL THEORY AND PEACE RESEARCH

Critical theory was articulated and applied to international relations in the 1980s. Central to its critique was the view that positivist methodology imported from the natural sciences lacked sufficient self-examination. As a consequence it was incapable of maintaining a check on the validity of the dogmatic assertions that it produced, such as that the world was defined exclusively by state actors and the quest for power based on the rational self-interested agent model. Robert Cox observed that it was necessary to guard against such dogmatic theoretical assertions because ultimately 'all theory is for someone and for some purpose'.[91] Critical international relations theory advocated an epistemology whose purpose was not merely to observe and document so-called irregularities in the empirical realm, but also sought to do so with the intention of exploring the possibility of reducing injustices between the actors in the global sphere.[92] Within this critical movement in international relations there was a plethora of contending attitudes and views. Nick Rengger notes that within critical theory 'there is a major, perhaps fatal, disagreement over the nature of the project, the kind of conclusions sought and therefore the aim of the enquiry called international political theory'.[93] For Andrew Linklater, critical theory's function was to 'invite observers to reflect upon the social construction and effects of knowledge and to consider how claims about neutrality can conceal the role knowledge plays in reproducing unsatisfactory social arrangements'.[94] For Chris Brown, critical theory seeks to contribute towards bringing about a metaethical and metatheoretical transition which attempts to ensure that 'international relations theory is no longer confined to its own, self-imposed ghetto'.[95]

The way international relations and a sub-field like peace research are studied is very much a product of the competing theories of knowledge that investigate them. Kant's work on perpetual peace suggested that it was necessary to conceive of a project for peace based on a propensity for moral criticism which challenged the dogmatic assertion about the timeless regularity and inevitability of war. Kant in a sense was in this way an early advocate of the ethics of peacebuilding. In effect, the underlying theme that this chapter seeks to emphasise is that a peace researcher requires 'an unending willingness to shift one's point of view, to take on other potential points of departure in thinking about the world and one's place and function in it, a willing commitment always to consider the otherwise'.[96] Linklater argues that a critical theory of international relations is premised on developing models for 'theory/ practice relationships' that endeavour to bring about the widening of the circle of community to include those who are currently separated by states. He notes that it also strives to improve social and political relations within the boundaries of existing societies.[97] The fact that this project is concomitant with peacebuilding suggests that critical theory and peace research are effectively striving to achieve the same objectives. A critical moral epistemology of peacebuilding should endeavour to bring about an understanding of the world that is simultaneously engaged in the process of envisioning alternative futures in which an emphasis is placed on the reduction and eradication of injustice which foments conflict. If there is a field that needs to be cognisant of the social construction and effects of knowledge and consider how knowledge plays a role in reproducing unsatisfactory social arrangements, it is the field of peace research. If peace research does not generate ideas for informing effective peacebuilding processes then it betrays its primary objective. Peace research does not directly resolve conflict, but it does provide legitimacy to the attitudes and views of researchers and peacebuilding practitioners as well as policy- and decision-makers. The relationship between knowledge and action is mutually reinforcing, which is why it is necessary to ensure that moral introspection and self-reflexivity prevail in peacebuilding. The willingness of parties to engage in a peacebuilding process is related to the perceived moral legitimacy of the process. By extension, it is paramount that once parties are engaged in a peacebuilding process, mechanisms and institutions have to be ethically oriented to work towards genuinely fostering peace. This means that the goal of ensuring that peacebuilding processes, mechanisms and institutions can achieve their objectives has to begin at the level of developing moral knowledge to guide them. Reid and Yanarella observe that in order for peace research to make a contribution to practice it is essential for it to be self-referential and self-questioning.[98]

MORAL KNOWLEDGE AND VALUE-ASSUMPTIONS ABOUT THE POSITIVE NATURE OF PEACE

Dower addresses the question as to whether peace itself is an ethical concept. He notes that there are in fact ethical norms that are internal to its pursuit and concludes that 'I take for reasons which will become apparent that peace is a positive value and war is a negative value.'[99] He does acknowledge, however, 'that this is not an uncontentious claim'.[100] The question then arises as to whether, if we accept a priori the positive value of peace, we need to demonstrate that this value can be grounded in a normative body of knowledge. Dower also suggests that 'there is a sense in which peace is necessarily the preferred state in most normal situations' and that 'peace is therefore not just something we all want. It is something which we all have reason to work for'. If there is this 'sense' that peace is a preferred state and that it is something that 'we all have reason to work for' then is it equally important to create an epistemological framework to justify these sentiments? This chapter sought to outline and discuss such an epistemological framework. It is important to demonstrate that our sentiments about the positive value of peace can equally emerge from a particular body of moral knowledge that is similarly imbued with normative prescriptions and value-assumptions about the ethical norms that are already implicit in researching peace in order to promote it more effectively. The objective of this chapter was to illustrate that there is a body of moral knowledge that can be drawn upon to explicitly and prescriptively advocate for the promotion of peacebuilding. This in effect ultimately leads us to the normative conclusion that is being sought in this chapter. This can then provide the reader with a basis upon which to make the necessary link between the deliberation and discussion in this chapter and the practical importance of accepting the value of peace and the conceptual virtues that are necessary to implementing peacebuilding on the ground.

CONCLUSION

This chapter developed an analysis of moral knowledge as it pertains to international relations and peace research. It explored the possibility of advancing a moral epistemology of peacebuilding knowledge. The chapter argued that in a very practical sense effective peacebuilding requires practitioners, parties and analysts to adopt a conceptual framework that is conducive towards promoting positive peace. Ultimately, these actors have to accept certain ethical values even though they have different theoretical moral positions. By acknowledging that we need to accept that peacebuilding is an activity that requires human agency, the chapter then assessed what theoretical perspectives should inform it. It also explored how positivism has impacted on peace research and by extension on the production of peacebuilding knowledge. It analysed whether peacebuilding should be informed by ethical egoism. Should peacebuilding proceed on the basis of how it impacts upon the greatest number of people? Third parties often initiate conflict resolution and peace processes because of their self-interest in securing a particular outcome, thus perpetuating a logic of ethical egoism in peace processes.

This chapter argued that there should be a much more profound moral basis for undertaking peacebuilding. It examined the theoretical perspectives that could inform the activity of peacebuilding and assessed the role of critical theory in creating the space for theoretical reflection on the development of moral knowledge. It also highlighted the criticisms of this approach articulated by various schools of thought, including the anti-foundationalist and post-structuralist critiques of knowledge.

This chapter also assessed whether the production of knowledge is gender biased, which would also imply that the current repertoire of peacebuilding knowledge is gender biased. It explored theoretical perspectives that argue for the importance of ensuring gender mainstreaming in the production of moral and peacebuilding knowledge.

Ultimately, this chapter emphasised the importance of recognising that critical international relations theory advocates an epistemology whose purpose is not merely to observe and document so-called irregularities in the empirical realm, but one that seeks to do so with the intention of exploring the possibility of reducing injustices between the actors in the global sphere. At the heart of this argument is whether we do in fact need to explicitly make the case for creating a body of moral knowledge that is imbued with a set of values which can serve the function of orienting human behaviour to achieve the desired goal of peace. This is the normative conclusion which this chapter sought to articulate. In effect it attempted to provide a philosophical understanding of the intrinsic ethical value of researching peacebuilding in order to determine the best way to implement it effectively.

NOTES

1. Steven Smith, 'The Forty Years' Detour: The Resurgence of Normative Theory in International Relations', *Millennium: Journal of International Studies*, vol. 21, no. 3, 1992, p. 489.
2. Jenny Teichman, *Social Ethics* (Oxford: Blackwell, 1996), p. 3.

3. Ibid.

4. Jonathan Dancy, 'Moral Epistemology', in Jonathan Dancy and Ernest Sosa (eds), *A Companion to Epistemology* (Oxford: Blackwell, 1992), pp. 286–90.

5. Nigel Dower, *World Ethics: A New Agenda*, 2nd edition (Edinburgh: Edinburgh University Press, 2007), p. 134.

6. Iain Atack, *The Ethics of Peace and War* (Edinburgh: Edinburgh University Press, 2005), p. 243.

7. For a more detailed treatment, see P. Guyer, 'Thought and Being: Hegel's Critique of Kant's Theoretical Philosophy', in F. Beiser (ed.), *The Cambridge Companion to Hegel* (Cambridge: Cambridge University Press, 1993), pp. 171–210. See also Jürgen Habermas, 'Hegel's Critique of Kant: Radicalisation or Abolition of the Theory of Knowledge', in Jürgen Habermas, *Knowledge and Human Interest* (Cambridge: Polity Press, 1987), pp. 7–24.

8. For general discussions on these three thinkers, see C. Guignon, *Heidegger and the Problem of Knowledge* (Indianapolis: Hackett, 1983); M. Clark, *Nietzsche on Truth and Philosophy* (Cambridge: Cambridge University Press, 1990); and Ludwig Wittgenstein, 'A Lecture on Ethics', in Stephen Darwall, Allan Gibbard and Peter Railton (eds), *Moral Discourse and Practice: Some Philosophical Approaches* (Oxford: Oxford University Press, 1997), pp. 65–70.

9. C. Guignon, 'Martin Heidegger', in Dancy and Sosa, *A Companion to Epistemology*, p. 171.

10. Friedrich Nietzsche, *The Gay Science*, trans. W. Kaufmans (New York: Random House, 1974), p. 354.

11. A. Nehamas, 'Friedrich Nietzsche', in Dancy and Sosa, *A Companion to Epistemology*, p. 304.

12. Wittgenstein, 'A Lecture on Ethics', p. 70.

13. Such views have been reformulated and rearticulated in Richard Rorty, *Philosophy and the Mirror of Nature* (Princeton: Princeton University Press, 1979) and Paul Feyerabend, *Against Method* (London: Verso, 1993).

14. For an extensive discussion, see E. Matthews, *Twentieth-Century French Philosophy* (Oxford: Oxford University Press, 1996), p. 154.

15. For a comprehensive treatment of this term see Jacques Derrida, *Of Grammatology*, trans. G. Chakravorty Spivak (Baltimore: Johns Hopkins University Press, 1976).

16. Raymond Morrow, *Critical Theory and Methodology* (London: Sage, 1994), p. 234.

17. Matthews, *Twentieth-Century French Philosophy*, p. 168.

18. See Michel Foucault, *The Archaeology of Knowledge*, trans. A. Sheridan Smith (New York: Pantheon Books, 1972); see also D. Ingram, 'Foucault and Habermas on the Subject of Reason', in G. Gutting (ed.), *The Cambridge Companion to Foucault* (Cambridge: Cambridge University Press, 1994), pp. 215–61.

19. Foucault, *The Archaeology of Knowledge*, p. 117.

20. Matthews, *Twentieth-Century French Philosophy*, p. 152.
21. Michel Foucault, 'What is Enlightenment?', in Paul Rainbow (ed.), *The Foucault Reader* (Harmondsworth: Penguin, 1986), p. 46.
22. Thomas McCarthy, 'The Idea of Critical Theory', in S. Benhabib, W. Bonss and J. McCole (eds), *On Max Horkheimer: New Perspectives* (Cambridge, MA: MIT Press, 1993), p. 133 (emphasis added).
23. Ibid.
24. Ibid (emphasis added).
25. Ibid.
26. H. Seigel, 'Relativism', in Dancy and Sosa, *A Companion to Epistemology*, p. 429 (emphasis added).
27. Ibid.
28. G. Pavlich, 'Contemplating a Postmodern Sociology: Genealogy, Limits and Critique', *The Sociological Review*, vol. 43, no. 3, August 1995, p. 563.
29. For a general discussion on critical theory and the Frankfurt School, see Max Horkheimer, *Critical Theory: Selected Essays* (New York: Seabury Press, 1972) and R. Wiggershaus, *The Frankfurt School* (Cambridge: Polity Press, 1994).
30. McCarthy, 'The Idea of Critical Theory', p. 134.
31. Ibid., p. 135.
32. For the various debates, see S. Harding and M. B. Hiutikka (eds), *Discovering Reality: Feminist Perspectives on Epistemology, Methodology and Philosophy of Science* (Dordrecht: Reidel, 1983).
33. Virginia Held, 'Feminist Transformations of Moral Theory', *Philosophy and Phenomenological Research*, vol. 50, Autumn 1990, pp. 321–44.
34. Genevieve Lloyd, *The Man of Reason: 'Male' and 'Female' in Western Philosophy* (Minneapolis: University of Minnesota Press, 1984), p. 104.
35. Held, 'Feminist Transformations of Moral Theory', p. 321.
36. Ibid.
37. L. Code, 'Feminist Epistemology', in Dancy and Sosa, *A Companion to Epistemology*, p. 138.
38. For a general debate on the various feminist epistemologies, see S. Harding, *Whose Science? Whose Knowledge? Thinking from Women's Lives* (Milton Keynes: Open University Press, 1991).
39. Kimberly Hutchings, *Kant, Critique and Politics* (London: Routledge, 1995) p. 168.
40. A comprehensive discussion is beyond the scope of this chapter. For a more detailed treatment, see S. Brown, 'Feminism, International Theory and International Relations of Gender Inequality', *Millennium: Journal of International Studies*, vol. 17, no. 3, Winter 1988, pp. 461–75.
41. Sterba, *Morality in Practice*, p. 5.
42. Ibid.
43. Teichman, *Social Ethics*, p. 7.
44. For a general discussion, see Thomas Nagel, *The Possibility of Altruism* (Oxford: Clarendon Press, 1970).

45. Teichman, *Social Ethics*, pp. 8–9.
46. B. Potter, 'David Davies: A Hunter for Peace', *Review of International Studies*, vol. 15, January 1989, pp. 27–36.
47. Michael Banks, 'The International Relations Discipline: Asset or Liability for Conflict Resolution?', in John Burton and Francis Dukes (eds), *Conflict: Readings in Management and Resolution* (London: Macmillan, 1990), pp. 51–70.
48. For discussion of positivism, see in chronological order Karl Popper, *The Poverty of Historicism* (London: Routledge and Kegan Paul, 1961); Jürgen Habermas, *Knowledge and Human Interests* (Cambridge: Polity Press, 1987); Jim George, *Discourses of Global Politics: A Critical (Re)Introduction to International Relations* (Boulder, CO: Lynne Rienner, 1994); Mark Neufeld, *The Restructuring of International Relations Theory* (Cambridge: Cambridge University Press, 1995); and Steve Smith, Ken Booth and Maria Zalewski (eds), *International Theory: Positivism and Beyond* (Cambridge: Cambridge University Press, 1996).
49. Neufeld, *The Restructuring of International Relations Theory*, p. 33.
50. It is argued elsewhere that it is possible to identify twelve varieties of positivism. However, for the purpose of this chapter these can be reduced to early and contemporary formulations. See P. Halfpenny, *Positivism and Sociology: Explaining Social Life* (London: Allen Unwin, 1982) and William Outhwaite, *New Philosophies of Social Science: Realism, Hermeneutics and Critical Theory* (London: Macmillan, 1987).
51. Auguste Comte, *A Discourse on the Positive Spirit*, trans. E. S. Beesly (London: William Reeves, 1903), p. 25.
52. Ibid., pp. 25–6.
53. Neufeld, *The Restructuring of International Relations Theory*, p. 25.
54. B. Stroud, 'Logical Positivism', in Dancy and Sosa, *A Companion to Epistemology* (Oxford: Blackwell, 1994), p. 262.
55. Ibid.
56. Ibid., p. 263.
57. Ibid., p. 263.
58. Banks, 'The International Relations Discipline: Asset or Liability for Conflict Resolution?', p. 57.
59. Ibid.
60. Ibid., p. 58.
61. Hans Morgenthau, 'The Nature and Limits of a Theory of International Relations', in W. Fox (ed.), *Theoretical Aspects of International Relations* (Notre Dame: University of Notre Dame, 1959), pp. 19–20 (emphasis added).
62. Hans Morgenthau, *Politics Among Nations: The Struggle for Power and Peace*, sixth edition (London: McGraw-Hill, 1985), p. 3 (emphasis added).
63. Smith, 'The Forty Years' Detour: The Resurgence of Normative Theory in International Relations', p. 489.
64. C. W. Kegley and E. R. Wittkopf, *World Politics: Trends and Transformations*, fifth edition (New York: St. Martin's Press, 1995), p. 26.

65. Stanley Hoffman, 'An American Social Science: International Relations', *Daedalus*, vol. 106, no. 3, 1977, p. 59.
66. Banks, 'The International Relations Discipline: Asset or Liability for Conflict Resolution?', p. 58.
67. Ibid.
68. Ibid.
69. Smith, 'The Forty Years' Detour: The Resurgence of Normative Theory in International Relations', p. 490.
70. For responses to the ethics of realism, see Alistair Murray, *Restructuring Realism: Between Power Politics and Cosmopolitan Ethics* (Keele: Keele University Press, 1997); and Roger Spegele, *Political Realism in International Theory* (Cambridge: Cambridge University Press, 1996).
71. For a general discussion, see Quincy Wright, *A Study of War* (Chicago, IL: University of Chicago Press, 1942) and T. Lentz, *Towards a Science of Peace: Turning Points in Human Destiny* (New York: Bookman Associates, 1955).
72. Peter Lawler, 'Peace Research and International Relations: From Divergence to Convergence', *Millennium: Journal of International Studies*, vol. 15, no. 3, 1986, p. 371.
73. Banks, 'The International Relations Discipline: Asset or Liability for Conflict Resolution?', p. 59.
74. John Vasquez, *The Power of Politics: A Critique* (London: Frances Pinter, 1983).
75. S. Touval, 'The Superpowers as Mediators', in Jacob Bercovitch and Jeffrey Rubin (eds), *Mediation in International Relations: Multiple Approaches to Conflict Management* (London: Macmillan, 1992), p. 232.
76. Christopher Mitchell, 'The Motives for Mediation', in Christopher Mitchell and Keith Webb (eds), *New Approaches to International Mediation* (Westport, CT: Greenwood, 1988), pp. 29–51.
77. William Zartman and Saadia Touval, 'International Mediation: Conflict Resolution and Power Politics', *Journal of Social Issues*, vol. 41, no. 2, 1985, p. 27.
78. See, for example, Robert Keohane and Joseph Nye, *Power and Interdependence* (Boston: Little, Brown & Co., 1977) and R. Mansbach, Y. Ferguson and D. Lampert, *The Web of World Politics: Nonstate Actors in the Global System* (Englewood Cliffs, NJ: Prentice-Hall, 1976).
79. James Laue and G. Cormick, 'The Ethics of Intervention in Community Disputes', in G. Bermant et al. (eds), *The Ethics of Social Intervention* (Washington, DC: Halstead Press, 1978).
80. John Burton, *World Society* (Cambridge: Cambridge University Press, 1972).
81. John Burton, 'Conflict Resolution as a Political Philosophy', in D. Sandole and Herve van der Merwe (eds), *Conflict Resolution Theory and Practice: Integration and Application* (Manchester: Manchester University Press, 1993), p. 55.

82. Ibid.

83. Ibid (emphasis added).

84. Ibid.

85. R. Yalem, 'Controlled Communication and Conflict Resolution', *Journal of Peace Research*, vol. III, 1971, p. 266.

86. A. J. R. Groom, 'Paradigms in Conflict: The Strategist, the Conflict Researcher and the Peace Researcher', in John Burton and Frank Dukes (eds), *Conflict: Readings in Management and Resolution* (New York: St. Martin's Press, 1990), p. 80.

87. This does not represent an exhaustive array of the branches of contemporary criticisms of knowledge; see, among others, Hans Georg Gadamer, *Truth and Method* (New York: Seabury, 1975); Richard Rorty, *Philosophy and the Mirror of Nature* (Princeton: Princeton University Press, 1979); and Paul Feyerabend, *Against Method*, third edition (London: Verso, 1993).

88. See Max Horkheimer, 'Traditional and Critical Theory', trans. M. O'Connell, in Max Horkheimer, *Critical Theory: Selected Essays* (New York: Seabury Press, 1972), pp. 188–243; see also a comprehensive treatise on the school in R. Wiggershaus, *The Frankfurt School* (Cambridge: Polity Press, 1994).

89. Thomas McCarthy, 'The Idea of Critical Theory', in S. Benhabib, W. Bonss and J. McCole (eds), *On Max Horkheimer: New Perspectives* (Cambridge, MA: MIT Press, 1993), p. 128.

90. Jay Bernstein, *Recovering Ethical Life: Jürgen Habermas and the Future of Critical Theory* (London and New York: Routledge, 1995), p. 14.

91. Robert Cox, 'Social Forces, States and World Orders: Beyond International Relations Theory', *Millennium: Journal of International Studies*, vol. 10, Summer 1981, p. 128.

92. See Mark Hoffman, 'Critical Theory and the Inter-Paradigm Debate', *Millennium: Journal of International Studies*, vol. 16, no. 2, 1987, pp. 231–49; Jim George and David Campbell, 'Patterns of Dissent and the Celebration of Difference: Critical Theory and International Relations', *International Studies Quarterly*, vol. 34, no. 3, 1990; and Andrew Linklater, *Beyond Realism and Marxism: Critical Theory and International Relations* (London: Macmillan, 1990).

93. Nick Rengger, 'Going Critical? A Response to Hoffman', *Millennium: Journal of International Studies*, vol. 17, no. 1, 1988, p. 84.

94. Andrew Linklater, 'The Achievements of Critical Theory', in Steven Smith, Ken Booth and Maria Zalewski (eds), *International Theory: Postivism and Beyond* (Cambridge: Cambridge University Press, 1996), p. 279.

95. Chris Brown, 'Turtles All the Way Down: Anti-Foundationalism, Critical Theory and International Relations', *Millennium: Journal of International Studies*, vol. 23, no. 2, 1994, p. 213.

96. Mark Franke, 'Immanuel Kant and the (Im)Possibility of International Relations Theory', *Alternatives*, vol. 20, no. 3, July–September 1995, p. 312.

97. Andrew Linklater, 'The Problem of Community in International Relations', *Alternatives*, vol. XV, 1990, p. 151.

98. H. Reid and E. Yanarella, 'Towards a Critical Theory of Peace Research in the United States: The Search for an "Intelligible Core"', *Journal of Peace Research*, vol. XIII, no. 4, 1976, p. 315.

99. Dower, *World Ethics: A New Agenda*, p. 142.

100. Ibid.

CHAPTER 3

THE MORALITY OF CONFLICT RESOLUTION: A CRITIQUE OF THE STATE SYSTEM AND ITS MANAGEMENT OF SUB-NATIONAL CONFLICT

INTRODUCTION

This chapter will revisit some of the issues in international relations relating to the morality of citizens, states and institutions. The morality of conflict resolution will be cast as an ethical imperative for all citizens, states and institutions whatever their geopolitical location. It explores the phenomenon of sub-national conflict and makes the argument that the current international system is ill-equipped in terms of processes, institutions and mechanisms to address this type of conflict. It also offers a typology of sub-national conflicts. The challenges of contemporary macro-level peacebuilding are complicated by the problem of how nation-states are invariably pitted against sub-national polities. Northern Somalia, or Somaliland, has asked the African Union (AU) to recognise its independence. South Ossetia and Abkhazia in Georgia have asked the United Nations (UN), Russia, the European Union (EU) and the Organization for Security and Cooperation in Europe (OSCE) to recognise their independence.[1] The international system still has an inherent bias towards the state and therefore there are no effective processes and institutions to enable sub-national polities to seek recourse to their grievances, which might explain the difficulties of consolidating peace. There is, however, tension within the sub-national groups between those who wish to form a new state and those who merely wish to be a properly recognised ethnos within the state. This chapter will also seek to address this issue and will argue that world citizenship in its embryonic form can best be articulated by a genuine concern for the welfare of others and a commitment to promoting the conditions for positive global peace. This chapter ultimately makes a trans-boundary ethical responsibility and universal duty of all to promote macro-level global peacebuilding.

HOW DOES CONFLICT RESOLUTION CONTRIBUTE TO PEACEBUILDING?

Effective peacebuilding in practice is successful conflict resolution. If there is a need to build peace then the resolution of conflict is at the heart of such an endeavour. Efforts to resolve conflict in the last four decades have taken on a more prominent place in international relations. Hurst Hannum suggests that 'ethnic conflict has replaced the Cold War as the primary interest of political and military theorists, and even conflicts that may be primarily political and economic in nature are frequently given an ethnic cast'.[2] Contemporary conflicts, however, cannot be delinked from the legacy of the Cold War. A significant number of these conflicts have their roots in this era or were exacerbated by the superpower geostrategic struggle for power and dominion. Specifically, the conflicts in Afghanistan, Bosnia and Herzegovina, Chechnya, Colombia, the Democratic Republic of Congo (DRC), Ethiopia/Eritrea, Kosovo, Lebanon, Nagorno-Karabakh, North Korea, Somalia and Sri Lanka were effectively part and parcel of a complex of 'proxy' wars fought by the superpowers and their client states in these countries. The mechanisms of conflict resolution were also influenced by the superpower politics of this era. Jaine Leatherman and Raimo Vayrynen observed that during 'the Cold War the strategies to manage and resolve inter-state conflicts relied, if feasible, on direct political negotiations and arms control between the great powers'.[3] As a consequence these mechanisms had a strong inter-state bias. This meant that trying to build peace in disputes involving non-state actors was more or less confined to, and to some extent constrained by, these statist institutions. The United Nations (UN), and other regional organisations like the European Economic Community (EEC – the present-day European Union), the Organization of African Unity (OAU – the present-day African Union), the Organization of American States (OAS) and the Association of South East Asian Nations (ASEAN), were generated by states and not ethnic groups; thus they had, and still have, limitations as far as relating to the concerns of sub-national groups[4] who are the primary actors in contemporary conflicts.[5]

The withering away of the Cold War and simultaneous transformation of political communities around the world presents new challenges as far as conflict resolution and peacebuilding are concerned. The emerging geopolitical terrain has increased the number of challenges to the legitimacy of the nation-state as the exclusive unit of political community. The creation of the EU and the AU have been experiments in relocating sovereignty upwards, whilst the fragmentation of erstwhile states like Somalia and Yugoslavia has illustrated that there are pressures inherent in the state construct to devolve power down to sub-national levels. At the heart of peacebuilding is the importance of ensuring that sub-national groupings and the nation-state are able to renegotiate the existing principles of association and establish more equitable norms and structures of political coexistence.[6]

At the heart of building peace therefore is the importance of effective conflict resolution strategies. Clearly, to be effective these strategies have to be informed by the morality of inclusion. The question then arises: whose responsibility is it to ensure that conflict resolution processes are ethically informed? Historically, instances in which states were in conflict with sub-national groups were viewed by the international system as internal or domestic matters to be left to the discretion of the state to resolve. In the current situation whereby governments and non-state groups are in conflict with each other, the priorities for conflict resolution and peacebuilding can no longer be defined in terms of the interests of nation-states.[7] On the increasing incidence of sub-national contestations of state power and the ability of existing institutions to address these concerns, David Carment notes that 'lagging behind this emergent reality are the world's mechanisms for the prevention of internal conflicts and the peaceful settlement of disputes within states'.[8] This chapter will argue that statist organisations like the UN, EU and AU need to rethink their relationship with sub-national groups. In the case of the UN, for example, it 'has confronted a paradox: how does the institution maintain the integrity of the state system from which its political existence is derived and also promote and protect the interests of minorities'?[9] Increasingly the focus needs to be on how to establish and promote a framework for conflict resolution which ensures that the interests of sub-national actors and nation-states are addressed. Such a framework is of necessity imbued by a global ethic of responsibility. Contemporary conflicts now have regional and international dimensions, meaning that their resolution is clearly a global responsibility. This issue will be addressed further later in this chapter.

SUB-NATIONAL CONFLICT FORMATION

Before addressing this question in depth it is worthwhile spelling out the nature of the conflicts that we are discussing. This is vital in order to draw out the challenges that peacebuilding initiatives are faced with. The fragmentation of former nation-states that we have witnessed in recent history has raised important questions about the assumptions inherent in the classical political realist tradition. The very term nation-state initially meant that the state's legitimacy was derived from the nation(s) or people composing it. The nation-state, in a sense, sought to express an aspect of citizenship entitlement to a unique territorial and political unit.[10] Today, less than 10 per cent of the world's countries are ethnically homogenous and only half the remainder contain more than a 75–per cent ethnic majority. The imperial break-up after the First World War, which became accentuated after the Second World War and the end of the Cold War, ensured the increasing permanence of the multi-national state in contemporary global society. Nation-states were initially attempts to force-fit governance and territory to outdated notions of national identity. As a consequence most of the emergent conflicts involve sub-national groups whose territorial ambitions and aspirations for legitimate governance are at odds with the existing state border or terms of rule.

CONCEPTUALISING ETHNICITY

The challenge of building peace by addressing the sub-national challenge is problematic from the outset in that it has at its core the essentially contested concept of 'ethnicity'. The term ethnic is utilised in this book as a convenient shorthand and nomenclature for ethnic, religious, linguistic and cultural associations. Michael Brown points out that 'the term "ethnic conflict" is often used loosely, to describe a wide range of intrastate conflicts that are not, in fact, ethnic in character'.[11] Nevertheless, it is necessary for the ensuing discussion to attempt to invoke a working definition of what a sub-national ethnic entity might entail.

Debates have raged as to whether these 'ethnic' divisions are timeless sociological givens or whether they are to some extent constructed. Anthony Richmond suggests that essentially there are two views concerning the fundamental nature of ethnicity:

one emphasises the ascriptive, or primordial, nature of ethnic group membership and the importance of early socialisation and primary group membership. The other insists that ethnicity is situationally defined, that ethnic group boundaries are malleable and permeable, and that ethnicity may be acquired or divested at will.[12]

Primordialism views ethnicity as a thing-in-itself. Anthony Smith describes an ethnic community or an *ethnie* as 'a named human population with a myth of common ancestry, shared memories, and cultural elements; a link with a historic territory or homeland; and a measure of solidarity'.[13] Smith argues that a distinction must be made between ethnic categories and ethnic communities. The former are characterised by external or objective cultural criteria such as customs, language and religion. Several thousand of these exist around the world. The latter, in a sense, emerge from the ethnic categories and by possessing or adopting the characteristics of a community (for example a distinct name, a shared ancestral myth, an ethno-history or a link with a territorial homeland) they take on an added aura of collectivity and identify themselves as ethnic communities.[14]

In an appraisal of the merits and demerits of these attempts to capture the fundamental nature of ethnicity Smith argues that they each in their own way are victim to conceptual limitations.[15] For instance, the primordialist position makes the assumption that human beings are differentiated by ethnic origins and cultures and then makes an attempt to explain these assumptions without acknowledging that there is no basis for such an assumption in the first place. In Smith's view primordialism 'fails to explain why particular ethnic communities emerge, change and dissolve, or why so many people chose to emigrate and assimilate to other ethnies'.[16] In addition, he further points out that it cannot 'explain why in some cases we witness a fierce xenophobic ethnic nationalism, and in others a more tolerant, multicultural national identity'.[17] In a similar vein the post-structuralist interpretation of the fundamental nature of ethnicity, according to Smith, 'tends to exaggerate the ability of elites to manipulate the masses and fails to explain why millions of people may be prepared to die for a cultural artefact'.[18] On the other hand, instrumentalism 'fails to explain why ethnic conflicts are so often intense and unpredictable, and why the "masses" should so readily respond to the call of ethnic origin and culture . . . and . . . be ready to lay down their lives for their nations'.[19] The most extreme form of a manifestation of this phenomenon was the Rwanda genocide of 1994. These divergent viewpoints make a useful contribution towards enhancing our conceptual efforts to come to terms with the complex phenomenon of ethnicity.

POLITICISED ETHNICITY

Despite this conceptual divergence there is more of a consensus on the view that whether or not ethnicity is pre-given or whether it is manufactured, it nevertheless serves as a powerful tool for mobilising human collectives. Charles Tilly proposes that 'ethnic groups serve as a basis for mobilisation and collective action when the actions of outsiders either threaten to exclude them from their share of collectively-controlled opportunities'.[20] Echoing this view, Immanuel Wallerstein has suggested that 'ethnic consciousness is eternally latent everywhere. But it is only realised when groups feel that it is an opportune moment politically to overcome longstanding denial of privilege'.[21] In an attempt to account for the mass participation in the Rwandan genocide, Ravi Bhavnani undertook a study into 'the emergence of ethnic norms – rules instituted and enforced of its members toward rivals'.[22] Thus, paradoxically, predatory and overbearing states rather than strengthening and consolidating their authority on the ethnic nations within them, tend to foment resistance against such authoritarianism. This predicament plants the seeds of 'unjust' political practices which in turn impinge on the perceived survival, by ethnic groups, of their socio-economic and cultural life. As Stavehagen surmises, 'numerous ethnic conflicts occur because the homogenising, integrating model of the nation-state, expressed in official ideologies, government policies of various sorts, dominant social attitudes and political behaviour, enter into contradiction with the ethnic and social identity of subordinate groups'.[23] Thus, understanding the nature of the challenge to redress this situation is vital to implementing effective peacebuilding. Stavehagen also notes that 'when the dominant nation-state ideology is incapable of accommodating cultural and ethnic diversity, the likelihood of protracted ethnic conflict increases. Cultural genocide or ethnocide, which frequently accompany such conflicts, are common occurrences in many parts of the world'.[24] Effective peacebuilding has to be morally underpinned by inclusive political and cultural accommodation and economic distributive justice.

TYPOLOGY OF SUB-NATIONAL GROUPS

Even though the phenomenon of intra-state conflicts has been a dominant feature of international relations since the end of the Cold War, the international community seems to have been caught off-guard by the proliferation of sub-national ethnic claims. In the intervening period, in Africa alone sub-national forces have since come to power in

Uganda, Ethiopia, Eritrea, Rwanda and the DRC. In Asia, sub-national groups have been contesting the legitimacy of the state in Kyrgyzstan, Tajikstan, Indonesia, Kashmir (India and Pakistan) and Nepal. In Latin America, sub-national challenges to the state are evident in Colombia and Ecuador. In the Middle East, sub-national contestation has persisted between Israel and the Occupied Territories as well as in Algeria, and currently in Lebanon. Europe is not immune to this phenomenon and sub-national claims are still being made in Spain's Basque country and in Cyprus.

Therefore, in all parts of the globe authoritarian and highly centralised, and often ethnicised, state regimes are finding it increasingly difficult to contain the claims for legitimacy, participation and cultural and economic security by the minority ethnic groups within their jurisdiction. Ted Gurr's *Minorities at Risk Project*,[25] a study of ethnic groups who as targets of discrimination, by the state or other ethnic groups, have organised to take political and/or military action to promote and defend their interests, has identified 233 communal groups. These are 'groups that were targets of discrimination or were organised for political assertiveness or both'.[26] However, Gurr is quick to make the point that 'these 233 politicised communal groups vary so widely in their defining traits, political status, and aspirations that it is useful to make some systematic distinctions among them'.[27] He makes the distinction between *national peoples* and *minority peoples*, the former being 'regionally concentrated groups that have lost their autonomy to expansionist states but still preserve some of their cultural and linguistic distinctiveness and want to protect or re-establish some degree of politically separate existence'.[28] Minority peoples, however, 'have a defined socio-economic or political status within a larger society – based on some combination of their ethnicity, immigrant origin, economic roles, and religion – and are concerned about protecting or improving their status. Gurr further suggests that 'national peoples seek separation or autonomy from the states that rule them; minority people seek greater access or control'.[29] Gurr goes on to propose that these groups include eighty-one *ethnonationalists*, relatively large and regionally concentrated national peoples who had a history of political autonomy and who have pursued separatist objectives at some time during the last half-century. These include, for example, the Quebecois, colonised by the British, the Karen of Burma, the East Timorese in Indonesia and the Kurds in Iran, Iraq and Turkey. Eighty-three *indigenous peoples* are also, according to Gurr, national peoples. They include Native Americans, Australian Aborigines and the Khoisan of Southern Africa. They tend to possess some ethno-nationalistic attributes but are usually distinct in that they are the conquered descendants of the original inhabitants of a region who tend to have cultures that differ significantly from the dominant groups or the state.

Minority peoples can also be further sub-divided into forty-five *ethno-classes* who tend to be 'ethnically or culturally distinct peoples usually descended from slaves or immigrants, with special economic roles, usually of low status'.[30] Notable groups include the Muslim minority in France, the Turkish in Germany and 'people of colour' in Britain and the United States. They typically demand more equitable treatment. Forty-nine *militant sects* also fall under the rubric of minority peoples and tend to be defined wholly or substantially by their religious beliefs, which in turn serves as the focal point of the politicisation of their cause against an authoritarian state regime. Examples of these polities include Arab citizens in Israel, Muslim minorities in the successor states of the former Soviet Union, Catholics in Northern Ireland and Kashmiris and Sikhs in India. Gurr's typology concludes with minority peoples who he refers to as *communal contenders*. Numbering sixty-six, these groups tend to be based on shared cultural, linguistic or geographical origins. Thus, identity is situated in 'tribes or clans', all of them vying for state power. Political power in the centre foments intense competition between these communal groups. Power tends to be exercised through intergroup coalitions which are 'usually dominated by a powerful minority that uses a mix of concessions, cooptation, and repression to maintain its leading role'.[31] The failure of power sharing among communal contenders has led to a spate of violent conflicts that we are witnessing around the world.

THE 'ETHNICISATION' OF INTERNATIONAL RELATIONS

Whether or not we concur with Gurr's typology of sub-national disputants it is worthwhile to note that the common theme that flows through these different categories is the centrality of the state apparatus, and its instruments of power, as a focal point for dispute. This tends to be based upon demands for more equitable treatment which oscillate between secessionist demands and claims for cultural and economic justice. Valery Tishkov describes the emergence of the global phenomenon of 'ethnic revival' as largely being

> due to the desire to eliminate the historical, social, and political injustice to which many peoples are subjected and which accumulated during the long periods of colonialist and neo-colonialist policies, and also discrimination against immigrant, racial, and ethno-religious groups in multi-ethnic states.[32]

The international community, however, seems to be suprisingly incoherent in determining how to go about responding to ethnic claims, particularly when they escalate into violent conflict and collapsed states. Brown observes that 'some of these conflicts, in the former Soviet Union and in Burma and Rwanda, for example, were never addressed in a serious way by the international community as a whole'.[33] This lack of coherence has proved to be costly to people around the world. Indeed, as Brown observes:

> this failure was particularly striking in Rwanda, where about 800,000 were killed in a four-month period between April and July 1994; distant powers did next to nothing while one of the worst genocides the world had seen in five decades was carried out.[34]

Similar failures were experienced in Bosnia, Somalia, Angola and Sri Lanka. Brown suggests that 'the credibility of the world's major powers, the multilateral organisations through which they often operate, and the international community in general has suffered'.[35] Gurr and Harff note that 'conflicts between minorities and states increased steadily from 1950 to 1989. The worldwide magnitude of ethnic rebellion, for example, increased nearly four-fold between the period 1950–1955 and the years 1985–1989'.[36] Thus, while the end of the Cold War may be a contributing factor to the plethora of sub-national disputes that we are witnessing, it is not the root cause. During the Cold War sub-national conflicts were both aggravated and contained in order to suit the interests of the superpowers. In the post-Cold War world geostrategic pre-eminence is no longer at stake and new international thinking is required to implement policies which can begin to deal with the explosion of sub-national conflicts.

Deng et al. observe that the end of the Cold War removed an external dimension which often served to constructively and destructively regulate the intensity of disputes between ethnic groups and the state.[37] More specifically, the end of the Cold War has left behind a 'struggle between the central government and dissident groups with minimal input from outside'.[38] In addition, 'since the state is usually the main beneficiary of the international system, the loss of strategic alliances has led to its weakening which, at least in part, accounts for the massive breakdown of law and order, and even the total or partial collapse of the state'.[39] Crucially, what is morally pertinent here is the way that the 'international system' impacts upon sub-national disputes. When ethnic factions want to consolidate their power, capturing the state-government apparatus is clearly motivated by the desire to 'benefit' from the privileged position of the state vis-à-vis the international system. Rwanda serves as a poignant illustration of this predicament. In

1994, the Tutsi sub-national group mobilised an armed militia, the Rwanda Patriotic Front, based in neighbouring Uganda, and mounted a decisive military campaign against the predominantly Hutu government.[40] This precipitated the eventual genocide that has left a moral scar on the African continent and the world as a whole. Hutu refugees fled to neighbouring DRC, which suggests that unless bold steps are taken to renegotiate the constitution of the state to ensure the genuine inclusion of Hutus, Tutsis and Batwa in the political, social and economic affairs of the country, then revanchist Hutu ambitions against the current government in Rwanda cannot altogether be dismissed.[41] The situation in Rwanda, as in other parts of the world, is thus articulated by Chaim Kaufman when he remarks that:

> regardless of the origins of the ethnic strife, once violence (or abuse of state power by one group that controls it) reaches the point that ethnic communities cannot rely on the state to protect them, each community must mobilise to take responsibility for its own security.[42]

In effect, this is a testament to the way in which the 'international system' is failing to provide the necessary security, at the institutional level, for the well-being of these sub-national groups. The international system itself seems to be exerting a constraining effect on the movement towards a political environment in which 'justice' for sub-state communities can be fostered. The existence of the multi-ethnic state around the world means that this issue is bound to continue to be a recurring problem for the international community and a challenge to efforts to promote and build peace.

THE MULTI-ETHNIC STATE IN CONTEXT

Benedict Anderson observes that in 'the 1770s the first nation-state was born in North America out of armed resistance to imperial Britain, but it was inwardly so divided that it subsequently endured the bloodiest civil war of the nineteenth century'.[43] A cursory glance across the terrain of international relations raises the interesting question of whether there has been a significant change in the nature of the power struggles within states or whether similar struggles are indeed still being fought. During the sixteenth and seventeenth centuries Europe witnessed the elaboration of the concept of sovereignty to explain and legitimise the evolution of the centralised and absolutist state. The Westphalian logic prevailed throughout the period of empires and found its ultimate expression in the aftermath of the Second World War with the collapse of the colonial empires of Belgium, Britain, France, Holland and Portugal and the creation of the UN. By 1970 the UN had approximately four times the membership of its predecessor the League of Nations about thirty years earlier. Essentially, the nation-state project represented from the outset 'a forlorn attempt to stretch the short tight skin of nationalism' over entities often incorporating an array of multi-ethnic, multi-religious and multi-linguistic communities.[44] The fact is that the absence of heterogeneity is rare; as Uri Ra'anan observes 'it has been one of the fallacies of contemporary political thought, particularly in the West, to assume that the international arena of the twentieth century is occupied largely, if not almost exclusively, by nation-states or nation-states-to-be'.[45] It is nevertheless a political 'fallacy' whose continued propagation has proved to have disastrous effects for humanity in the twentieth and twenty-first centuries. Instead, it would be more appropriate to think of the nation-state as a political system which

> assumes a diversity of political ideas, power centres and the separation of state from civil society; it is a political arrangement for the articulation, expression and mediation of differences; it assumes the existence of conflict rather than a utopian end to all conflict.[46]

In a sense conflict and consensus are characteristic of the nation-state. Recognising the socio-political diversity both within groups and between sub-national groups is essential to ensuring that the nation-state becomes an instrument for maintaining peace. Failure to recognise this fact leads to dissension and fragmentation. Ultimately, genuine democratic institutions need to be predisposed to the politics of accommodation rather than the politics of domination if they are to stand a chance of reinforcing the stability of the contemporary multi-ethnic state.

THE CENTRALISED PREDATORY STATE AND THE INSTITUTIONALISATION OF DOMINATION

The genesis of ethnic groups in conflict, as with conflict between states, cannot be explained using single causal models.[47] In essence, a multitude of factors such as socio-economic inequality, corruption, the legacy of external interference and colonialism are all contributory factors. It is vital to explore how sub-national conflicts can emerge uniquely from the predatory machinations of state authority.

Anita Singh makes the observation that 'whether cultural diversity enriches a society or whether it will foment separatism depends on how it is handled'.[48] This has been demonstrated periodically by authoritarian rulers who rejected the seeking of consensus and subsequently fomented instability in their multi-national states by aggravating the differences between ethnic groups. This includes, for example, Presidents Suharto of Indonesia who fomented secession by Timor-Leste; Tito of Yugoslavia whose misrule laid the foundations for the dissolution of the country into Serbia, Croatia and the still contested Bosnia and Herzegovina; and Said Barre of Somalia whose departure led to the collapse of centralised sovereign authority in that country. Singh also notes that the 'political structures of any state partly reflect the ideas that have inspired its elites'.[49] Leaders who subscribe to 'exclusivist' or 'assimilationist' concepts of an ethnic nation-state are less inclined to forge institutions premised on the politics of accommodation. In effect, 'by identifying with one nation [or ethnic group], a professedly democratic government restricts both intellectual and political pluralism and political participation for minorities'.[50] Elizabeth Crighton and Martha MacIver emphasise this point when they argue that the instrumental utilisation of 'democratic' institutions for the purpose of sub-national manipulation and subjugation occurs 'when one ethnic group manages (often with the help of outside powers and creative gerrymanders) to establish its political dominance through institutions which protect its identity'.[51] This has several consequences, one of which is the 'institutionalisation of domination' which

> may take different forms, but occurs most readily where a demobilised mass public offers no challenge to the political order. Dominant institutions tend, therefore, to control conflict in a manner of 'coercive regimes', which enjoy high compliance but low support.[52]

The privileging of one ethnic group or a coalition of ethnic groups in this type of situation in effect means the negation of the politics of accommodation. The resultant 'inflexibility' and 'exclusiveness' spawns sub-national groups willing to challenge the institutionalised system of ethnic dominance leading ultimately, in a significant number of cases, to the ignition of conflict exacerbated by pre-existing social issues.

Pierre van de Berghe argues that 'the fiction of the nation-state is seldom innocuous. It often contains a prescription for the cultural destruction of a people through state policies of more or less compulsory assimilation and, at the limit, for genocide'.[53] Anderson reinforces this view and notes that the guarantor of the reality and the idea of popular sovereignty was, and continues to be, a national army. Faced with dissension in internal politics 'militaries largely armed and trained from the outside were even more likely to turn inwards', culminating in a situation confronting a large portion of humanity in which there is a proliferation of 'national armies that have never fought an external enemy, but continue to torment their own fellow citizens'.[54]

POLITICISED ETHNICITIES AND THE COLLAPSE OF STATES

More often than not minority groups find themselves politically 'handicapped' by the state, and by extension the state system, in their attempts to ensure their own economic and cultural survival. As a consequence mobilisation against the state becomes politicised. As Milton Esman remarks, 'ethnicity in a modern guise has emerged as a powerful group mobiliser and weapon of social conflict, not only in most Third World societies but also in the post-Soviet bloc, and in many advanced industrialised countries'.[55] For example, in May 2007, the Scottish National Party (SNP) won the majority of seats in the Scottish Assembly, a devolved regional government within the United Kingdom. The SNP's tacit objective is for an independent Scotland based on the parochial mobilisation of 'Scottish' ethnicity to counter the dominance of the British government based in London. Thus, while this phenomenon is global it possesses greater volatility in developing regions where 'the boundaries of most states were created by European colonial powers and have little meaning for many peoples who are divided by them, or who live within them along with many other peoples'.[56]

THE DE-LEGITIMATION OF THE NATION-STATE

As discussed above, ethnic polities that find themselves marginalised by other ethnic groups that have coopted the governing instruments of a state are denied the ability to articulate their political will. This creates a volatile situation in which the actions of the state in effect de-legitimate it in the eyes of the sub-national group. The state in this case is defined as 'a system of government exercising supreme authority, having a monopoly over the legitimate use of military and other coercive agencies within a clearly defined territory, and whose sovereignty is recognised by other states'.[57] As Kumar Rupeshinge, the former Secretary-General of International Alert, a non-government organisation which monitors conflicts around the world, argues, for a given internal dispute 'the state itself has often been party to the ethnic conflict or has been partisan or has escalated the conflict by imposing authoritarian strategems'.[58] A state holding a monopoly over the instruments of violence is in a strong position to reinforce its coercive regime and undermine the ability of ethnic groups to participate equally in national political life. If such a situation emerges the ensuing conflict is effectively a dispute that is bound to undermine the stability of the institution of the state. This was evident in the case of Somalia and the former Yugoslavia. Rupeshinge further notes that:

> contrary to theories which define the state, particularly in the Third World, as an arbitrator or a neutral actor, it is important to bear in mind that the state is neither an arbitrator nor neutral: it is itself a focal point of competition, an actor in the conflict.[59]

SECESSION VS RECOGNITION: THE TENSION BETWEEN STATE FORMATION AND ETHNIC AUTONOMY

It is important to recognise that there is tension within the sub-national groups between those who wish to form a new state and those who merely wish to be a properly recognised ethnos within the state. The first situation challenges the idea of the state system in favour of a new conception of relevant community in a global polity. The latter situation, however, does not challenge the state system as such, merely its failure to take seriously secessionist tendencies. However, the cases of Kosovo, Eritrea and Somaliland are informative in this regard. In the case of Kosovo a protracted struggle for ethnic recognition and accommodation was fought by the Kosovo Liberation Army (KLA) after the breakdown of the Yugoslav state in the early 1990s. For at least two decades the sub-national grievances in Kosovo were not addressed and the international community was significantly implicated in trying to resolve the situation in the country whilst at the same time prolonging it. In the emerging configuration of geopolitical power Russia, a staunch ally of Serbia, did not countenance the secession of Kosovo, because this would have implications for its own internal situation. Meanwhile, US and British interests gave tacit approval to the Kosovo Albanians to secede, which led to the pronouncement in February 2008 of Kosovo's independence. Eritrea underwent a similar trajectory. It was initially incorporated into the Ethiopian nation-state as a constituent state as a result of colonial compromise between the Italian and Ethiopian authorities. Eritreans for the most part did not recognise themselves as a constituent state of Ethiopia. Eritrea engaged in a protracted war with the Ethiopian regime that led to the country's independence in 1993 when the Marxist regime of Mengistu Haile Mariam collapsed. In the case of Somaliland, it was, and some argue still remains, a sub-national component of Somalia as a result of the decision to merge former British and Italian colonial parts of Somalia. With the effective dissolution of the Somali state in 1991 following the collapse of the regime of Siad Barre, Somaliland, also referred to as northern Somalia, broke away and ultimately declared its independence. In 2005, Somaliland submitted a request to the African Union to be recognised as an independent country. However, as of 2008 the AU has not recognised Somaliland because of the concern within the Pan-African organisation as to whether this would potentially open a pandora's box of future claims for secession on the African continent.

Thus, if the international system does not effectively resolve a subnational conflict situation then this can cause the objectives of the groups to significantly alter. Failure to address demands for ethnic autonomy can lead to a build-up of pressure that ultimately leads to demands for secession and independence. One reason why governments of nation-states are concerned about granting a significant degree of ethnic autonomy is because they often see this as the first step towards the demand for independence and ultimately secession. Paradoxically, it is the refusal to grant autonomy that can lead to the fragmentation of the state. This is a conundrum that the international system has not yet managed to address effectively.

The UN's *Agenda for Peace* is pragmatically against secessionist tendencies because they would portend the end of the current state system. As a club of nation-states the UN has reason to want to downplay secessionism, which would potentially lead to the further unravelling and fragmentation of the Westphalian system. The declaration of independence by Kosovo in February 2008 and the pressure on the international system to bestow a state on the Palestinians suggests that this issue cannot be swept under the carpet. There is a need to begin exploring alternative conceptions of global, national and sub-national community. In terms of peacebuilding an ethical predisposition towards resolving disputes actually demands that these alternative conceptions of the international system be assessed. If the tensions that arise from the persistent sub-national pressure on the nation-state system is not addressed, and effective mechanisms for addressing the grievances of ethnic groups within states are not established, then instability will prevail.

THE MORALITY OF CONFLICT RESOLUTION AND THE INTER-STATE SYSTEM

Conflict resolution between divided groups within states is a complex moral matter, one that requires us to alter our ethical perceptions of the problem and accept a range of options that can facilitate durable solutions and sustainable peace. To a large extent, previous and current attempts to come to terms with sub-national conflicts, in which state governments are clearly participating as belligerents, have framed the problem in terms of breakaway secessionist groups seeking to undermine the structure of the state. The state is thought of as being concrete and immutable according to the moral-legal principles of the UN Charter. Thus, the conventional reading and analysis of these problems begins from the a priori assumption that the nation-state is indivisible and the subsequent efforts to resolve the sub-national dispute should focus on how to put the state back together again. However, we need to recognise that the establishment of the post-colonial state in Africa, Asia, Latin America and Eastern Europe was an arbitrary attempt to force-fit a system of governance onto human populations. Once we have accepted this, then we can discuss whether these arbitrary efforts were a success or a failure. In fact for the most part one could argue that these post-colonial attempts at nation-building did in fact end in failure. So today the misnomer 'failed state' actually should refer to a failure to establish the state in the first place. Within the embryo of nascent post-colonial states lay the problems that today have led to their de-legitimation. Writing about the post-colonial political trends in African states in 1961, Frantz Fanon argued that 'this tribalising of the central authority, it is certain, encourages regionalist ideas and separatism. All the decentralising tendencies spring up again and triumph, and the nation[-state] falls to pieces, broken in bits'.[60] To complement this view, Ali Mazrui notes 'that Africa is experiencing a high-risk rebellion not only against the colonial state but sometimes against the state per se as a mode of governance. Many African societies are ill at ease with the state as a system of governance'.[61] The fragmentation of states is, however, not exclusively an African phenomenon. The secession of Timor-Leste from Indonesia, the potential irredentism of the Kurds from Turkey, Iran and Iraq as well as the potential secession of Kosovo from Serbia all illustrate the potential contagion of collapse that exists today.

In a seminal volume entitled *Collapsed States*, edited by William Zartman, this internal implosion is described as a condition in which

> the basic functions of the state are no longer performed, as analysed in various theories of the state. As the decision-making center of government, the state is paralysed and inoperative: laws are not made, order is not preserved, and societal cohesion is not enhanced.[62]

Furthermore, a collapsed state 'as a territory . . . is no longer assured security and provisionment by a central sovereign organisation. As the authoritative political institution, it has lost its legitimacy, which is therefore up for grabs, and so has lost its right to command and conduct public affairs'.[63] Therefore when disintegration affects a state fuelled by sub-national conflict then the moral 'legitimacy' and the moral 'right' of the 'state' to exercise authority are substantially diminished. In this context, conflict resolution and peacebuilding become a deeply moral issue. Sustainable peacebuilding will only be achieved when the international community can begin to ethically entertain alternatives and innovative forms of political association. The solutions should not be pre-given, since it may be the case that the majority of ethnic groups may embrace a statist framework. Rather, a more ethical way forward would be to ensure that conflict resolution and peacebuilding processes also accept the possibility of establishing and constituting post-statist or post-national frameworks which would fundamentally alter the traditional understanding of the state. Only by enabling sub-national groups working in tandem with governments to frame a system of political coexistence can we begin to genuinely address the issue of peacebuilding.

STATE-CENTRIC MECHANISMS FOR CONFLICT RESOLUTION AND PEACEBUILDING

As mentioned in the introduction to this chapter, traditionally the international mechanisms for conflict resolution and peacebuilding have a strong inter-state bias which means that disputes involving non-state actors are more or less confined to, and constrained by, these approaches. Mark Hoffman suggests that:

> the substance of deep-rooted conflicts beneath the contours of Cold War confrontation had direct implications for the approaches taken toward conflict management. During the Cold War, complex conflicts were handled through the traditional means of coercive diplomacy and crisis-management in the context of superpower rivalry and competition.[64]

These conflict resolution mechanisms sought to contain rather than resolve conflicts. As Hoffman further notes:

> the efficacy of the approaches needs to be seriously questioned. The flawed assumptions on which they are based, the inherent contradictions they entail and their largely unsuccessful history in promoting sustainable solutions to violent conflict are part of the legacy of the former Cold War system.[65]

As such, these mechanisms could not adequately address the 'underlying sources' of conflicts and often exacerbated them.[66]

It is clear that today, as during the Cold War, the international peace and security issues generated by the legitimate claims of sub-national groups are not adequately being addressed. As Carment notes, realist 'theories of international relations view ethnic conflict as an epiphenomenon – a by-product of the interaction between the processes of state building and an anarchical system'.[67] As a consequence the privileging of one group of actors (states) in the international system over another arrested the development and evolution of effective conflict resolution mechanisms. The former Special Representative of the UN Secretary-General for the former Yugoslavia, Yasushi Akashi, makes a similar point when he observes that 'because the role of the United Nations in conflict resolution has been expanding and has become increasingly complex, there is a need for a strategy to cope with the new challenges . . . the complex underlying causes of the [Yugoslav] conflict have often been obscured'.[68] In the particular case of Yugoslavia there was a proliferation of mandates that were difficult or impossible to implement because they were not clearly defined. Fred Riggs argues that 'at the state level, all members of the United Naions now belong to a self-preservation club in which the maintenance of existing state boundaries has become a top priority'.[69] With the demise of interstate conflict and the significant increase in intra-state conflict the international system's official conflict resolution mechanisms have not kept up with these geopolitical transformations. For example, the 1993 Declaration of the Assembly of Heads of State and Government of the Organization of African Unity (OAU – the predecessor to the African Union), on the establishment of a mechanism for conflict resolution, revealed its statist bias by noting that 'the mechanism will be guided by the objectives and principles of the OAU Charter, in particular, the sovereign equality of Member States, non-interference in the internal affairs of States'.[70] Elsewhere, this author has criticised the inability of this mechanism to genuinely address sub-national conflicts.[71] In particular, the mechanism was compelled to respect 'the sovereignty and territorial integrity of Member States, their inalienable right to independent existence, the peaceful settlement of disputes as well as the inviolability of borders inherited from colonialism'.[72] In the long run the legacy of such a policy can only serve to exacerbate conflict. The lack of a clearly defined approach to addressing the emergent reality of sub-national groups in conflict with states can only lead to the inefficacy of conflict resolution mechanisms which, according to Kamal Shehadi, lack 'the track record and the credibility to reassure a communal group that it will not be left at the mercy of a more powerful group or state'.[73] Contemporary inter-governmental conflict resolution processes are inherently 'incapable of effectively mediating complex international disputes'.[74]

CHARTING A POLITICAL ETHIC OF RESPONSIBILITY: TOWARDS A MORAL FRAMEWORK FOR CONFLICT RESOLUTION AND PEACEBUILDING

The changing context of contemporary international relations is currently confronted with a geopolitical realm that is simultaneously unipolar and multipolar as well as both globalising and fragmenting. This chapter so far has sought to demonstrate that the global community is witnessing the emergence of sub-national conflicts which are by definition more amorphous than wars between states. These conflicts often involve ethnic groups fighting each other, in addition to the ethnic groups challenging the authority of the state. In the post-Cold War context intergovernmental mechanisms for resolving disputes are faced with major limitations when they attempt to address sub-national conflicts. This is illustrated for example in a conflict between a national government and a sub-national group where 'the government may not want to imply recognition of the insurgent groups through engaging in official talks with them'.[75] Clearly, in such a situation in which communities comprised of both governments and non-state groups come into conflict with each other, the priorities can no longer be defined in terms of the nation-states' interests if sustainable solutions are to be crafted. This directly challenges the moral authority of intergovernmental organisations like the UN to mediate and build peace. Therefore, it is necessary to engage in a normative critique of this intergovernmental mechanism of dispute settlement.

In particular, cosmopolitan notions of creating a moral community can inform international conflict resolution and peacebuilding approaches. Only mechanisms that are morally inclusive can receive the generic consent of the warring parties in the emerging twenty-first-century theatres of conflict. In the context of this transforming global order, conflict resolution and peacebuilding processes need to be submitted and subjected anew to a moral legitimation process. Specifically, conflicts that are fuelled by processes that have de-legitimated the state can only be addressed by mechanisms that do not legitimate what are perceived, by sub-national groups, to be illegitimate states. This is with the intention of informing policy development that will lead to the establishment of structures, procedures, actions and policy decisions for dispute settlement that possess a quality of just and efficacious international relations.

Such mechanisms will necessarily have to adopt a moral posture of universal inclusion if they are to be effective. In effect, the possibility of peacebuilding in the post-Cold War environment has to be underpinned by a legitimation process and would herald the institutionalisation of moral egalitarianism. The work of the Enlightenment philosopher Immanuel Kant developed a notion of responsibility. Kant believed that through greater interaction human beings are in a process of creating the idea of 'universal community', whereby the 'violation of the rights in one part of the world is felt everywhere'.[76] In this regard, Kant viewed 'international relations as an historical evolutionary process'.[77] In his understanding of the way in which 'peace' could be sustained 'perpetually' Kant held the view that 'peace ought to function as a matter of duty'.[78] In addition, Kant proposed that a 'constitution of perpetual peace' could only be achieved through 'a partnership of independent states and by the lawful rational consent of what the individuals therein ideally will'.[79] This encapsulates and relates to the nature of a framework that can underpin the norms and mechanisms for resolving conflict in a world polarised by disparate competing identities; in essence 'the validity of all norms has to be tied to the discursive formation of the will of the people potentially affected'.[80] This theme has been picked up in the contemporary philosophy of Jürgen Habermas, who attempts to ground a conception of justice and obligation towards the other in something more profound than the convictions of a maturing global society and culture. He argues that our basic moral intuitions are rooted in something deeper and more universal than the particularities of our own traditions. Habermas concedes that basic moral intuitions are acquired in the process of socialisation, though he maintains that they include an 'abstract core' that is not culture- but species-specific.[81] Thus, in claiming rights as autonomous entities worthy of these rights, sub-national and national groups have to necessarily recognise the other's legitimate right to exist. The respect for an autonomous entity is tied to the freedom of each entity to act on the norms that govern the general interaction of individuals.

It could be argued that Kant favours an individualist rather than a collectivist approach. In particular, he maintains that individuals have obligations towards human beings in other parts of the world or the broad cosmopolitan view. Kant believed in respecting the rational agency of other human beings. As Dower observes, Kant 'advocates some kind of world ethic for individuals, as belonging to one global moral community – where community is defined in terms of the claimed moral relations'.[82] The issue then would be how to advocate a collectivist approach to peacebuilding when one is drawing upon a tradition that emphasises an individualist tradition. Ultimately, peacebuilding is carried out by individuals either through institutions or through their own agency. Therefore, the need to ground peacebuilding as a global moral responsibility is not contradictory with a position that advocates recognising the obligation of individuals towards each other. In fact, as Dower notes, Kant 'recommends a moral framework for international relations going beyond what was established on or acted on' and his concern was 'the duty of hospitality for foreigners, that is as citizens of the world we owe certain things towards any human being'.[83]

The broader issue is the fact that the relations between states and towards the wider global population can also be justified in terms of a cosmopolitan view. In terms of advocating the need for an ethic of conflict resolution, this book adopts this position and proposes that building peace is in fact a moral obligation of every citizen of the world towards each other. Dower notes that:

> individual human beings need to take seriously their identity as world citizens, since in principle there is a layer of obligation which might well require of them actions which go beyond, and even in some cases, are in conflict with, what is required of them as citizens of their own states.[84]

More specifically, the solidarist-pluralist conception of cosmopolitanism advocates 'solidarity throughout the world for promoting the essential conditions of well-being . . . it is essentially the approach adopted by many thinkers, especially in NGOs, who are activated by concerns about poverty, economic inequality and environmental problems'.[85] The solidarist-pluralist conception of cosmopolitanism also provides the foundation upon which to make the case for an ethics of peacebuilding predicated on the global moral responsibility of all world citizens to achieve this condition.

In the emerging global context a mechanism or institution that seeks to address intractable ethnic conflicts would then require a framework in which

> the 'arrangements and accommodations that emerge out of the interaction between the parties themselves, that address the basic needs of both parties and to which the parties are committed . . . [ultimately] . . . only this kind of solution is capable of transforming the relationship between societies locked into a protracted conflict that engages their collective identities and existentialist concerns.[86]

It is therefore necessary to explore and outline a framework for international conflict resolution and peacebuilding which promotes this moral ethos. This is vital in the realm of policy-making, practice and research to find ways of promoting sustainable solutions and avoid protracted chaos and instability.

The escalation of sub-nation conflict and the transformative dynamics sweeping international relations provide a unique opportunity for conflict resolution theory and practice. Sub-national conflict resolution is an issue that requires transnational global ethos but with a local understanding of the conflicts. Chipman observes that:

> ethnic conflict has become a universal security dilemma . . . a consistent failure to manage ethnic conflict could contribute to the . . . [frustration of] . . . efforts to build regional security more on the basis of enforceable norms of acceptable behaviour and less on balance-of-power arrangements with no inherent moral content.[87]

He further argues that 'all ethnic conflict is testimony to some prior failure of political arrangements'.[88] Chipman also believes that 'general guidelines of principle and policy should be available to negotiators of political settlements'.[89]

THE CHALLENGE OF GLOBAL GOVERNANCE: TRANSFORMING MICRO-/MESO-LEVEL PRINCIPLES TO THE MACRO LEVEL

Translating the grassroots peacebuilding initiatives from the micro- and meso-levels to the macro- level is in effect a challenge of how to ensure effective global governance. Rosenau defines governance as 'a more encompassing phenomenon than government. It embraces governmental institutions, but it also subsumes informal, non-governmental mechanisms whereby those persons and organisations within its purview move ahead, satisfy their needs, and fulfil their wants'.[90] Global governance is therefore the process and the institutional framework that enable the international system to function. There must be an interplay between grassroots, national and international actors in order for global governance to function. Specifically, Dower notes that people 'working in NGOs as part of what is called "global civil society", do now in some sense participate in global governance'.[91] Therefore, by engaging in micro- and meso-level peacebuilding, NGOs are already contributing towards the governance at a macro-level; thus the linkage between these levels is implied in such activity. In effect through their localised and regionalised peacebuilding initiatives civil society is contributing towards bringing order to global public affairs. Therefore by extension they are involved in translating micro- and meso-level peacebuilding into the level of international relations.

In addition peacebuilding is an activity that implicates actors at the grassroots, national and international levels. Ali and Matthews observe that the neglect of the international community of national and grassroots peacebuilding efforts can have a detrimental impact on sustaining peace.[92] If the global community does not remain involved in a local peacebuilding process and ensure that there is adequate development to meet the challenges of consolidating peace, there is a risk of the escalation of conflict. Ali and Matthews note that:

> peacebuilding is essentially a domestic activity. Civil wars begin and are fought in countries that then strive for peace . . . the international community's role should be a facilitative one, supporting and encouraging local actors to achieve their goals, not imposing its preferred vision of a peaceful society.[93]

The global governance of peacebuilding should be about ensuring that international conditions are conducive for local actors to establish the conditions that will enable them to build peace. Therefore, global networks of administration and governance are implicated in the need to consolidate peacebuilding.

International involvement in peacebuilding, however, remains a double-edged sword because uncoordinated and ad hoc intervention by the global community can also undermine local peacebuilding processes. This is why there needs to be a more harmonious relationship between sub-national, national and international efforts at peacebuilding. For example, in Somalia the international community has currently not been able to find a durable solution to the crisis in the country. The heavy-handed US-led UN military peace enforcement initiative in the early 1990s further exacerbated the situation in the country, which has yet to secure peace. This UN initiative 'lacked adequate knowledge about Somalia, ignoring or failing to appreciate Somali distrust and fear of any centralised government'.[94] This suggests that there is a need to rethink how global governance on the issue of peacebuilding can be restructured in order to address the issue of coordination. This issue will be discussed in Chapter 7 with reference to the UN Peacebuilding Commission.

CONCLUSION

This chapter discussed how ethnicity has been mobilised to generate sub-national contestations to the nation-state around the world. It examined a typology of sub-national groups and discussed their claims against states. Central to this analysis is the recognition that sub-national claims against nation-states form the majority of disputes afflicting international relations at this point in time. Whereas traditional theories of international relations understood sub-national conflicts in terms of a state-centric analysis this chapter sought to demonstrate that there are substantial grounds for challenging this conceptual categorisation. It demonstrated that sub-national conflicts are more amorphous than wars between states since they pit loosely defined populations with shifting leadership coalitions against one another. The parties to conflict are often communal groups diametrically opposed to governments of nation-states. As such the traditional state-centric mechanisms present significant limitations to the effective resolution of sub-national conflicts. In particular, the existing state system concretised in the Cold War can be viewed as having exacerbated the situation concerning these sub-state entities. By continuing to privilege the state and its institutions the international system has promoted a logic of exclusion which is increasingly viewed as lacking in legitimacy and authority.

This chapter also assessed how when sub-state entities seek to reinforce and consolidate their separateness the resistance that they encounter from the state often serves to foment further rebellion, through the invention of identity or the politicisation of ethnicity. It examined how the resurgence of sub-national claims can manifest through the onset of violent conflict, up to and including the collapse of the state. In effect these conflicts signal the loss of authority and the growth of radical and demagogic counter-elites, and lead to the eventual breakdown of governing institutions as witnessed in the case of Somalia. Central to the demands of the majority of sub-national conflicts are claims for more egalitarian forms of political association. Therefore, sub-national conflict can be viewed as an emerging international security dilemma.

In order for international mechanisms to be able to address these conflicts a moral framework that can respond to the transformed international context is necessary. The chapter further suggested that there are insights that could be gained from a neo-Kantian Habermasian tradition which emphasises entities recognising each other as legitimate interlocutors. Contemporary mechanisms of conflict resolution have to give the representatives of communal groups an egalitarian standing on which they can believe in and engage in the conflict resolution and peacebuilding process. Or, as Alex Heraclides notes, 'only if we are both principled and pragmatic can we be in the position to cope with what is one of the most intractable problems of our post-bipolar world and provide imaginative solutions to facilitate conflict resolution'.[95]

To speak of appropriate mechanisms of peacebuilding one has to address the limitations inherent in contemporary mechanisms for conflict resolution and global governance in order to sub-national conflict.

This chapter ultimately argued that there has to be an ethical orientation to address the significant role in the imagination and innovation of an alternative framework predicated on the politics of inclusion.

NOTES

1. Security Council Report, *Kosovo – Update Report*, no. 1, 10 March 2008, p. 5.
2. Hurst Hannum, 'The Specter of Secession: Responding to Claims of Ethnic Self-Determination', *Foreign Affairs*, vol. 77, no. 2, March/April 1998, pp. 13–18.
3. Jaine Leatherman and Raimo Vayrynen, 'Conflict Theory and Conflict Resolution: Directions of Collaborative Research Policy', *Cooperation and Conflict*, vol. 30, no. 1, 1995, p. 55.
4. The term 'sub-national' will be used as a convenient shorthand for ethnic, religious, linguistic and cultural. The phrase 'ethnic groups in conflict' is also used throughout this book in a generic sense. However, this book registers the problematic nature of both terminologies.
5. Stephen Ryan, 'Emerging Ethnic Conflict: The Neglected International Dimension', *Review of International Studies*, vol. 14, Winter 1988, pp. 161–77.
6. Andrew Linklater, 'Community, Citizenship and Global Politics', *Oxford International Review*, vol. 5, 1993, p. 6.
7. K. Deonandan, 'Learning from Somalia', *Peace Review*, vol. 6, no. 4, 1994, p. 453.
8. David Carment, 'The Ethnic Dimension in World Politics: Theory, Policy and Early Warning', *Third World Quarterly*, vol. 15, no. 4, 1994, p. 552.
9. David Carment and Patrick James, 'The United Nations at 50: Managing Ethnic Crises Past and Present', *Journal of Peace Research*, vol. 35, no. 1, 1998, p. 63 (61–82).
10. David Horowitz, *Ethnic Groups in Conflict* (Berkeley, CA: University of California Press, 1985), p. 186.
11. Michael Brown, 'Causes and Implications of Ethnic Conflict', in Michael Brown (ed.), *Ethnic Conflict and International Security* (Princeton: Princeton University Press, 1993), p. 4.
12. Anthony Richmond, 'Ethnic Nationalism: Social Science Paradigms', *International Social Science Journal*, vol. XXXIX, no. 1, February 1987, p. 3 (3–18).
13. Anthony Smith, 'The Ethnic Sources of Nationalism', in Brown, *Ethnic Conflict and International Security*, pp. 28–9.
14. For an extensive discussion see Joanne Nagel, 'The Ethnic Revolution: The Emergence of Ethnic Nationalism in Modern States', *Sociology and Social Research*, vol. 68, no. 4, 1983, p. 428.
15. Anthony Smith, 'Culture, Community and Territory: The Politics of Ethnicity and Nationalism', *International Affairs*, vol. 72, no. 3, 1996, p. 446 (445–58).

16. Ibid.
17. Ibid.
18. Ibid.
19. Ibid.
20. Charles Tilly, 'Ethnic Conflict in the Soviet Union', *Theory and Society*, vol. 20, no. 5, October 1991, p. 574 (569–80).
21. Immanuel Wallerstein, *The Capitalist World-Economy* (Cambridge: Cambridge University Press, 1979), p. 184.
22. Ravi Bhavnani, 'Ethnic Norms and Interethnic Violence: Accounting for Mass Participation in the Rwandan Genocide', *Journal of Peace Research*, vol. 43, no. 6, 2006, p. 652 (651–69).
23. Rodolfo Stavehagen, *Ethnic Conflicts and the Nation-State* (London: Macmillan, 1996), p. 120.
24. Ibid.
25. Ted Robert Gurr, *Minorities at Risk: A Global View of Ethnopolitical Conflict* (Washington, DC: United States Institute of Peace Press, 1993) and Barbara Harff, *Ethnic Conflict in World Politics* (Boulder, CO: Westview, 1991), p. 5.
26. Ted Gurr and Barbara Harff, *Ethnic Conflict in World Politics* (Boulder, CO: Westview, 1991), p. 5.
27. Gurr, *Minorities at Risk*, p. 15.
28. Ibid.
29. Ibid.
30. Ibid.
31. Ibid., p. 22.
32. Valery Tishkov, 'Glasnost and the Nationalities within the Soviet Union', *Third World Quarterly*, vol. 11, no. 4, October 1989, p. 200 (191–207).
33. Brown, *Ethnic Conflict and International Security*, pp. 10–11.
34. Ibid., p. 11.
35. Ibid., p. 11.
36. Gurr and Harff, *Ethnic Conflict in World Politics*, p. 11.
37. Francis Deng, Sadikiel Kimaro, Terrence Lyons, Donald Rothchild and I. William Zartman, *Sovereignty as Responsibility: Conflict Management in Africa* (Washington, DC: Brookings Institution, 1996), p. 68.
38. Ibid., p. 69.
39. Ibid., p. 69.
40. See Scott Straus, *The Order of Genocide: Race, Power, and War in Rwanda* (Ithaca, NY: Cornell University Press, 2006) and James Waller, *Becoming Evil: How Ordinary People Commit Genocide and Mass Killing* (Oxford: Oxford University Press, 2002).
41. Gerald Prunier, *The Rwanda Crisis: History of a Genocide* (London: C. Hurst & Co., 1995), pp. 322–8.
42. Chaim Kaufman, 'Possible and Impossible Solutions to Ethnic Civil Wars', in Michael Brown, Owen Cote, Sean Lynn-Jones and Steven Miller (eds), *Nationalism and Ethnic Conflict* (Cambridge, MA: MIT Press, 1997), p. 276 (265–304).

43. Benedict Anderson, 'The New World Disorder', *New Left Review*, no. 193, May/June 1992, pp. 3–14.

44. Ibid., pp. 4–5.

45. Uri Ra'anan, 'The Nation-State Fallacy', in Joseph Montville (ed.), *Conflict and Peacemaking in Multiethnic Societies* (Lexington, MA: Lexington Books, 1990), p. 5 (5–20).

46. Anita Singh, 'Democracy and Ethnic Diversity: A New International Priority?', *World Today*, vol. 57, no. 1, January 1996, p. 21.

47. Hidemi Suganami, *On the Causes of War* (Oxford: Oxford University Press, 1996).

48. Singh, 'Democracy and Ethnic Diversity', p. 21.

49. Ibid., p. 22

50. Ibid., p. 22.

51. Elizabeth Crighton and Martha MacIver, 'The Evolution of Protracted Ethnic Conflict: Group Dominance and Political Underdevelopment in Northern Ireland and Lebanon', *Comparative Politics*, January 1991, p. 128.

52. Ibid.

53. Pierre van den Berghe, 'Introduction', Pierre van den Berghe (ed.), *State Violence and Ethnicity* (Niwot, CO: University Press of Colorado, 1990), p. 6.

54. Anderson, 'The New World Disorder', pp. 11–12.

55. Milton Esman, 'Political and Psychological Factors in Ethnic Conflict', in Monteville (ed.), *Conflict and Peacemaking in Multiethnic Societies*, p. 58 (53–64).

56. Jason Clay, 'Epilogue : The Ethnic Future of Nations', *Third World Quarterly*, vol. 11, no. 4, October 1989, p. 225.

57. Richmond, 'Ethnic Nationalism: Social Science Paradigms', p. 5.

58. Kumar Rupeshinge, 'Internal Conflicts and their Resolution: The Case of Uganda', in Kumar Rupeshinge (ed.), *Conflict Resolution in Uganda* (Oslo: The International Peace Research Institute, 1989), p. 4 (1–23).

59. Ibid., p. 3.

60. Frantz Fanon, *The Wretched of the Earth* (London: Penguin, 1990), p. 148.

61. Ali Mazrui, 'The African State as a Political Refugee', in David Smock and Chester Crocker (eds), *African Conflict Resolution: The US Role in Peacemaking* (Washington, DC: United States Institute of Peace Press, 1995), p. 25 (9–26).

62. William Zartman, 'Introduction: Posing the Problem of State Collapse', in William Zartman (ed.), *Collapsed States: The Disintegration and Restoration of Legitimate Authority* (London: Lynne Rienner, 1995), p. 5 (1–14); see also Gerald Helman and Steven Ratner, 'Saving Failed States', *Foreign Policy*, no. 89, Winter 1992–3, pp. 3–20.

63. Zartman, 'Introduction', p. 5.

64. Mark Hoffman, 'Third-party Mediation and Conflict in the Post-Cold War World', in John Baylis and Nicholas Rengger (eds), *The Dilemmas of World Politics: International Issues in a Changing World* (Oxford: Clarendon Press, 1992), p. 262.

65. Ibid.

66. Ibid.
67. Carment, 'The Ethnic Dimension in World Politics', p. 553.
68. Yasushi Akashi, 'The Limits of UN Diplomacy and the Future of Conflict Mediation', *Survival*, vol. 37, no. 4, Winter 1995–6, pp. 87–90.
69. Fred Riggs, 'Ethnonationalism, Industrialisation and the Modern State', *Third World Quarterly*, vol. 15, no. 4, 1994, p. 604.
70. Organization of African Unity, *Declaration of the Assembly of Heads of State and Government on the Establishment within the OAU of a Mechanism for Conflict Prevention, Management and Resolution* (Cairo, Egypt, June 1993), pp. 7–8.
71. See Tim Murithi, 'The OAU Mechanism for Conflict Resolution: Contextualising the Sub-national Problematic', *Africa World Review*, March 1998, pp. 18–21.
72. Organization of African Unity, *Declaration of the Assembly*, pp. 7–8.
73. Shehadi, 'Ethnic Self-Determination and the Break up of the State', p. 63.
74. Saadia Touval, 'Why the UN Fails', *Foreign Affairs*, vol. 73, no. 5, September/October 1994, p. 45.
75. F. Mawlawi, 'New Conflicts, New Challenges: The Evolving Role of Non-Governmental Actors', *Journal of International Affairs*, vol. 46, no. 2, 1993, p. 396.
76. Immanuel Kant, 'Perpetual Peace: A Philosophical Sketch', in H. Reiss (ed.), *Kants Political Writings*, second edition, trans. H. B. Nisbet (Cambridge: Cambridge University Press, 1991), pp. 107–8.
77. John Macmillan, 'A Kantian Protest Against the Peculiar Discourse of Inter-Liberal State Peace', *Millenium: Journal of International Studies*, vol. 24, no. 3, 1995, p. 560.
78. M. Franke, 'Immanuel Kant and the (Im)possibility of International Relations Theory', *Alternatives*, vol. 20, no. 3, July–September 1995, p. 308.
79. Ibid.
80. Jürgen Habermas, 'What does a Legitimation Crisis Mean Today? Legitimation Problems in Late Capitalism', in William Connolly, *Legitimacy and the State: Readings in Social and Political Theory* (Oxford: Blackwell, 1984), p. 154.
81. Jürgen Habermas, *Moral Consciousness and Communicative Action*, trans. C. Lenhardt and S. Nicholsen (Cambridge, MA: MIT Press, 1990).
82. Nigel Dower, *World Ethics: A New Agenda*, second edition (Edinburgh: Edinburgh University Press, 2007), p. 25.
83. Ibid., p. 84.
84. Ibid., p. 22.
85. Ibid., p. 27.
86. N. Rouhana and H. Kelman, 'Promoting Joint Thinking in International Conflicts: An Israeli-Palestinian Continuing Workshop', *Journal of Social Issues*, vol. 50, no. 2 1994, p. 154.
87. John Chipman, 'Managing the Politics of Parochialism', in Brown (ed.), *Ethnic Conflict and International Security*, p. 239.

88. Ibid., p. 239.
89. Ibid., p. 240.
90. James Rosenau and Ernst-Otto Czempiel, *Governance without Government: Order and Change in World Politics* (Cambridge: Cambridge University Press, 1992), p. 4.
91. Dower, *World Ethics: A New Agenda*, p. 79.
92. Taisier Ali and Robert Matthews (eds), *Durable Peace: Challenges for Peacebuilding in Africa* (Toronto: University of Toronto Press, 2004), p. 404.
93. Ibid., p. 408.
94. Ibid., p. 405.
95. Alex Heraclides, 'Secession, Self-Determination, and Non-intervention: In Quest of a Normative Symbiosis', p. 420.

CHAPTER 4

THE UTILITY OF NEGOTIATION AND MEDIATION

INTRODUCTION

This chapter will look at the ethical dimensions of negotiation and mediation processes. It will discuss the ethical norms of negotiation and mediation that were established by macro-level institutions such as the League of Nations and the United Nations (UN). It will then examine how recent trends in macro-level global politics are beginning to erode these norms. The chapter will argue for a revitalisation of the values and norms that animated the creation of these peacemaking and peace-building institutions that currently exist. It will assess the normative drive behind the efforts of peacebuilding actors like the Quakers, at the meso or national level in Nigeria. The chapter will then seek to draw out the common philosophical links between the approaches of these actors and institutions to establish the ethics of negotiation and mediation in its historical and contemporary context. In addition, this analysis will provide valuable insights into some of the challenges and successes that have been achieved in the field of negotiation and mediation.

THE ETHICS OF NEGOTIATION AND MEDIATION

In seeking to understand the ethical dimensions of negotiation and mediation processes, we need to initiate the discussion with reference to Article 33 of Chapter VI of the UN Charter which states that 'the parties to any dispute, the continuance of which is likely to endanger the maintenance of international peace and security, shall, first of all, seek a solution by negotiation, enquiry, mediation, conciliation, arbitration, judicial settlement'.[1] Negotiation is a process involving two or more parties that necessitates direct interaction and dialogue between the parties to find a solution to a common problem. Mediation is a form of third-party intervention that seeks to assist two or more disputing parties to find a mutually acceptable settlement.[2] Negotiation proceeds between parties generally without substantial external assistance and guidance; mediation is therefore negotiation with the added dimension of a third party facilitating the interaction between the parties. This is why mediation is sometimes referred to as assisted negotiation. Mediation can best be thought of as a dynamic and ongoing process that begins with a pre-mediation process and continues up to the post-mediation implementation and monitoring phase. The underlying ethic of negotiation and mediation processes is to find an agreement or a resolution that is considered by all the parties involved to be beneficial to them.[3] As such, negotiation and mediation initiatives are highly ethical processes. Kevin Gibson argues that 'mediators need more grounding in philosophical ethical theory'.[4] A key obstacle to successful negotiation and mediation is the corruption, cooptation and instrumentalisation of a process to suit the self-interests of one particular party at the expense of the other parties. The unethical abuse of negotiation and mediation processes by the parties themselves or by interested secondary actors is therefore a challenge that has to be addressed in order to improve the chances of effective peacebuilding in the future.[5]

CONTEXTUALISING NEGOTIATION AND MEDIATION

The nature of conflict resolution and management activities in the international arena is diverse. Marieke Kleiboer surmises that 'there are many forms of third party intervention, so many, in fact, that it is often confusing to try to figure out which is which'.[6] George Levinger and Jeffrey Rubin note that 'conflicts at every level can lead to one of two broad kinds of solutions: settlement or resolution'.[7] They further observe that 'settlement refers to behavioural change, as when two sides find a way to reach agreement, but their basic attitudinal opposition remains largely unchanged. Resolution not only implies a change in behaviour but also a convergence in underlying attitudes'.[8] Richard Rubenstein, a former Director of the Institute for Conflict Analysis and Resolution at George Mason University, suggests that 'the conflict resolver's skill lies in assisting severely alienated parties – groups representing contending ethnic communities, social classes, religions, or nations – to identify their basic needs and interests and to create mutually acceptable systems capable of satisfying them'.[9] For some analysts conflicts are essentially subjective even though they may appear to the parties affected as being objective. A. J. R. Groom contends that 'conflict is subjective, in structure but not in perception . . . conflict is objective only because the parties choose to see it as such and their perceptions are subject to change'.[10] If a third party proceeds on this premise then it is evident that the central task of all peacemaking and peacebuilding processes is to draw the attention of the disputants to the importance of reconceptualising their positions in relation to each other. One can argue that this then requires a third party to adopt an ethical stance with respect to that party's responsibility to make peace.

THE MORALITY OF PACIFIC DISPUTE SETTLEMENT AND THE LEAGUE OF NATIONS

It is useful to examine how the League of Nations sought to institutionalise an ethical mechanism for settling conflict.[11] In particular, it will be useful to look at how the League, in its short-lived existence, sought to address the pressing issue of conflict through arbitration, negotiation and mediation, primarily between nation-states but also in response to the claims of sub-national groups. The League effectively tried to promote the moralisation of international politics and even institutionalised a mechanism for the pacific settlement of disputes. This was evident in the significant but limited success that occurred when the League administered the resolution of disputes through the Mandates Commission and through plebiscites in Upper Silesia, the Åland Islands and the Saar region.

THE ESTABLISHMENT OF THE LEAGUE OF NATIONS

With the end of the First World War the founding Covenant of the League of Nations, established through the Treaty of Versailles of 1919, sought to enshrine a system of international security. The rise of nationalism brought with it the need to address how to determine the basis of political community. Over time the principle of national self-determination gained currency. Driven by liberal notions of self-development, in the context of human freedom, this principle sought to invoke a new order which would balance the interests within and between communities. Issues such as the relationship between the individual and the nation had to be addressed. The issue of the relationship between the sovereignty of a state and how this would accommodate the rights and integrity of minority and indigenous cultures also had to be addressed. Thus, as John Macmillan notes, 'early liberals supported national self-determination as a concept that would lead to the establishment of political communities in which individuals could live freely in relation to one another'.[12] However, the nation-state sovereignty model brought with it several problems. Various assumptions were made about the viability of the state. Primarily, the dominant view maintained that to become a member of the family of nations a state needed to have a settled government capable of carrying out essential government services. Such services included establishing, keeping and building public peace as well as maintaining its own political independence and territorial integrity. As a logical corollary to this assumption emerged the view 'that some peoples were not yet ready for statehood'.[13] This attitude was based on the conclusion that the world was a dangerous place. Events such as the 'Bulgarian Horrors' and the massacre of the Armenians helped to foment the notion that in such a world non-state peoples needed protection. Such protection, in keeping with the principle of self-determination, should ideally be provided for by a state belonging to the people. But following on from the position that some people were not ready for statehood then this protection would have to be mandated to other states and administered by the League. This led to the formulation of the League's mandates system.

Responsibility for particular non-state peoples was assigned to the various mandatory powers who in turn had to make regular reports to the League Council and in particular the League's Permanent Mandates Commission.[14] The mandates system initially encompassed sixteen states through various treaties and formal declarations of intent, including Poland, Austria, Estonia, Latvia, Lithuania, Finland (with reference to the Åland Islands) and Germany (with reference to Upper Silesia).[15] Yet in most of these mandates minorities existed alongside other minorities and with the intervention of conationals or coreligionists in neighbouring countries competition for resources and dominance could easily erupt. In some instances groups would challenge the plans of the mandate system and demand the right to determine their own political future. The Commission gradually came to assume the function of arbitrator and mediator to the claims of minorities; however, it was not endowed with the military power necessary to implement and consolidate mandates. Instead, 'it relied on persistence, persuasion and a non-confrontational approach'.[16] This was very much in keeping with its ethical approach to dispute settlement. A more detailed analysis of the League's efforts follows.

THE LEAGUE'S EFFORTS IN FORGING AN ETHICAL PEACE IN THE ÅLAND ISLANDS

One situation presented itself to the League in July 1920. Under the provisions of Article 11 of the League's Covenant, Great Britain brought before the Council the question of the Åland Islands, which span the exit of the Gulf of Bothnia into the Baltic Sea. The islanders had been of Swedish descent since the Middle Ages and were ceded by Sweden to Russia in 1809, after which they were governed as part of the Grand Duchy of Finland. Finland declared independence from Russia in 1917 and at the conclusion of the First World War the Åland Islands were held by Finland and claimed by Sweden. The islands were closer to Finland than to the Swedish mainland and were joined to Finland by a field of ice during the winter months, thus enhancing their strategic value to the Finns. With the support of the Swedish authorities the islanders claimed their right to self-determination and this eventually led to a situation in which both sides were prepared to engage in war.

Finland granted autonomy to the Islands in 1920 but this did not decrease the tension. When the League became involved, at the behest of Great Britain, the Finns argued that the dispute was domestic and did not concern the League. The Swedish, on the other hand, demanded a plebiscite counting on the majority of the islanders to vote in their favour. Both Finland and Sweden were present at the League Council meetings concerning the dispute. The League had adopted an ethical position of favouring the use of consent rather than coercion in resolving disputes. Finland was not at the time a member of the League but it nevertheless had the same rights and obligations as Sweden for the purposes of the disputes settlement machinery. The League put under scrutiny Finland's reservations about its involvement and came to the conclusion the Islands were subject to Finnish sovereignty and disputed by Sweden, thus the dispute fell under international jurisdiction. In September 1920 the Council, following the course of action described in the Covenant, appointed a three-man group of rapporteurs to work out a settlement. It is important to note that for all intents and purposes both nations were at this stage demonstrating a certain degree of restraint as far as the movement towards war was concerned. The League's machinery for dispute settlement, for one thing, provided them with an avenue through which they felt that their claims would at least be given fair and ethical treatment.

It is apparent that the League of Nations at the time, like the UN later on, did not recognise sub-national groups as political actors. The League of Nations, however, gave a minority protection guarantee to the Swedes in the Åland Islands through which they could exert the right to maintain their religious, cultural and linguistic identity.[17] The recommendations were adopted by the League Council in June 1921 and remained in effect until the Second World War.

The key useful insights that emerge from the League's mediatory role include the fact that both sides of the dispute consented to the body's ruling. Clearly, Sweden did not in the end make any gains and Finland was willing to accommodate the wishes of the islanders. The Swedes could have turned to war, which was their original position, and the Finns could have declined to grant the islanders their request. Consistent with the theme being explored in this book, the viability of the moral process as far as settling disputes is concerned helped to generate a solution acceptable to all sides. It is possible to argue that the two parties were prepared to compromise on this issue partly because of the moral authority of the League of Nations and the legitimacy of the dispute settlement machinery. Other variables can also be factored in, such as the isolation of Sweden in the League, its weak domestic government and the difficulties it would have had in acting unilaterally. In the final analysis, the League's ability to provide a forum where parties felt that they had moral parity may have had a role to play in assuaging the fears of marginalisation, domination and exclusion held by the disputants.

PACIFIC DISPUTE SETTLEMENT IN UPPER SILESIA

Another case involved the region of Upper Silesia which stretched across the new borders of both Poland and Germany and had in 1920 a population of two million people. The region was claimed by both Poland and Germany. To complicate matters the great powers at the time were intimately engaged in the situation, with France backing Poland and Britain supporting Germany. There were twice as many Poles as there were Germans but given that local communities were so mixed, with Germans living among Poles and Poles living among Germans, there was no way to draw borders along national lines.

Given that population removal was ruled out, the situation seemed at the outset insoluble. Ethnic hatred was rife and mistrust and suspicion escalated into conflict between well-organised Polish and German subnational militias. Unable to find a solution through direct negotiation, Britain and France decided to submit the problem to the League on 21 August 1921. The report to the Commission on Upper Silesia was produced by Jean Monnet (subsequently a leading architect in the formation of the European Economic Community).[18] The report recommended setting up two joint bodies to run the region for fifteen years on both sides of a proposed borderline. One body consisted of a mixed Polish–German Managing Commission and the other was an Arbitration Tribunal. Though there was a plethora of issues arising from the proposed body a Polish–German convention was signed on 15 May 1922, in Geneva, Switzerland. For the full fifteen years mandated by the convention the Polish and German minorities in Upper Silesia had access to a well-developed mechanism for handling complaints of discrimination guaranteed by a right of appeal to an international forum.[19] Thus, the League's efforts provide us with evidence to substantiate the argument that the ethical reformulation of political relations within and between communities on the basis of consent can be sustained. This is, of course, dependent on the collective willingness of the parties concerned to see the arrangement succeed.

PLEBISCITES AS A MORAL MECHANISM FOR MANAGING TENSION: THE SAAR REGION

In addition to its efforts to mediate, the League also relied on plebiscites, or referenda, to ascertain the political will and consent of minority populations in nation-states. The plebiscite was a mechanism utilised to enable the ethic of self-determination to be expressed. This principle held that people had a right to choose their own rulers and system of governance under which they would live. Thus, inhabitants of territories would be given the opportunity in free plebiscites to make this decision.

One such plebiscite fixed by the Treaty of Versailles was related to the Saar region.[20] The Saar was a rich industrial region situated on the north-eastern border of France and Germany. After the First World War, France demanded that the Saar, largely populated by ethnic Germans, should become part of the territory as compensation for the devastation inflicted on France by the German Army. Britain and the USA rejected this claim and proposed instead that the region would be held under the administrative authority, or trusteeship, of the League for a period of fifteen years, after which the Saarlanders would be called upon to indicate the sovereignty under which they would prefer to live through a free plebiscite. However, France was granted ownership of the coal mines and allowed to establish industries.

The plebiscite would seek to express whether the people of the Saar would prefer to continue to: i) remain under the trusteeship of the League; ii) join in a union with France; or iii) join in a separate union with Germany. After the fifteen-year period a Plebiscite Commission of three members and an expert adviser was set up. It also included fifty inspectors to oversee the plebiscite. As Yves Beigbeder records, the 'plebiscite took place on 13 January 1935, "with perfect discipline and dignity". On 14 January, the ballot boxes, guarded by detachments of the International Force, were carried to Saarbrucken, where 300 neutral tellers counted them'.[21] As far as the result was concerned, 90 per cent of the electorate (477,119) voted for reunion with Germany, whilst 46,615 voted to maintain the League's trusteeship and only 2,124 voted for union with France.

France accepted the results and the League's Council following the recommendation of the Plebiscite Commission decided that the territory would be united with Germany and this duly took place on 1 March 1935. According to Beigbeder

> the plebiscite itself was a political and operational success for the League, in implementing a commitment written in the Treaty of Versailles 35 years before. Signatory countries respected their word, including Germany, no longer a League member. All observers were impressed by the fairness and efficiency with which the plebiscite had been organised.[22]

Thus, the ethical framework espoused by the League's principle of consent, in this case generated through plebiscites, was shown to be capable of bringing about the peaceful transition in political community.[23]

It is, however, important to acknowledge that the League was not always in a position to effectuate peaceful settlements. It failed to settle disputes between Poland and Lithuania in 1921 and between Bolivia and Paraguay in the Chaco War between 1932 and 1935.[24] In the course of events that led to the onset of the Second World War there was an extensive debate over the reasons for the failure of the League. In 1919 there was a significant degree of support for the League even amongst nation-states like Germany and Italy. However, by the late 1930s both these countries had descended into totalitarianism and, according to Murray, were effectively trampling on the 'corpse' of liberal internationalism.[25]

THE ETHICS OF THE LEAGUE'S PACIFIC DISPUTE SETTLEMENT FRAMEWORK

In his pessimistic strictures on utopian thinking Carr viewed international morality in an epiphenomenal and instrumental way. He believed that great powers would only support so-called universal principles when they served to legitimise their position.[26] According to Carr, it was misguided for the pro-League utopians to insist that the establishment of a machinery for settling disputes with 'morally right' procedures would allow for the appropriate reconciliation of divergent national interests.

What insights can be gained from the League of Nations' activities in terms of contemporary conflict resolution and peacebuilding? Firstly, prudence must be invoked in any attempt to offer valid analogies or applicable lessons based on the League's history.[27] An investigation into the League's works in peacebuilding provides us with four useful insights that are relevant to contemporary conflict resolution efforts. Firstly, it illustrates that it is possible to establish a framework for international peacebuilding based on moral principles. Secondly, in the contemporary global environment defined by a marked decrease in inter-state conflict and a concomitant increase in intra-state disputes, a mechanism based on generating the consent of the parties is bound to meet with problems similar to those that the League encountered. Thirdly, taking cognisance of and managing the crude egotistical imperatives of powerful nations can enable a third party to encourage the other parties to engage in a peace process. And finally, the League's experiences demonstrate that it is only when disputants recognise each other as ethical interlocutors within a consensual framework that the possibilities for generating sustainable agreements become more likely. This was particularly demonstrated by the experiences in the Åland Islands, Upper Silesia and the Saar region.

The moral principles that shaped the formulation of the League of Nations in the uneasy twenty-year pre-Cold War era have become part of both our intellectual and our institutional inheritance.[28] In a study of ethics and peacebuilding there is undoubtedly a case to be put for examining the role that the League played in this field. From a historical perspective, clearly the period of the League's existence and evolution turned out to be a period of experimentation. The international experiment in conflict resolution is ongoing and the concepts and principles that prevailed at the inception of the League can still offer valuable insights. The League effectively established an ethical framework for resolving disputes and building peace, even though it subsequently succumbed to the forces of nationalism which undermined the moral and political foundations on which it was built. The League's efforts, however, are to be noted for their attempt to establish ethical internationalism and the use of consensus-building mechanisms to resolve international disputes.

THE LIMITS OF THE LEAGUE OF NATIONS' PACIFIC DISPUTE SETTLEMENT MECHANISM

The League of Nations was in many ways ahead of its time and ultimately it did not succeed in maintaining peace in the face of authoritarian regimes that fomented the Second World War. In her book *The Illusion of Peace: International Relations in Europe 1918–1933*, Sally Marks observes that 'the League was so much weaker than the powers which dominated it'.[29] In particular, Britain and France still had imperial interests over territories under their tutelage. These interests conflicted with the attempt by the League to achieve genuine peace. When the League failed 'to bolster the peace, European diplomats fell back on the more traditional approach of defensive alliances'.[30] The League Council, the highest decision-making organ of the organisation, was fractured by imperial interests since Britain, France, Italy and Germany had permanent seats on the Council. The League Council was mandated to determine the violation of any treaties. However, the mechanics of this process were complicated. Marks observes that 'Britain insisted that there should be no obligation to act until the Council had declared a violation. Given French, British, Italian, and German permanent seats on the Council and the unanimity require-ment' this provision would have made decisive and judicious action hostage to a balance of interests among the so-called 'great' powers.[31] After Germany joined the League in 1926, the politics of its Council threatened to undermine the activities of the organisation. The distinc-tion between countries that had permanent seats and those that held non-permanent seats, and the dominance of European great powers in the Council led to 'Brazil and Spain declaring their intention to with-draw from the League'.[32] In 1927 Brazil indeed effectively withdrew from the League. In 1928 the League members signed an International Treaty for the Renunciation of War as an Instrument of National Policy, which was also known as the Kellogg–Briand Pact. As Marks suggests, that 'pact was indicative of a deep yearning to put the war and the post-war into the past and to enter upon a long, golden era of peace.'[33] She observes that 'eager advocates convinced themselves that the flimsy foundation of the Pact was firm and that its empty verbiage could provide a genuine basis for true peace'.[34] In fact, 'the Kellogg–Briand Pact contributed to the illusion of peace, not its reality, and proved completely ineffectual whenever it was invoked in the years to come'.[35] Ultimately, Marks concludes that 'for all its defects the Pact did constitute the first formal renunciation of war as an instrument of national policy in the annals of mankind and the first step toward the slowly spreading view that war is immoral'.[36] In this sense the League was definitely ahead of its time, and as of 2008 humankind is still trying to internalise these moral principles.

Even though Article 16 of the League Covenant called for sanctions against aggressors, the organisation was unable to prevent the re-armament race that strengthened the position of Germany vis-à-vis other imperial powers. In January 1930, the last French troops left German soil, and on 14 September 1930, Adolf Hitler's Nazi Party became the second largest party in the German Reichstag.[37] The intervening years were defined by German revisionism and re-arma-ment. The rise of the Nazis and the *Anschluss*, or annexation of Austria, subsequently gave way to a Nazi-led German invasion of Poland in 1939. In October 1933 Hitler withdrew Germany from the Disarmament Conference and from the League of Nations. Elsewhere the incursion of Japan into China in September 1931 compelled the Chinese Nationalist government to appeal 'to the United States under the Kellogg–Briand Pact and to the League under Article 11 of the Covenant, which did not automatically require League action'.[38] However, no significant action was forthcoming. This series of events effectively terminated the per-ception and reality of the League of Nations as a mechanism for preventing disputes. White observed that 'the League of Nations had failed to keep world peace primarily because the idea of collective security was far weaker than the individual States' desires to protect their national interests'.[39]

DOES THE UNITED NATIONS HAVE AN ETHICAL FRAMEWORK FOR PEACEMAKING?

Following the subjugation of the fascist and totalitarian powers at the end of the Second World War the wartime allies decided to construct a new framework for the post-war world order. The United Nations organisation was the progeny of this endeavour and its primary purpose was to ensure that there was an institutional mechanism that would encourage its members to 'settle their international disputes by peaceful means in such a manner that international peace and security, and justice are not endangered'.[40] Through the mechanisms of the Security Council and the General Assembly the UN was provided with the ability to oversee the peaceful settlement of disputes through an array of processes including negotiation, mediation, conciliation, arbitration and judicial settlement. In a similar way to the mechanisms that the League established, these processes were also predicated on forging the consent of the warring parties. The question that we need to address is

whether these institutions of the UN constituted an ethical framework
for building peace.

White notes that 'a collective security system entails the centralisation
of a society's coercive mechanisms'.[41] In the context of international
society 'the UN Charter contains all the rudiments of such a system,
whereas the League of Nations did not'. According to White, it was the
'partial institutionalisation of the concept of collective security in the
League of Nations [that] gave way to the old system of competing
interests and rival alliances'.[42] The Charter of the UN contains 'quite
elaborate provisions in Chapter VI for the pacific settlement of disputes,
the "teeth" of the Charter were contained in Chapter VII which granted
the Security Council the unprecedented power to take mandatory
economic and military action against an aggressor'.[43] However, what
seemed initially to be a resourceful array of mechanisms and processes
to resolve conflict were soon to be confronted by the structural limitations and the egotistical imperatives of the superpowers that dominated
the Cold War era. The superpowers (the USA and USSR) and their
client states within the UN framework formed de facto alliances along
ideological lines and institutionalised an oligarchy of power. This
appropriation of global power manifested itself through the dominance
of the Security Council in all major decisions and meant that the UN's
ability to resolve conflicts and build peace became structurally paralysed. Rarely, if at all, did the interests of the USA or the USSR
converge. The greatest threat to international peace and security therefore arose from the conflict between its most powerful members. The
Cold War period witnessed over 150 armed conflicts which claimed
approximately 25 to 30 million lives. In this climate of East–West
competition the mechanisms and strategies to manage and resolve
conflicts relied on coercive political negotiations in the context of the
prevailing superpower rivalry. Leatherman and Vayrynen concur with
this view and further suggest that the 'involvement of collective security
organisations and other third parties was possible only in conflicts in
which the great powers did not have a direct stake or in which they had
shared interests'.[44] So even though the UN established what could have
served as an ethical framework for building peace it was severely
undermined by the exigencies of egotistical superpower politics.

ETHICAL EGOISM, POWER POLITICS AND THIRD-
PARTY INTERVENTION IN THE COLD WAR

Power politics, premised on ethical egoism, as discussed in Chapter 2,
infiltrated into mechanisms of international conflict resolution and

either coopted the UN or effectively marginalised it. The legacy of this era to a large extent retains its currency in contemporary international relations. Stephen Chan and Vivienne Jabri observe that 'some researchers emphasise the vital role played by coercive or leveraged mediation and suggest that this form of mediation is the most suited to the Hobbesian international system'.[45] They further note that 'advocates of this approach adopt a realist interpretation of the international system and suggest that outcomes to mediated conflicts are solely amenable to interpretation using a power-political framework'.[46] The realist approach contends that the intervening third party needs 'power in order to bring the disputants to the point where they will accept mediation'.[47] William Zartman argues that mediators can manoeuvre the disputants into perceiving that a moment is 'ripe' for engaging in an attempt at resolution. However, he points to the necessity of having the second characteristic mentioned above, 'leverage' or power as a mediator in order to bring about this state of affairs. Zartman partly derived his theoretical prescription from the archetypal realist statesman, Henry Kissinger, who proclaimed 'never treat crises when they're cold, only when they're hot'.[48] Thus, a key assumption about conflict management within a power-political framework is that power can be applied to re-orient the behaviour of the disputants. In a study of Kissinger's contribution to the Arab–Israeli peace process, Brian Mandell and Brian Tomlin concluded that a third party could employ 'substantial incentives, or punishments, to encourage behavioural change in the antagonists sufficient in degree and nature to support the transition to cooperative norms'.[49] For this approach certain preconditions have to be met before a dispute can be viewed as feasible for resolution. Either the parties are coerced into accepting a settlement process or they reach a point at which they consider themselves to be locked into what Saadia Touval and William Zartman have described as a 'mutually hurting stalemate'.[50] The problematic nature of such a 'stalemate' in terms of who is supposed to recognise it and whether it self-evidently presents itself or if it can be 'created' continues to be debated amongst analysts and practitioners of peacemaking.[51] What emerges from this discussion is a sense in which political realism in theory and practice conceptualises conflict resolution as a realm in which power politics is fundamental, if not all-encompassing. In effect realism contends that 'third parties themselves are often motivated to intervene because their own interests are threatened by the continuation of the dispute'.[52] This reveals an adherence towards implementing the principles of ethical egoism discussed in Chapter 2. A central tenet of realism is that the primary actors in the international system, nation-states, are first and foremost self-interested rational actors. Power-political third parties 'are often allies of one or both disputants, and the dispute may threaten such third parties in, or may threaten the entire system of alliances'.[53] The Cold War emphasised the maintenance of a balance of power regime as witnessed in the Middle East conflict in 1973 and the efforts to contain it, lest it spilled over and ignited a global confrontation. Realists consider that a conflict between two weaker entities can potentially 'threaten' the interests of the powerful third party. The process of conflict resolution is 'important' to the mediator primarily because it has an interest in securing a particular outcome. Therefore, little or no attention is paid to the moral interests of the disputants. This philosophical approach to third-party intervention exposes its fundamental limitation in that mediators are interested parties in a negotiation process and they can, and do, undermine the chances of resolving the conflict to the satisfaction of the other parties.

ILLUSTRATIONS OF POWER-POLITICAL INTERNATIONAL MEDIATION

The infiltration of the percepts of realism into the sphere of conflict resolution during the Cold War has left a legacy in international mediation that is proving to be inadequate with regard to laying the foundations to build peace between sub-national ethnic groups fighting their states, as discussed in Chapter 3. In his examination of the USA's mediation role between the Israelis and the Lebanese during the Cold War, Efraim Inbar observed that 'it is much more dangerous to estrange a superpower in an intermediary role than less powerful international actors. Indeed, the array of "sticks" and "carrots", which is at the essence of international interactions is invariably greater at the super-power level'.[54] Here, Inbar makes reference to the 'danger' that can befall a disputant resisting the power manoeuvres of the superpower; this is a clear reference to the 'arm twisting' potential of such a third party. Thus, an array of 'sticks' and 'carrots' was employed to achieve a settlement and the cessation of overt hostility; it remains, however, questionable as to what extent the underlying causes of the conflict were addressed. At the core of the US involvement in mediation initiatives during the Cold War was a 'concern that a conflict between two states may provide opportunities for the Soviet Union to increase its influence, by intervening on behalf of one side or the other'.[55]

Mark Katz suggests that given the relative unimportance of the so-called 'Third World' to the USA and the USSR they employed these mechanisms in several regional conflicts without much consideration for the moral consequences of the communities affected by the outcome. Katz observes that 'although the superpowers did not cause the many conflicts in Asia, Africa, and Latin America, their involvement often exacerbated them'.[56] Marianne Spiegel argues that with respect to US involvement in the Namibian dispute settlement process, it became evident that the US preoccupation 'with global or regional politics or with ideology can so bias American negotiators that their mediation efforts actually become counterproductive'.[57] Zalmay Khalilzad observes that in the case of Afghanistan the US misperception of the nature of the conflict and an assumption on its part that the Kabul government was a proxy for Soviet military control was exposed for its short-sightedness. After the Soviets withdrew the conflict remained, and continues to remain, unabated with devastating consequences for socio-political stability. Khalilzad proposes that in the coercive framework of conflict management established by Moscow and Washington through the medium of the UN in 1982, the negotiations 'were merely a continuation of conflict by other means. They were perceived by both sides as an adjunct to their military policies'.[58] Central to Khalilzad's contention is the view that the superpowers' larger interests blinded them to the very real conflict over substantive issues in Afghanistan and other parts of the world. To a large extent the mechanisms employed to address these disputes were ineffectual and often left the conflict in an unstable condition with the possibility of future re-escalation.

Touval adopts a different analysis and suggests instead that 'we can assume that American and Soviet mediation was more effective than the mediation of other international actors. This almost follows from the quality of being superpowers: they possess superior resources and carry more influence than other states'.[59] However, she subsequently concedes that there are in effect no established criteria on which to conclusively base such a judgement. Elsewhere, Zartman and Touval acknowledge that 'even where basic issues were resolved, the mediation provided conditions by which the parties could learn to live together, but did not effect any deep reconciliation of the parties or a restructuring of their perceptions of each other'.[60] In contrast, this should be the objective of all ethical approaches to peacemaking and peacebuilding.

THE UN'S ATTEMPT TO OPERATIONALISE ETHICAL PEACEMAKING

The UN did, however, manage to undertake peacemaking operations in situations where great power interests were not as salient. Through the office of the UN Secretary-General and in particular through the deployment of the Special Representatives of the UN Secretary-General a number of peacemaking efforts were made.[61] Notable relative successes include UN efforts in El Salvador, Guatemala, Cambodia, Namibia and Mozambique, where peacemaking and the transition to peacebuilding was effectively operationalised. Conflict situations in these countries were resolved through negotiated peace agreements led or supported by the UN and other international actors. According to Dower, 'over the years the UN has played its part in containing violent conflict, whether through the often unnoticed "good offices" of the Secretary-General and his colleagues, or through the intervention of peacekeeping forces'.[62] In this regard, the UN was on a certain level able to operationalise an ethical framework for peacemaking. However, this was clearly constrained by the geopolitical interests of global powers and regional hegemons.

The cases mentioned above reveal that where conditions permitted and when there was consensus between the powerful members of the UN, the organisation was able to implement its ethical mandate of the pacific resolution of conflicts. This suggests that the UN could only selectively operationalise its ethical framework for mediation. The UN provides an ethical framework for resolving disputes which is often flouted or undermined by its member states, who tend to advance their parochial self-interests rather than promote the global interest. Even after the end of the Cold War, the UN is still dominated by statist-realist assumptions which limit its effectiveness. In this regard, the UN can still be reclaimed by internationalists and cosmopolitanism provided there is a conscious effort to do so.

Internationalism, according to Dower, sees

> the present world order of states as a value worth preserving. The society of states is itself of vital importance, both for the preservation of nation-states within it and because such a system of states is the only realistic way of organising human affairs.[63]

In this context, internationalists would view the UN as 'primarily an instrument for the maintenance of world order, peace, and security . . . it is essentially a statist organisation, dedicated to preserving the state-system'.[64] By contrast, cosmopolitanism, which has also been discussed substantively in this book in Chapter 3, assesses the utility of an international organisation based on 'how well it allows and enables human beings to achieve well-being and moral agency'.[65] Based on this cosmopolitan approach, while the UN is an embodiment of global values, the fact that it does not effectively ensure the well-being of all humans means that it should be reformed. As Dower notes:

if the UN can be changed to be more effective towards realising these goals, then it should be changed. If in changing the UN to become more effective the freedom of action of member states becomes more limited because of the strengthening of international law, then that is to be accepted.[66]

The form of cosmopolitanism advocated in this book proceeds largely along these lines. Therefore, recent efforts to transform the UN from within to improve its performance in mediation, peacemaking and peacebuilding (see Chapter 7) are a welcome strategy.

EFFORTS TO REVIVE THE UN'S THIRD-PARTY ROLE IN THE POST-COLD WAR ERA

Subsequent to the corruption of its conflict management and resolution institutions and processes during the Cold War, there was an attempt to revitalise the norms that initially animated the UN. The former UN Secretary-General Boutros Boutros-Ghali published in 1992 *An Agenda for Peace*, a report which argued for proactive peacemaking and humanitarian intervention.[67] It outlined suggestions for enabling the UN to respond quickly and effectively to threats to international peace and security in the post-Cold War era. In particular, four major areas of activity were identified, namely: preventive diplomacy; peacemaking; peacekeeping; and post-conflict peacebuilding.

Preventive diplomacy is 'action to prevent disputes from arising between parties, to prevent existing disputes from escalating into conflict and to limit the spread of the latter when they occur.'[68] Peacemaking is 'action to bring hostile parties to agreement, essentially through such peaceful means as those foreseen in Chapter VI of the Charter of the United Nations'. Peacemaking therefore includes using mediation to persuade parties in a conflict to cease hostilities and to negotiate a peaceful settlement to their dispute. Generally, preventive diplomacy, which also includes the use of mediation, seeks to resolve disputes before they become violent. Peacemaking is employed to stop ongoing conflicts and to find solutions that can preserve peace.

The UN Department for Political Affairs (DPA) is responsible, within the UN Secretariat, for conducting peacemaking and preventive diplomacy. It needs, therefore, to have an in-house repository of mediation expertise. As the Cold War came to a close, new opportunities emerged for negotiating peace agreements. A number of conflicts were brought to an end, either through direct UN mediation or by the efforts of other third parties acting with the support of the UN.[69] This includes disputes in El Salvador, Guatemala, Namibia, Cambodia, Mozambique,

Tajikistan, Bougainville, Afghanistan, Sierra Leone, Burundi and, more recently, the North–South conflict in the Sudan. In addition, an undetermined number of potential disputes have been deffused through preventive diplomacy and other forms of conflict prevention.

The end of the Cold War brought about a shift in the geostrategic imperatives of the superpowers and many governments were faced with challenges from within their states. Today, the legacy of this era still persists and many countries are having to deal with sub-national armed resistance movements. The most difficult situations include internal disputes in Colombia, Côte d'Ivoire, the Democratic Republic of the Congo (DRC), Israel and the Occupied Territories, Kosovo, Nepal, Somalia, Sri Lanka, the Sudan and Western Sahara, to name but a few. In addition, there are still inter-state conflicts between India and Pakistan on the Kashmir issue and the as-yet unresolved tensions between Ethiopia and Eritrea. As a result, the demands placed on the UN have increased. The High-Level Panel on Threats, Challenges and Change noted that the demand for the UN's 'good offices' and mediation in particular had 'skyrocketed'.[70]

THE UN MEDIATION SUPPORT UNIT: PROSPECTS FOR REVITALISING ETHICAL MEDIATION

Given this increase in dispute situations requiring third-party mediation and the demands placed on the DPA, it became necessary to increase the capacity of the department as a matter of urgency[71]. The Mediation Support Unit was established as a centre of expertise and a resource on mediation for the DPA and UN system, following the Outcome Document of the UN General Assembly in September 2005. The MSU serves as a focal point for interaction with other third-party mediation efforts in which the UN can play a supporting role. The MSU also provide mediation support services through its mediation support officers and has established a system to identify and recruit the best possible mediators to serve as mediation support officers. The unit also provides mediation training through its mediation training officers. It has adopted a long-term strategy and strives to nurture future generations of special envoys of the UN. The MSU also seeks to equip regional divisions with the necessary knowledge of the most effective strategies for mediation in the specific political, cultural and geographic realities that they encounter. The Unit has further assessed the potential of interfacing with indigenous mediation systems so as to encourage the ownership by local populations of the process.[72]

The MSU serves as a centre of expertise on mediation. It briefs UN officials who are about to embark on mediation processes and provides support services for ongoing mediation efforts. From its cadre of mediation support officers, the MSU can deploy mediation experts to assist UN envoys and other officials in field missions. Mediation support officers need to have the requisite knowledge of the cultural, socio-economic and political contexts of the conflicts that they are designated to address and therefore have to be skilled practitioners with a knowledge of, and a background in, international relations.

The MSU also seeks to develop and enhance the knowledge and skill of DPA staff by providing an efficient and effective training and development service within the department. Mediation training officers assess the training needs of the DPA to identify opportunities for improved mediation strategies. The mediation training officers develop, facilitate and conduct training programmes on conflict analysis, negotiation and mediation procedures. Mediation training officers also provide UN mediators with advice on UN standards and operating procedures. They also provide a briefing on the UN peacemaker website and demonstrate how it can be utilised by partners active in peacemaking efforts around the world including member states, regional organisations, civil society and non-governmental organisations; they therefore need to have some experience in a training environment. Other issues include how the activities of the MSU can be mainstreamed throughout the Department of Political Affairs.

Resource mobilisation for the MSU is a vital issue. The High-Level Panel concluded that there was a chronic 'under-resourcing' of the Department of Political Affairs. The Panel noted that 'the deliberate under-resourcing' of the Department 'by member states is at odds with these same states' professed desire for a strong United Nations.' The Panel urged that the DPA be provided with additional resources. The DPA has, however, been able to carry out its invaluable initiatives thanks to the voluntary contributions to its two main trust funds: the Trust Fund for Special Missions and Other Activities Related to Preventive Diplomacy and Peacemaking and the Trust Fund for Preventive Action. With reference to the potential activities of the MSU, the Terms of Reference for the Trust Fund for Preventive Diplomacy and Peacemaking notes that it was established to 'support peacemaking activities' including the 'mediation activities of Special Envoys or Special Representatives of the Secretary-General'. The terms of reference also note that these funds would be utilised to provide

long-term and systematic education and training of appropriate personnel including government personnel, United Nations personnel, mediators, regional organisations and NGO personnel, and representatives of parties to conflict, with the goal of improving capacity for early warning, mediation and conflict resolution.[73]

There is a need to determine where funding for the MSU should come from. Given that the decision to establish the Unit was taken with the consent of member states, the meeting should assess whether new funds should be sourced directly from the regular budget rather than depleting the limited trust funds. Beyond the need to mobilise resources it is important to identify the potential constraints on the effective operationalisation of the MSU.

The MSU's primary objective is to put the mediation efforts of the DPA on a much more robust and ethical footing in order to increase the likelihood of generating sustainable agreements between parties.[74] The medium- to long-term strategy of the MSU includes empowering countries to establish their own national mediation offices because differences are bound to emerge in the future and it is much more economical and ultimately sustainable for countries to manage their own affairs.[75] This also enables the DPA to build local relationships and the trust required for ethical diplomatic interventions.

NON-OFFICIAL THIRD-PARTY INTERVENTION EFFORTS

Even though the UN was structurally paralysed there were other principled efforts at peacemaking. It is useful to assess other conflict resolution frameworks that existed outside the UN framework, particularly during the Cold War when superpower imperatives impeded the effective implementation of ethical policies. Intervention and mediation activities during the Cold War were undertaken by a variety of third parties including the Holy See, Moral Re-Armament (MRA), the International Negotiation Network (INN), ecumenical bodies such as the Quakers as well as a number of academic researchers in peace and conflict studies.[76]

MORAL MEDIATION: QUAKER INTERVENTIONS DURING THE COLD WAR

This section will assess the ethical basis of the peacebuilding efforts of the Quakers. Sydney Bailey describes non-official mediation as 'mediation in international disputes by persons who are not employed by or responsible to a national government or an inter-government organisation'.[77] The Quakers have throughout their history been involved in conflict resolution and mediation. They have developed a social activist programme predicated on pacifism and the practice of consensual decision-making. By seeking to apply the central tenets of their religious beliefs to the realms of international and domestic politics, the Quakers have endeavoured to sustain the principles of peace, justice and reconciliation in the difficult and often frustrating task of mediation.[78] It is therefore useful to engage in an analysis of the philosophical foundation and the practical application of the Quaker approach to international relations. This will involve briefly tracing the origins of their activities and examining their methodology in dealing with various problems culminating in an investigation of how their ideas were put into practice in the Nigeria–Biafra civil war of 1967–70. This section will also assess the moral dimension of Quaker mediation efforts.

ORIGINS OF THE QUAKER BELIEF SYSTEM

The Quakers have been instrumental in establishing the modern peace movement. In 1647 George Fox, the founder of the Society of Friends, refused to take up arms in the English civil war. Fox's stance was based on his conviction that there was a fundamental contradiction between the spirit of Christ and the spirit of war. He in effect provided the embryonic core for the pacifist position that the Quakers subsequently adopted.[79] As described by the historian Arnold Lloyd, Fox 'was oppressed by the discrepancy between Christian profession and Christian practice; he sensed a failure of Christian faith in the very outbreak of civil war, and he was conscious of frustration and futility in his own Christian living'.[80] Lloyd further notes that Fox 'got a deeper impression of the intellectual and moral chaos which accompanied the war, and of the disillusion which was becoming more and more apparent in Puritan ranks'.[81] Furthermore, after several years of searching for a solution in new notions and ideas, Fox described an experience in which an inner voice spoke to him, telling him that there is an 'inward teacher' in everyone in the form of Jesus Christ who can and will 'speak to thy condition'.[82] Fox subsequently pondered this revelation and felt a calling and responsibility to direct men to their inward teacher. Fox came to the understanding that if people 'would discipline themselves to listen to this voice, they would be guided in all their perplexities, theoretical and practical'.[83] The evolution of the Quaker society can best be understood in terms of the communication of moral advice and of helping to solve practical problems.[84] The tradition of Quaker peacemaking can be traced back to the efforts of William Penn to reach a peace agreement with the native Americans living near the newly formed colony of Pennsylvania in the eighteenth century.[85]

THE QUAKER APPROACH TO INTERNATIONAL MEDIATION

The Quaker ethos advocates peace, tolerance and goodwill as illustrated by Bailey when he says that because

> Quakers believe that there is that of God in all people to which others may respond, they not only hope for the best but they expect the best, believing that bad situations are likely to get better with the input of a little honest goodwill.[86]

Bailey further suggests that with reference to conflict resolution the Quakers did not necessarily have any 'special aptitudes or skills as mediators'; rather they endeavoured to sympathise with both sides in international disputes because they felt that both were 'usually victims of past mistakes'.[87] John Volkmar, a Quaker mediator who helped with the peacebuilding efforts in the Nigerian civil war of the late 1960s, reinforced this view when he suggested that with regard to conflicts 'no problem is ever resolved by war. War only postpones the problem, and it is destructive, expensive, and painful. Ultimately you will have to sit down together'.[88] Quakers adhered to four key elements in their approach to international conflict resolution which are relevant to the central theme of this book, namely:

1. The view that the use of power for the purpose of dominating others is detrimental to human communities;
2. A belief that opening the lines of communication between disputants is vital to correcting misperceptions and reducing mistrust;
3. There has to be a commitment towards refraining from being judgemental about the activities of the parties that one seeks to mediate between;
4. There has to be a commitment to maintaining a presence at the grassroots level which to Quakers is an indispensable criterion for gaining trust and helping to foster consent between disputants.

An integral component of the Quaker philosophy was a critique of the use of power for the purposes of domination in human affairs. Quakers believe that the use of force nearly always only serves to create more problems than it can solve. They held the view that as peacemakers their commitment was to peace and justice without ulterior motives. Bailey, however, emphasises that far from being out of touch with the realities of their environment, Quakers always renounced the use of armed force irrespective of the consequences for themselves and others, yet they could understand why people were driven to take the military option when peaceful means failed.[89] The fact that Quaker initiatives some-times found themselves at odds with certain parties, when they declined to partake in practices that contravened their belief system, served to remind them that they were not dislocated from the attitudes of human prejudice and egocentric passion that prevailed during the execution of wars.

Even though religion has often been a divisive factor in international relations, religions and spiritually oriented non-official mediators have been prominent actors in conflict resolution.[90] Quakers embodied this orientation in the way they brought their spiritual resources to bear on the difficult and often frustrating problem of international conflict. They developed a style and moral approach to mediation which, whilst retaining some generic principles with the majority of other non-official mediating parties, were tempered by the uniquely Quaker method which traces its historical lineage to the late seventeenth and early eighteenth centuries. When intervening in a conflict situation their activities were wholly geared towards opening lines of communication, reducing fears and misperceptions and advocating for a negotiated settlement while supporting the official conflict resolution efforts.[91]

The Quaker approach emphasised the necessity of direct negotiations between parties whenever possible. Bailey notes that 'Quakers are reluctant to believe that direct contacts between the parties do not always make things better'.[92] In attempting to establish effective pro-cesses 'they considered the contacts across political barriers, in the right circumstances, lead to greater human understanding, and that under-standing of those on the other side should facilitate the resolution of the dispute or conflict'.[93] The late Adam Curle, a distinguished Quaker mediator, described the faulty perceptions, distrust and poor commu-nications that accompany deteriorating relations during a conflict and pointed out that the role of the mediator in this scenario is to reverse these damaging trends by correcting misperceptions, reducing distrust and improving communications. Curle further describes how he felt compelled to do what was possible through reason and persuasion so as to create an atmosphere in which reasonable discussions could be sustained and rational bargaining be successfully implemented.[94] To transmit messages and to understand the attitudes, perceptions and fears of the parties meant that a mediator had to have a cultivated skill of listening. For the Quaker mediator, listening also served a spiritual function as described by Curle when he notes that:

> to listen attentively is to act autonomously . . . thus as in prayer, so in listening we
> try to reach a deeper part of our being . . . the importance of listening then, is not

only that we 'hear' the other in a profound sense but communicate with him or her through our true nature.[95]

Therefore, 'very strong and positive feelings are often aroused in both the listener and the one listened to. In this way peacemakers may reach the part of the other person that is really able to make peace, outwardly as well as inwardly'.[96] Thus, a fundamental tenet of the Quaker approach to conflict resolution is that they morally refrain from being judgemental about the activities of the parties involved. As mediators, the Quakers do not necessarily have to agree with any proposal submitted by the parties in dispute. Their role as mediators is not to advance personal opinions but to help the parties find common ground so long as this activity does not contravene their values and objectives.[97] Allied to this position is the Quaker insistence that each side has the 'ability to terminate the Quaker intervention at will without repercussions'.[98] For the Quakers, this condition of consent is necessary so that neither party feels coerced into the process, as this would go against their moral beliefs. This attitude was captured by Mike Yarrow, in his comprehensive study of the Quakers, when he concluded that it was not simply a matter of being impartial; the Quakers had to be *seen* as being impartial.[99] This is an indispensable element for any consensual mechanism of conflict resolution. In the realm of international relations where power-oriented strategic behaviour is so prevalent amongst most of the actors, non-official mediators working through a mechanism predicated on consent must continually, in the words of Thomas Princen, 'demonstrate to others that they are not like most other actors'.[100] Quaker mediators have demonstrated patience and perseverance in dealing with often complex disputes, which attests to their ability to gain the trust and consent of the disputants.

The Quakers have often maintained a presence at the grassroots level to help with famine relief efforts, refugee settlement or generic development projects. However, they did not maintain 'a panel of expert mediators in some key location, ready to be dispatched to an area of conflict' when the need arose.[101] Often the Quaker mediators would not even know the representatives of the parties in conflict or have a sound understanding of the issues in dispute. They usually became involved in the conflict situation because they were already involved in the aforementioned problems in the area and felt that they could play a role having gained the respect of a certain party in the dispute or if they were called upon by a governmental organisation to undertake mediation.[102] The Quaker stance, in effect, was one of dealing with each situation within its localised context. The approach to most conflicts was generic only to the extent that they maintained an ethical commitment to acknowledging and recognising the substantive security concerns of the warring groups. The Quakers brought to their process of conflict resolution an attitude of tolerance and moral egalitarianism which in turn encouraged the genuine and consensual relationship that existed between them, as mediators, and the parties in dispute. Having discussed the four elements which Quakers aspire to, we can briefly examine an example of a Quaker effort to mediate in the Nigerian civil war, also known as the Biafran war.

QUAKER MEDIATION IN BIAFRA: A CASE OF ETHICAL MEDIATION IN NIGERIA, 1967–70

The Quakers have been involved in a supportive role in many major conflicts since 1945, including conflicts in the Middle East in 1955 and 1967; work between East and West Germany following the construction of the Berlin Wall from 1962 to 1973; mediation between India and Pakistan in 1965; and the Nigeria–Biafra civil war in 1967–70. Due to the scope and purposes of this chapter only one of these cases will be examined as it adequately serves the purposes of highlighting the main theme of this book, namely the ethics of building peace. The Nigeria–Biafra civil war also contributes to a sub-theme of this book, which is the importance of establishing more ethical processes for dealing with the emergence of sub-national conflicts in a world of nation-states. Biafra was a sub-national group seeking to negotiate its autonomy from Nigeria.

Nigeria achieved independence from Britain through a peaceful decolonisation process. However, the British left behind a young state which was deeply divided along regional, ethnic and religious lines.[103] The Eastern and Western regions of Nigeria, where Christianity and traditional religions prevailed, were economically more dominant than the Northern region, which was predominantly Muslim and also politically dominant. Because of the inadequacies of the Nigerian constitution in providing for the demands of sub-national groups in the country, political patronage and corruption led to the destabilisation of the fragile government. The conflict in Nigeria locates its genesis in the ethnic and religious cleavages in a nation-state held together by regional divisions dating from the period of colonisation.[104] Nigeria has approximately two hundred and fifty distinct language groups; however two-thirds of the population is composed of three groups of approximately equal numbers. The Hausa-Fulani is situated generally in the North, the Yoruba in the West and the Ibo in the East. These three groups dominate, to a larger extent than other groups, the economic and political activities in the country, a factor which has as a consequence spawned competition amongst them. Because of the colonial practices of the British, the East and West were relatively more advanced than the North in education, development and representation in the civil service and the officer ranks of the military. The North in turn dominated Nigerian politics.[105]

After independence there were widespread allegations of fraud and violence by government officials and in 1966 there were two military coups. The first coup in January saw the Ibos' attempt to capture power. While they were unsuccessful in this objective, they eliminated a significant number of the country's political leadership, which included most Northerners. The attempted coup was eventually quelled by another Ibo, Major-General Aguyi-Ironsi, who assumed the mantle of head of state of a federal military government. Ironsi's cabinet was ethnically mixed but he surrounded himself with Ibos in the top positions. He neglected to bring the coup plotters, his fellow Easterners, to trial even though they were jailed. Through a series of miscalculations Ironsi faced a growing tide of opinion against him. Many Nigerians, particularly in the North, saw the counter-coup as an attempt by the Ibo to take over the government. As a consequence, demonstrations in the North against Ironsi's policies turned violent and the Eastern Ibos residing in the region were targeted, hundreds of people dying in the process.[106]

Another coup in July 1966 orchestrated by Northerners eliminated Ironsi and his military clique and installed a Northerner, Lieutenant Colonel Yakubu Gowon, as head of state. Gowon convened a constitutional conference to make recommendations on an appropriate form of civilian government for Nigeria. Before the completion of its work, in September 1966, there were orchestrated massacres against Ibos living in the predominantly Fulani North which brought about retaliation against the Fulanis living in the predominantly Ibo East. This development fuelled and served to spread the violence into central Nigeria. Government military forces were involved in the pogroms in which approximately ten thousand Ibos were killed. An estimated 1.5 million Ibos fled the North for their Eastern home region.[107] In return the Eastern military Governor, Lieutenant Colonel Chukwuemeka Ojukwu, ordered the expulsion of all non-Ibos from the region on the grounds that he could not ensure their safety.

At this point in time Nigeria was sliding towards civil war. In January 1967, an attempt to find a compromise on governance was attempted by the head of state of neighbouring Ghana with little success. On 30 May

1967, Ojukwu, backed by the Eastern Consultative Assembly, declared the Eastern region of Nigeria as the sovereign republic of Biafra. The Nigerian federal army initiated 'police action' against the secessionist movement. The Biafran army responded with a military incursion into the Mid-west region of Nigeria. At this stage the federal government instituted a campaign of total war against the secessionists in a conflict that was eventually resolved militarily thanks to the vast resources at the disposal of the federal government. Ultimately, the attempted secession was quelled and the region was reinstated into the federation.

Despite the outcome of the conflict it is nevertheless beneficial for the purposes of understanding the multilateral dimension of conflict resolution to engage in an analysis of the role played by the various third parties in attempting to resolve the conflict. It is worthwhile to note that the Quakers were not the only third parties involved in trying to resolve this particular conflict. The Quaker mediation efforts over the course of the conflict ran parallel to those of the Organization of African Unity and the Commonwealth, as well as British and American political leaders. Thus, any attempt to specifically judge the effects of any one of these interventions would be inconclusive. What can be analysed is the mechanism of conflict resolution that a certain party utilised and the nature of its interaction with the parties in dispute. In light of this, an analysis of Quaker mediation in the Nigeria–Biafra dispute will examine how the Quakers brought their spiritual values and their practical resources to bear on this seemingly protracted conflict.

The strength of the Quaker contacts in West Africa and their interaction with Nigerian and Biafran officials – through Quaker conferences for diplomats – enhanced the probability for starting the process of mediation in the conflict.[108] Adam Curle, who had, in late 1996, just returned from a Quaker mediation mission in India and Pakistan, contacted the Quakers' UN headquarters in New York to see if his experience could be of use in the Nigeria–Biafra conflict. He managed to meet with the Nigerian ambassador to the UN who indicated to Curle that Nigerians were sensitive to external intervention. The feelers put out to the Nigerian and Biafran authorities were generally received favourably and coupled with clearances from the headquarters of the Quaker committees in Philadelphia and London. Curle was given the go-ahead to set the mediation machinery in motion.[109] In doing so he appealed to a key element in the Quaker approach with regards to opening the lines of communication between belligerents.

The nature of the Quakers' ethical commitment to sustaining impartiality, another of their mediation objectives, came to the fore when Curle was accompanied by John Volkmar. In any given conflict it is often difficult for a third-party entity to remain 'morally neutral' in the sense that during the course of a lengthy process of conflict resolution a mediator can develop an 'underlying empathy with one side [more] than the other'.[110] Bailey suggests that to counteract this tendency and in order to make the mediation team more versatile the Quakers tend to entrust mediator work to at least two representatives.[111] Curle and Volkmar toured Nigeria and Biafra for four weeks in April and May 1967, in what were essentially reconnaissance visits to establish contact with the leaders of the two parties and to offer to gather and transmit information in a way that would seek to alleviate tensions. In the East they met with Ojukwu and in the federal republic they met with two officials, Okoi Arikpo, the Commissioner for External Affairs, and Hamzat Ahmadu, a Principal Secretary to Gowon.[112]

The conflict was underway by 1967 and the Quakers initially decided to support an African initiative to resolve the conflict. The OAU formed a consultative committee comprised of six African heads of state in September of that year. Some of the members of this committee were themselves facing secessionist movements and instead of seeking to address the substantive concerns of both sides, the committee opted to side with Gowon and called on the Biafrans to renounce secession and to accept reinstatement into a united Nigeria.[113] The Quakers viewed these developments as counter-productive and began to explore a different approach to the situation. With the collusion of the President of neighbouring Niger, the Philadelphia branch of the Quakers decided to set up secret low-level meetings, thus bringing to the fore their commitment towards fostering direct communication, which would essentially be unofficial and would seek to establish talks that would eventually lead to negotiations.[114] Curle, at the time, argued that in the interests of influencing policy the meetings should be aimed at involving high-level officials, but the Philadelphia committee felt that lower-level meetings would be most effective. There was, however, a general agreement to proceed 'as the way opened' and in a quintessentially Quaker approach with trips to both sides to attempt to open lines of communication and reduce fears and misperceptions.[115]

By the time that their mission was reactivated in January 1968 Curle and Volkmar felt that if they revealed too much to lower-level officials about their intentions to convene a meeting, extremists on either side would have the opportunity to scuttle their efforts. They realised that an early meeting with Gowon was essential if any effective measures were to result. When a communiqué to the Principal Secretary Ahmadu proved to be inconclusive, they approached the Minister for External Affiars, Edwin Ogbu, who thought that there might be a role for the

Quakers and arranged a meeting with Gowon in February 1968. Gowon was favourable to their proposal for a secret meeting, though sceptical because a previous meeting had failed. He pointed out that the Biafran propaganda machine had systematically misconstrued his overtures for peace and he felt that the Quakers would be subjected to a similar form of manipulation. Nevertheless, Gowon sanctioned the Quakers' attempt to pursue the idea with the Biafrans. Although he did not oppose the Quaker trip to Biafra he informed them that he could not guarantee their safety, as it was the federal government's policy to shoot down all aircraft in Biafran airspace. When the Quaker representatives declined to attempt to rescind their peacemaking mission in the light of the risks involved Gowon offered them a concession which they could present to the 'rebels'. Gowon suggested that together with the secret meetings he was also prepared to stop his troops' advance if Ojuwku agreed to a ceasefire, and he would even entertain the presence of a third of the forces to police the frontlines. From the outset, the government had maintained that the war was a domestic affair and publicly it re-articulated this position. By agreeing to accept an external peacekeeping force, Gowon was demonstrating a commitment to de-escalating the conflict which in turn provided the Quakers with hope and encouragement in their efforts to resolve the dispute.[116] Gowon's actions were intriguing given the fact that he had previously spurned similar efforts at mediation by the Vatican, the World Council of Churches and the Presbyterian Church of Canada who he viewed as predominantly pro-Biafran. This impression may have been engendered by the papal envoys and church delegations to the predominantly Catholic region of Biafra and the ensuing highly publicised reception by Ojukwu (for the purposes of propaganda in Gowon's view) proffered to these parties.[117]

At the meeting in March Curle, accompanied this time by Walter Martin, informed Ojukwu of their contact with Gowon and the proposal for a secret meeting. Ojukwu responded favourably to the idea of having a meeting on neutral ground and emphasised that the presence of a 'non-official' organisation like the Quakers was important. Curle and Martin were aware that Ojukwu had certain reservations about the peace terms being issued by the federal government and did not insist on his response.[118] At this stage the Quakers had achieved significant reactions from the warring parties, which illustrated that their objective of reducing suspicion and exploiting possible compromises was on the verge of acquiring impetus. Their subsequent activities for the duration of this drawn-out conflict were similar in nature and in the majority of cases the warring parties demonstrated their willingness to engage in meetings that were mediated impartially by the Quakers.

In what was essentially a protracted sub-national conflict, the issues at stake were diametrically opposed. On the question of either unity or secession the conflict was, in Princen's view 'strictly zero sum and the bargaining range consisted of only two mutually exclusive points'.[119] The mechanisms of conflict resolution had to contend with a particular equation. While the OAU and the British negotiators adopted a partisan stance in Nigeria's favour, the Quaker approach remained vigilant to their spiritual principles and sought to sustain their moral legitimacy in the eyes of both parties and thus encourage a genuine ethical engagement between them. The Quakers sent groups of representatives to Biafra that included two people on four separate occasions in which they met with Ojukwu twice and with federal officials eight times including meetings with Gowon on six occasions. In addition, the Quakers met with representatives of the two sides in New York, Washington, London, Paris, Geneva, Lisbon, Kampala, Addis Ababa and Niamey. The federal government with its relatively more substantial resources was in a better position to sustain war and eventually managed to overwhelm the Biafran secessionists and reinstate the region into Nigeria. Gowon, however, took a principled stand against any possible federal occupation and retribution against the Ibo people in the Eastern region by allowing them to fully integrate into the Nigerian way of life and participate as citizens in a united country. Throughout these developments the Quakers' ethical commitment to peace and justice helped them to earn the trust, goodwill and consent of the parties.

ASSESSING QUAKER ETHICS OF MEDIATION

As mentioned previously, even though the Quakers were not entirely successful in bringing about a secession of hostilities in the Biafran conflict their approach provided useful insights into mediation and peacebuilding. The Quaker mediators were non-official actors and did not presume to take the lead in the official dispute settlement efforts. They operated largely in a supportive role and in concert with the OAU, the British government and the Commonwealth Secretariat, who undertook the official negotiations. As alluded to previously, it is difficult to quantify the degree to which the parallel and intersecting efforts of the third-party entities either complemented each other or negated each other's efforts. In light of this, an exercise in the analysis of the conflict resolution mechanisms in terms of their 'results' is a difficult and arguably highly contentious undertaking. However, an assessment of their particular approach and the dynamic that it engendered from the disputants can be undertaken.

The reactions of the Nigerian and Biafran representatives to the Quaker efforts help to shed light on how the parties assessed their motives. Gowon and Ojukwu both exhibited a degree of trust in the Quakers when they accepted the principle to partake in secret meetings. This was an activity which the Quakers believed would lead them along the road to 'greater human understanding' and thus 'facilitate the resolution of the dispute'. Thus a fundamental feature of any moral mechanism striving to build peace is:

1. its ability to inculcate the consent of the parties involved;
2. its spatial proximity to the disputants in an environment devoid of obstacles and barriers to the cultivation of understanding.

The Quakers were consciously aware that even the most vigilant individual could easily be swayed by the more persuasive argument of one party or repulsed by the atrocities of another. In an effort to remain non-partisan and flexible in their approach to making peace the Quakers endeavoured, where possible, to use two representatives. Also important to the Quaker approach was the belief that the channels of communication, once established among the parties, would only be effective if they involved representatives that had any say in the formulation of policy. Thus, the Quakers would endeavour to rely on the endorsed consent of the leaders of both parties and they were not judgemental even though they were aware of the atrocities being committed by both sides. As noted earlier, their ethical approach viewed all sides involved in a conflict as having been victims at some point in the past. The Nigerian authorities that suppressed the Biafrans, for example, had historically been victims of British colonialism.

INSIGHTS FROM QUAKER MEDIATION

Useful insights are to be gained from the Quakers' unofficial approach to mediation particularly the fact that they were 'not employed by or responsible to a national government or an inter-governmental organisation'.[120] The Quakers carried distinct moral credentials and endeavoured to implement their philosophical principles. Their unofficial status brought with it freedom from the constraints of governmental and intergovernmental protocol and the pronounced sensitivity that accompanies the diplomatic interaction in mediation processes. Mawlawi captures the ethical essence of these approaches when he observes that practitioners of moral mediation processes 'cite their commitment to a long-term solution that is equitable to all of the conflicting parties –

as opposed to a settlement at all costs – as a primary reason for their success in informal mediation',[121] to the extent that their 'lack of coercive power frees them from being perceived as arm twisters, their military or political weakness paradoxically translates into a mediatory strength'.[122] Ultimately, the ethical dimension of such mediation approaches is based on the process which 'lays the groundwork for their acceptance as impartial ambassadors of goodwill and enables them to inspire trust and confidence among the parties to the conflict'.[123] Such approaches operationalise a methodology of ensuring that the concerns of the parties are listened to. They emphasise, as an integral component to the process, the clarification of all the underlying interests so as to ensure that the fears and concerns that lead to misperception are minimised. Quaker mediation in particular is a normative approach that demands consensus. In other words, it is an approach that cannot proceed without the consent of all the parties involved. These approaches effectively recognise the 'psycho-subjective' nature of a conflict and accordingly they temper their design to effectively address and resolve the dispute. This was evident in the words of Curle when he was reflecting on the nature of Quaker mediation, which he described as 'essentially an applied psychological tactic'.[124] For Curle the issues that separated people were on the whole not impossible to overcome; he believed that the real difficulty lay in trying to change people's perception or in helping them to re-perceive their enemies, themselves and the situation in its entirety. Curle notes that:

> however genuine, the causes of the quarrel are psychological: fear, fury, ignorance, the demonisation of the enemy and the glorification of one's own side, pride, dread of losing face, resentment, vanity, guilt for the destruction being caused and many other negative emotions and attitudes.[125]

These approaches to mediation ultimately advance our understanding when compared to the League of Nations' efforts in dispute settlement in the pre-Cold War era. The League of Nations attempted to institutionalise morality in its conflict resolution processes. It sought to do this by designing and concretising an ethical framework within which the parties interacted. In informal approaches, such as Quaker mediation, parties to a conflict are drawn into a process of defining and demarcating the moral 'norms' of interaction between themselves and the intervening third party. Normatively and ethically driven third-party interventions in Princen's view seek 'to promote alternative norms between disputants'.[126] By partaking in a mediation process through their own will and consent parties are in effect involved in the process of *validating* the ethical norms of interaction.

THE MENNONITES AND INTERNATIONAL PEACEBUILDING

It would be misleading to give the impression that only the Quakers have developed methods and processes of peacemaking directly derived from their moral beliefs. There are a range of such traditions not only within Christianity but also in other faiths. The Mennonites also developed an approach to peacemaking and have always been adherents to the global peace movement. The Mennonites were established as a religious grouping in 1561 by a former Frisian Catholic priest, Menno Simons, in the northern Netherlands, as an offshoot to the Anabaptists. The Anabaptists based in Munster had tried to create a peaceful community by force. This caused Menno to ask, 'how can Christians fight with the implements of war?'[127] This led him 'towards the enunciation of a fully non-violent stance' like George Fox of the Quakers.

Like most pacifist movements at the time, Mennonites believed that 'they must wait patiently for the change in men's hearts, and tried in the meantime to dissociate themselves where possible from the evil of war and the society contaminated by it'.[128] Pacifists already possessed a cosmopolitan sentiment in this regard, because they believed in an universalisable moral objection to all war. Mennonites adopted these principles to the point of objecting to being drafted into armies. In Holland in 1575, Prince William of Orange accorded an exemption to the Mennonites from being drafted into armies in return for their undertaking some form of civilian service.[129] This was the first recorded instance of a government giving leeway to conscientious objectors. This tradition has since left a legacy in history with conscientious objectors also resisting partaking in the First and Second World Wars.

The Mennonites settled in Germantown, Pennsylvania, in the mid-seventeenth century and maintained their traditions. During the Second World War, through their participation in Civilian Public Service (CPS) camps, Mennonites were able to avoid partaking in war activities. Thus, the Mennonites can be lauded with having launched the modern conscientious objectors movement which continues to have resonance in war-affected countries like Israel.

In more recent times the Mennonites have contributed towards ethical peacebuilding in international affairs. An extensive and comprehensive treatment is beyond the scope of this section; suffice to note that, through the Mennonite Central Committee and its International Conciliation Service, they have been involved in promoting micro- and meso-level peacebuilding in South Africa, Northern Ireland, Colombia, Nicaragua, Somalia, Liberia, Haiti and Israel.[130] John-Paul Lederach, in his book *From the Ground Up: Mennonite Contributions to International Peacebuilding*, notes that there is an increasing recognition of the role of religious leaders, transnational religious movements and faith-based NGOs in the post-Cold War era.[131] In this regard, Mennonites have contributed significantly towards an ethic of peacebuilding from both a philosophical and a practical point of view.

ETHICAL NEGOTIATION IN THE CONTEXT OF ONGOING VIOLENT CONFRONTATION

A key challenge to promoting ethical stances is the fact that violence between the parties generally accompanies negotiation and mediation processes, suggesting that it is a challenge to adopt such progressive values. Violence often coexists simultaneously with the claims by the parties of their willingness to embark on a route to seek alternative ways to achieve a settlement, or as Timothy Sisk notes, to 'foment violence at critical turning points in order to demonstrate that the negotiations themselves are unworkable and should be abandoned for a return to a zero-sum pursuit of the conflict'.[132]

Violence, however, can also be pursued to prevent marginalisation. This is carried out by 'political actors who support negotiation, but fear exclusion from political power in the new order, [and] may foment violence at critical turning points in the negotiations to ensure that their interests are protected in the final agreement'. Also, violence may be used to destabilise the opponent in response to a perception of the opponent's strength. The objective in this case is to enhance one's

own power in an effort to strike a more favourable deal at the table. Demonstrating the capacity to frustrate the negotiations process through instigating political violence is expected by actors engaging in such tactics to strengthen the hand of negotiations who otherwise may be perceived as relatively weak.[133]

Such tactics invariably emerge in most sub-national conflicts. The extremist groups in the Palestinian resistance against Israeli occupation of their lands have been known to perpetuate acts of violence against the Israeli state, which is in a more powerful position as far as negotiations are concerned, in an attempt to compel it to concede to their demands.

Violence may accompany a mediation effort throughout its different stages and serves as a fallback position when disputants feel that they are not making any progress in negotiation. The long-running factional conflict between Protestants and Catholics in Northern Ireland involving the British and Irish states is an example of this. A ceasefire declared by the Catholic Irish Republican Army (IRA) collapsed after eighteen months when the movement felt that the British government had not made any genuine efforts to move the peace process forward. The ceasefire was restored in July 1997. Prior to that the Chairman of the Negotiations on the Future of Northern Ireland, the US Senator George Mitchell, maintained that 'political violence, from whatever source, is morally wrong. It's counterproductive. It deepens divisions. It increases hatred. It hurts innocent people. It makes peace and reconciliation more difficult to attain'.[134] In order to move beyond the violence in most cases there will need to be what Robert Dahl referred to as a 'mutual security agreement'.[135] This consists of establishing non-belligerent contact through available communication channels and creating norms which set out principles which the parties can endorse with a view to guaranteeing each other's reciprocal security, which in turn provides a basis for negotiations to proceed. Efforts in Somalia to establish such mechanisms are meeting with mixed results. During his sojourn in the country in 1992, the UN Special Representative to Somalia, Mohamed Sahnoun, managed to negotiate several ceasefire agreements among the warring factions but a national mutual security agreement remained, and continues to remain, elusive. A similar scenario is evident in Angola and the UNITA insurgents, and the Muslim leadership of Sudan and the Christian sub-national faction the Sudanese People's Liberation Army. A significant level of moral exclusion still remains between the factions. Historically, in Cambodia such an agreement was initiated by Indonesia, under the auspices of the Association of South East Asian Nations (ASEAN), in July 1988 and subsequently signed on February 1989. This agreement is also referred to as the Jakarta Informal Meeting (JIM), signed between all four factions to the dispute on terms and conditions which would allow the peace process to move forward. Ultimately, violence can only be transcended provided that the disputants acknowledge that the socio-political norms that they create to foster communal coexistence must be acceptable to all those who will be affected by them.

MEDIATION AS MORAL LEARNING

Based on the insights gained from the above examples, the mediator's role is one of bringing to the attention of the disputing parties the fact that they have different moral perspectives from the other. The overall process of conflict resolution is one of helping them to begin to appreciate the moral world-view held by their opponent. To this extent an element of moral learning is discernible in the process of mediation. Gradually, as the mediator feels that the parties are moving closer to a common moral location, the mediator needs to adopt a more hands-off approach and let the disputants progressively become their own moral educators. This becomes more likely when parties make a conscientious effort to extend the parameters of their moral community. Throughout the duration of such a process parties become increasingly more caring, non-violent and conscious of the relational needs of the other. Rotham has alluded to this as 'a kind of learning that is especially important because the dynamics of conflict create a strong tendency to dismiss the occurrence and the possibility of change on the part of the adversary'.[136]

CONCLUSION

This chapter began with the premise that negotiation and mediation are vital processes in efforts to promote peace. The importance of parties and mediators maintaining ethical stances in their interactions with each other cannot be understated. Ethical processes are essential in order to achieve sustainable peace processes. However, there is a school of thought drawn from the realist tradition that maintains that mediators can coerce, leverage, manipulate and sanction parties in order to secure an 'agreement'. This viewpoint makes the mediator an interested party in the processes and exposes the ethical egoism that underpins such an approach. The Cold War was defined by power-political approaches to mediation due to the geostrategic rivalry that existed between the USA and the Soviet Union. The UN was either coopted or marginalised by the exigencies of superpower politics. There is therefore a strong case to make for the revitalisation of the values and norms that animated the creation of the UN's peacemaking and peacebuilding institutions. Contrasted to this approach were the examples of the League of Nations and the Quaker mediators. The League of Nations operating on a macro-level sought to institutionalise an ethical system of dispute resolution as a basis for meso-level and micro-level peacebuilding between communities, with mixed results. Similarly, the Quakers employed a moral approach to mediation because they believed that this was the most effective way of achieving peace. Ultimately, the utility of negotiation and mediation to peacebuilding cannot be underestimated. These processes are vital for the laying of foundations for effective peacebuilding and for creating a climate in which forgiveness and reconciliation between former warring parties can take root.

NOTES

1. United Nations, *Charter of the United Nations and Statute of the International Court of Justice* (New York: United Nations, 1945).

2. See Christopher Moore, *The Mediation Process: Practical Strategies for Resolving Conflict* (San Francisco: Jossey-Bass, 2003); Morton Deutsch and Peter Coleman (eds), *The Handbook of Conflict Resolution: Theory and Practice* (San Francisco: Jossey-Bass, 2000); and R. Fisher, *International Mediation: A Working Guide* (New York: International Peace Academy, 1978).

3. R. van Es, *Negotiating Ethics: On Ethics in Negotiation and Negotiation in Ethics* (Delft, Netherlands: Eburon, 1996).

4. Kevin Gibson, 'The Ethical Basis of Mediation: Why Mediators Need Philosophers', *Mediation Quarterly*, vol. 7, no. 1, Fall 1989, pp. 41–50.

5. Leda Cooks and Claudia Hale, 'The Construction of Ethics in Mediation', *Mediation Quarterly*, vol. 12, no. 1, Fall 1994, pp. 55–76.

6. Marieke Kleiboer, *The Multiple Realities of International Mediation* (London: Lynne Rienner, 1998), p. 6.

7. George Levinger and Jeffrey Rubin, 'Bridges and Barriers to a More General Theory of Conflict', *Negotiation Journal*, vol. 10, no. 3, July 1994, p. 204.

8. Ibid.

9. Richard Rubenstein, 'Dispute Resolution on the Eastern Frontier: Some Questions for Modern Missionaries', *Negotiation Journal*, vol. 8, no. 3, July 1992, p. 209.

10. A. J. R. Groom, 'Paradigms in Conflict: The Strategist, the Conflict Researcher and the Peace Researcher', in John Burton and Frank Dukes, *Conflict: Readings in Management and Resolution* (London: Macmillan, 1990), p. 73.

11. F. Walters, *A History of the League of Nations* (Oxford: Oxford University Press, 1952).

12. John Macmillan, *On Liberal Peace* (London: I. B. Tauris, 1998), pp. 127–8.

13. Dorothy Jones, 'The League of Nations Experiment in International Protection', *Ethics and International Affairs*, vol. 8, 1994, p. 85 (77–95).

14. Ibid., p. 81.

15. Documents Relating to the Protection of Minorities, *League of Nations Official Journal*, spec. supp. 73 (Geneva: League of Nations, 1929), pp. 48–49.

16. Jones, 'The League of Nations Experiment in International Protection', p. 83.

17. Ibid., p. 96.

18. See Jean Monnet, *Memoirs* (Garden City, NY: Doubleday & Co., 1978), pp. 87–91; for a more detailed discussion see F. Duchene, *Jean Monnet: The First Statesman of Interdependence* (New York: Norton, 1994), p. 41.

19. For a comprehensive discussion see George Kaeckenbeeck, *The International Experiment of Upper Silesia* (London: Oxford University Press, 1942).

20. Sarah Wambaugh, *The Saar Plebiscite* (Cambridge, MA: Harvard University Press, 1940).

21. Yves Beigbeder, *International Monitoring of Plebiscites, Referenda and*

National Elections: Self-determination and Transition to Democracy (Dordrecht: Martinus Nijhoff, 1994), p. 85.

22. Ibid., p. 86.
23. Sarah Wambaugh, *Plebiscites Since the World War* (Washington, DC: Carnegie Endowment for International Peace, 1933).
24. Ibid., pp. 7–12.
25. G. Murray, 'The Inevitable League', *Agenda*, vol. 1, no. 3, July 1942, p. 196.
26. W. T. Fox, 'E. H. Carr and Political Realism: Vision and Revision', *Review of International Studies*, vol. 11, 1985, p. 9.
27. F. P. Walters, 'The League of Nations', in E. Luard (ed.), *The Evolution of International Organisation* (London: Thames & Hudson, 1966), pp. 25–39.
28. Z. Steiner, 'Introductory Essay', in *The League of Nations in Retrospect*, Proceedings of the Symposium organised by the United Nations Library and the Graduate Institute of International Studies, Geneva, 6–9 November, 1980, p. 14.
29. Sally Marks, *The Illusion of Peace: International Relations in Europe 1918–1933* (London: Macmillan, 1976), p. 60.
30. Ibid., p. 61.
31. Ibid., pp. 67–8.
32. Ibid., p. 79.
33. Ibid., p. 100.
34. Ibid., p. 100.
35. Ibid., p. 100.
36. Ibid., p. 100.
37. Ibid., p. 100.
38. Ibid., p. 123.
39. N. D. White, *Keeping the Peace: The United Nations and the Maintenance of International Security*, second edition (Manchester: Manchester University Press, 1997), p. 3.
40. United Nations, *The Charter of the United Nations and Statute of the International Court of Justice*, article 2, paragraph 3.
41. White, *Keeping the Peace*, p. 5.
42. Ibid., p. 5.
43. Ibid., p. 6.
44. Leatherman and Vayrynen, p. 55.
45. Stephen Chan and Vivienne Jabri, *Mediation in Southern Africa* (London: Macmillan, 1993), p.xiv.
46. Ibid., p.xiv.
47. W. Smith, 'Power Ripeness and Intervention in International Conflict', *Negotiation Journal*, vol. 10, no. 2, April 1994, p. 148.
48. Cited in William Zartman, *Ripe for Resolution: Conflict and Intervention in Africa*, second edition (New York: Oxford University Press, 1989), p. 220.
49. Brian Mandell and Brian Tomlin, 'Mediation in the Development of Norms to Manage Conflict: Kissinger in the Middle East', *Journal of Peace Research*, vol. 28, no. 1, 1991, p. 46.

50. Saadia Touval and William Zartman (eds), *International Mediation in Theory and Practice* (Boulder, CO: Westview, 1985), p. 16.

51. See an analysis of this debate in Marieke Kleiboer, 'Ripeness of Conflict: A Fruitful Notion?', *Journal of Peace Research*, vol. 31, no. 1, 1994, pp. 109–16.

52. Smith, 'Power Ripeness and Intervention in International Conflict', p. 149.

53. Ibid., p. 149.

54. Efraim Inbar, 'Great Power Mediation: The USA and the May 1983 Israeli–Lebanese Agreement', *Journal of Peace Research*, vol. 28, no. 1, 1991, p. 72.

55. Saadia Touval, 'The Superpowers as Mediators', in Jacob Bercovitch and Jeffrey Rubin (eds), *Mediation in International Relations: Multiple Approaches to Conflict Management* (New York: St. Martin's Press, 1992), p. 233.

56. Mark Katz, 'The Future of Superpower Conflict Resolution in the Third World', in Mark Katz (ed.), *Soviet-American Conflict Resolution in the Third World* (Washington, DC: United States Institute of Peace Press, 1991), p. 170.

57. Marianne Spiegel, 'The Namibia Negotiations and the Problem of Neutrality', in Touval and Zartman, *International Mediation in Theory and Practice*, p. 138.

58. Zalmay Khalilzad, 'Soviet-American Cooperation in Afghanistan', in Katz, *Soviet–American Conflict Resolution in the Third World*, p. 70.

59. Touval, 'The Superpowers as Mediators', p. 246.

60. Zartman and Touval, *International Mediation in Theory and Practice*, p. 44.

61. Peck, C. *Sustainable Peace: The Role of the United Nations and Regional Organizations in Preventing Conflict* (Lanham, MD: Rowman & Littlefield, 1998).

62. Nigel Dower, *World Ethics: A New Agenda*, second edition (Edinburgh: Edinburgh University Press, 2007), p. 193.

63. Ibid., p. 197.

64. Ibid., p. 197.

65. Ibid., p. 199.

66. Ibid., p. 199.

67. Boutros Boutros-Ghali, *An Agenda for Peace: Preventive Diplomacy, Peacemaking and Peacekeeping* (New York: United Nations, 1992).

68. Ibid., paragraph 20.

69. Mark Malan and Joao Gomes-Porto (eds), *Challenges of Peace Implementation: The UN Mission in the Democratic Republic of the Congo* (Pretoria: Institute for Security Studies, 2003), pp. 140–1.

70. High-Level Panel on Threats, Challenges and Change, *A More Secure World: Our Shared Responsibility* (New York: United Nations, 2004).

71. Tim Murithi and Judi Hudson, *United Nations Mediation Experience in Africa* (Cape Town: Centre for Conflict Resolution, 2006), p. 15.

72. Ahmed Yusuf Farah, 'Traditional Approaches to Negotiation and Mediation: Examples from Africa – Roots of Reconciliation in Somaliland', in

L. Reychler and T. Paffenholz (eds), *Peacebuilding: A Field Guide* (Boulder, CO and London: Lynne Rienner, 2001), pp. 138–45.

73. United Nations, *Terms of Reference: Trust Fund in Support of the Special Missions and Other Activities Related to Preventive Diplomacy and Peacemaking* (New York: United Nations, 1997).

74. Connie Peck, *Sustainable Peace: The Role of the UN and Regional Organisations in Preventing Conflicts* (Lanham, MD: Rowman & Littlefield), 1998.

75. CDR Associates, *Designing Dispute Resolution Systems* (Boulder, CO: CDR Associates, 1992).

76. F. Mawlawi, 'New Conflicts, New Challenges: The Evolving Role of Non-Governmental Actors', *Journal of International Affairs*, vol. 46, no. 2, 1993.

77. Bailey, 'Non-official Mediation in Disputes: Reflections on Quaker Experience', p. 205.

78. Mawlawi, 'New Conflicts, New Challenges: The Evolving Role of Non-Governmental Actors', p. 395.

79. M. Janis (ed.), *The Influence of Religion on the Development of International Law* (London and Dordrecht: Martinus Nijhoff, 1991), pp. 224–5.

80. Arnold Lloyd, *Quaker Social History 1669–1738* (London: Longmans, Green & Co., 1950), pp. viii–ix.

81. Ibid., p.ix.

82. Ibid., p.ix.

83. Ibid., p.ix.

84. Ibid., p.ix.

85. Hugh Miall, The Peacemakers: *Peaceful Settlement of Disputes Since 1945* (London: Palgrave Macmillan, 1992), p. 76.

86. Bailey, 'Non-official Mediation in Disputes: Reflections on Quaker Experience', p. 208.

87. Ibid.

88. Cited in C. Sampson, 'To Make Real the Bond Between Us All: Quaker Conciliation during the Nigerian Civil War', in D. Johnson and C. Sampson (eds), *Religion: The Missing Dimension of Statecraft* (Oxford: Oxford University Press, 1994), p. 97.

89. Bailey, 'Non-official Mediation in Disputes: Reflections on Quaker Experience', p. 214.

90. Mawlawi, 'New Conflicts, New Challenges: The Evolving Role of Non-Governmental Actors', p. 395.

91. Sampson, 'To Make Real the Bond Between Us All: Quaker Conciliation during the Nigerian Civil War', p. 94.

92. Bailey, 'Non-official Mediation in Disputes: Reflections on Quaker Experience', p. 212.

93. Ibid.

94. Adam Curle, *Making Peace* (London: Tavistock, 1971), p. 177.

95. Adam Curle, *Tools of Transformation: A Personal Study* (Stroud: Hawthorn Press, 1990), pp. 50–1.

96. Ibid.

97. Bailey, 'Non-official Mediation in Disputes: Reflections on Quaker Experience', p. 218.

98. Thomas Princen, *Intermediaries in International Conflict* (Princeton: Princeton University Press, 1992), p. 208.

99. Mike Yarrow, *Quaker Experience in International Conciliation* (New Haven and London: Yale University Press, 1978), p. 164.

100. Princen, *Intermediaries in International Conflict*, p. 30.

101. Bailey, 'Non-official Mediation in Disputes: Reflections on Quaker Experience', p. 208.

102. Ibid., p. 208.

103. Sampson, 'To Make Real the Bond Between Us All: Quaker Conciliation during the Nigerian Civil War', p. 94.

104. A detailed history and analysis of the Nigeria–Biafra civil war, and the Quaker mediation thereof, is beyond the scope of this section. Instead this study seeks to draw out the fundamentals of the Quaker approach in this conflict and superimpose these strategies onto a discussion of the ethics of peacebuilding.

105. Sampson, 'To Make Real the Bond Between Us All: Quaker Conciliation during the Nigerian Civil War', p. 94.

106. J. de St. Jorre, *The Nigerian Civil War* (London: Hodder & Stoughton, 1972), pp. 30–64.

107. Ibid., p. 87.

108. Sampson, 'To Make Real the Bond Between Us All: Quaker Conciliation during the Nigerian Civil War', p. 92.

109. Princen, *Intermediaries in International Conflict*, p. 188.

110. Ibid., p. 209.

111. Ibid., p. 209.

112. Sampson, 'To Make Real the Bond Between Us All: Quaker Conciliation during the Nigerian Civil War', p. 93.

113. Princen, *Intermediaries in International Conflict*, p. 189.

114. Ibid., p. 189.

115. Yarrow, *Quaker Experience in International Conciliation*, p. 194.

116. Princen, *Intermediaries in International Conflict*, pp. 191–2.

117. Ibid., p. 190.

118. Ibid., p. 193.

119. Ibid., p. 193.

120. Bailey, 'Non-official Mediation in Disputes: Reflections on Quaker Experience', p. 205.

121. Mawlawi, 'New Conflicts, New Challenges: The Evolving Role of Non-Governmental Actors', p. 401.

122. Ibid., p. 401.

123. Ibid., p. 401.

124. Adam Curle, 'Peacemaking: The Middle Way', *Bridges: Quaker International Affairs Report*, vol. 92, no. 3, April 1992, p. 2.

125. Ibid., p. 2.

126. Thomas Princen, *Intermediaries in International Conflict* (Princeton: Princeton University Press, 1992), p. 29.
127. Peter Brock, *A Brief History of Pacifism: From Jesus to Tolstoy* (Syracuse: Syracuse University Press, 1992), p. 14.
128. Martin Ceadel, *Pacifism in Britain 1914–1945: The Defining of a Faith* (Oxford: Clarendon Press, 1980), p. 22.
129. Brock, *A Brief History of Pacifism*, p. 18.
130. John-Paul Lederach, *From the Ground Up: Mennonite Contributions to International Peacebuilding* (Oxford: Oxford University Press, 2000).
131. Ibid., p. 1.
132. Timothy Sisk, 'The Violence-Negotiation Nexus: South Africa in Transition and the Politics of Uncertainty', *Negotiation Journal*, vol. 9, no. 1, January 1993, p. 84 (74–94).
133. Ibid., p. 84.
134. George Mitchell, 'Peace is Not Impossible', *Newsweek*, 30 June 1997, p. 11.
135. Robert Dahl, *After the Revolution* (New Haven: Yale University Press, 1970).
136. J. Rotham, *From Confrontation to Cooperation: Resolving Ethnic and Regional Conflict* (London: Sage, 1992), p. 30.

CHAPTER 5

THE VIRTUE OF
FORGIVENESS

INTRODUCTION

Forgiveness is more than a synonym for pardon, which several theological teachings advocate. Ethically speaking, forgiveness can more appropriately be thought of as sacrifice; it is the giving up of one's self for the sake of others. In this sense forgiveness is in effect an ethical virtue. This chapter will assess the notion of forgiveness prior to assessing some illustrations of forgiveness. A major challenge that confronts the consolidation of peacebuilding in war-affected countries is putting in place effective and sustainable processes of forgiveness and reconciliation. Forgiveness is a major component of the reconciliation process. However, victims, perpetrators and observers alike consider achieving forgiveness to be a very difficult and sometimes impossible process in the context of situations where grave human rights atrocities are committed.

The processes and mechanisms of peacebuilding need to be informed by the issue of how to enable victims, in what are increasingly violent sub-national conflicts, to move from a condition in which they morally exclude their perpetrators as valid interlocutors to a situation in which they morally include and acknowledge the claims of the 'other'. As seen in Chapter 3, these foundations for an ethical approach to peacebuilding are not yet in place in the international system, which practises a de facto bias towards nation-states. Chapter 3 demonstrated that in the prevailing institutional arrangements the Westphalian system already 'morally' excludes sub-national groups from articulating their ethical claims against nation-states in an internationally and legally sanctioned forum.

This chapter will highlight some of the obstacles to achieving forgiveness. It will suggest that one way to reinforce the forgiveness process is to root it within a moral framework that acknowledges our common humanity. The foundation for forgiveness can only be established when victims adopt a perspective that morally includes the perpetrators. The frameworks of moral discourse developed by Jürgen Habermas and those of moral development articulated by Lawrence Kohlberg will be assessed. This is not straightforward because when perpetrators in violent conflict situations commit atrocities they operate on the basis of the moral exclusion of their victims. In order for forgiveness to take place victims are called upon to extend the parameters of their moral community to perpetrators who previously victimised them. This chapter will conclude by looking at the forgiveness forums convened by the Moral Re-Armament group which brought together victims and perpetrators from Cambodia in an example of micro-level peacebuilding.

THE ETHICS OF FORGIVENESS

Given the atrocities that have been committed in previous and current conflicts and those that will be committed in future conflicts there will be a need to put in place effective processes for achieving forgiveness.[1] Forgiveness requires bringing people together in a non-coercive framework of interaction to create better understanding and a basis for reconciliation through the validation of any sense of grievance and harm done to them. Ethically, forgiveness only becomes possible when victims can extend the parameters of their moral community to include their perpetrators. Since this is a highly subjective process, not all victims can bestow forgiveness. However, some victims are capable of perceiving their erstwhile tormentors and oppressors as members of the same moral community and are therefore able to grant them mercy for the harm they have caused. One way to reinforce the forgiveness process is to root it within a moral framework that acknowledges our common humanity.

A PHILOSOPHICAL BASIS FOR GRANTING FORGIVENESS: MORAL EXCLUSION AND THE NEED FOR FORGIVENESS

The ability to grant forgiveness requires a significant degree of moral development on the part of the victim. There are a variety of sources from which a victim can draw a philosophical basis from which to grant forgiveness, including religion, spirituality or ethics. This section will assess philosophical frameworks that provide some explanation of the nature of moral exclusion and how moral development might proceed to the point where individuals can grant others forgiveness for harm done.

The ethnicisation of the state, discussed in Chapter 3, demonstrated when a dominant ethnic group, or a coalition of ethnic groups, usurps the state apparatus and exploits other groups, perpetuates moral exclusion. The international community tends to tacitly side with the state government, which may be nothing more than a collectivity of dominant ethnic groups. Now more than ever, the blanket legitimation of the 'state' in regions affected by sub-national conflict needs to be reconsidered. Far from being a focal point for a moral political community the state in these regions and situations generates social-political inequalities and even the moral exclusion of some parts of its population by concretising enemy images among its citizens and groups. In this particular context, moral exclusion can be defined as excluding other individuals or groups from one's 'moral community', which involves viewing them as outside the boundary within which moral values and rules of justice and fairness apply.[2] Susan Opotow notes that 'those who are morally excluded are perceived as non-entities, expendable, or undeserving; consequently, harming them appears acceptable, appropriate, or just'.[3]

In international relations moral exclusion is evident in a range of issues, such as the deployment of nuclear weapons, the design and implementation of immigration policies, and environmental action or inaction. This is 'because our position on these issues [as policy makers, researchers or simply citizens] depends on whom we include in or exclude from our moral boundaries'.[4] Peacebuilding can also be analysed in terms of moral exclusion. Conflict, and in particular ethnic groups in conflict with nation-states, is premised on the construction of ethnicity which 'instructs by moral exclusion'. It is driven by a particular sub-state group, or group of states, proclaiming the moral boundaries which tend to exclude other groups. Through the centralisation of bureaucratic state power in the hands of a dominant group, moral exclusion gradually becomes concretised and institutionalised. Other ethnic groups within the state are not privy to the rules of justice or fairness. Thus, the ethnicised state presides over its own moral exclusion by sub-national groups. These ethnic polities, by constructing their own moral communities, create a boundary which in turn depicts the state as a 'non-entity, expendable and undeserving' of their political loyalty, in the figurative sense. Therefore, in sub-national conflicts moral exclusion is functional in a bidirectional sense. The state, which has through its repressive activities morally excluded parts of its population, is in a reciprocal sense morally excluded by these collectivities once they become organised and mobilise to resist the dominion of the state.[5]

Moral exclusion once consummated creates conditions which provide communities with the mindset necessary 'to dehumanise, harm, and act with incredible cruelty towards others'.[6] In situations where ethnic groups are in conflict, genocide is illustrative of moral exclusion in the extreme. For example, the depiction of fellow humans as other than human and in particular as cockroaches in the Hutu/Tutsi conflict laid the foundations for extreme moral exclusion and the Rwandan genocide. Similarly, the depiction by the Nazis of the Jews as 'rats' set the scene for the Holocaust. These processes of extreme moral exclusion have been commonplace in the history of human confrontation and conflict. Opotow observes that 'danger, conflict, and stress reinforce group boundaries and change information processing strategies and the choice of justice rules. As conflict escalates, cohesion within groups increases, but concern for fairness between groups shrinks'.[7] She further notes that 'because moral constraints on behaviour are weak for those outside the scope of justice, outsiders are increasingly endangered. Dominance can take extreme forms, such as exploitation, slavery, and extermination'.[8] This process of moral exclusion therefore makes the effort to forge forgiveness very difficult. This is due to the enemy images that are constructed and exploited in the process for fomenting moral exclusion.[9] According to Kurt and Kati Spillmann, 'images of the enemy are thus formed by a perception determined solely by negative assessment'.[10] This includes distrust of everything originating from the enemy; placing guilt on the enemy; always anticipating harm from the enemy; zero-sum thinking in which anything which benefits the enemy conversely harms one's moral community and vice versa. It also includes the refusal of empathy with the enemy, which emphasises the absence of common attributes, refusal to change the enemy image, and a rejection of any human feelings and ethical criteria with reference to the enemy.[11] Thus, Spillmann and Spillmann note that the enemy image is fairly 'non-rational' and resilient which means that 'a purely rational appeal for "more empathy" will thus not reach the actual roots of the image of the enemy, and consequently will have little chance of success'.[12] In effect, to promote forgiveness, actors that have been on opposite sides of the equation of moral exclusion, harbouring strong enemy images of the other, have to find a way to bridge the gap and redraw the boundaries of their moral communities to include the other.

MORAL DEVELOPMENT AS THE BASIS FOR FORGIVENESS: HABERMAS AND THE ETHICAL CONFLICT RESOLUTION

It is therefore necessary to develop conceptual frameworks which enable us to understand how moral exclusion can be deterred and moral inclusion engendered.

Jürgen Habermas has developed a communicative ethics model which proposes a way of conceiving how a process of moral discourse can ensure the validation of social and political norms. According to Donald Moon, 'discourse-based approaches offer a set of procedures that, if followed, would yield principles legitimating social practices and institutions'.[13] Habermas developed a theory of communicative action which reconstructs the basic rules governing speech situations. In the preconditions that enable actors to participate in communicative encounters Habermas identifies certain communicative practices geared toward consensus and understanding. From these he makes the assertion that 'our communicative practices are constitutive of our forms of relationship, and our forms of relationship reveal our ethical commitments'.[14] Morality, therefore, is rooted in the structure of communicative action. Thus, Habermas establishes a discourse-based morality. He invokes the principle of discourse ethics (D) which states that 'only those norms can claim to be valid that meet (or could meet) with the approval of all affected in their capacity as participants in a practical discourse'.[15] Habermas has also explicated his principles of discourse ethics with reference to the 'discourse principle' and the 'moral principle'. The discourse principle states that 'just those action norms are valid to which all possibly affected persons could agree as participants in rational discourses'.[16] This principle aspires to ground a framework of justice which encompasses social actors 'whose interests are touched by the foreseeable consequences of a general practice'.[17] The discourse principle can further be determined in a 'principle of morality' whereby 'the moral principle first results when one specifies the general discourse principle for those norms that can be justified if and only if equal consideration is given to the interest of all those who are possibly involved'.[18] The discourse principle 'is only intended to explain the point of view from which norms of action can be impartially justified'.[19] To this extent it functions as a principle of universalisation. For a moral norm to be valid it must be, in principle, freely acceptable to everyone affected by the norm. In this way it 'functions as a rule of argumentation for deciding moral questions rationally . . . and . . . operates at the level at which a specific form of argumentation is internally constituted'.[20]

Hence, Habermas's analysis of the dimensions of a discourse-based morality facilitates our understanding of how the validity of norms can be tested in social and political interaction. Ursula Wolf notes that for Habermas, 'moral norms are defined by the fact that they are social norms in need of justification'.[21] Douglas Rasmussen also remarks that 'the function of discourse ethics is to justify norms that will determine the legitimate opportunities for the satisfaction of needs. It deals primarily with questions of international justice'.[22]

Habermas has suggested that the underlying objective of 'moral-practical discourse is an agreement concerning the *just resolution of conflict* in the realm of norm-regulated action'.[23] Seyla Benhabib concurs that 'communicative ethics anticipates non-violent strategies of conflict resolution . . . it is a matter of political imagination . . . to project institutions, practices, and ways of life which promote non-violent conflict resolution strategies and associative problem-solving methods'.[24] By appealing to a discourse-based morality Habermas seeks to develop the normative criterion with which to judge existing institutional arrangements and expose the exploitative and exclusionary power relationships which they may be perpetuating. Moon observes that 'it should go without saying that the judgements of many are never articulated and sometimes are not even formed in the first place. The silence is often due to the suppression of certain voices by structures of domination and oppression'.[25] Thus, the silencing of the voices of the 'many' in affairs which concern and affect them reduces their status to mere objects of instrumental gain. They become the means by which the oppressors consolidate and entrench their structural positions of power to achieve certain ends. The relationship between ethnicised states and marginalised sub-national groups with reference to the state system is a case in point as this book has argued throughout.

Critics have often challenged Habermas's contention of the feasibility and practicality of a proposed norm being 'accepted by all'. The issue here is one of whether or not discourse-based morality with its insistence on 'generalisability' suppresses individual difference. In response Habermas has made the distinction between moral questions and ethical questions.[26] Ethical questions are evaluative questions of what constitutes the 'good life'. They are based upon our individual identities which are in turn derived from the culture in which we live and into which we are socialised; thus they fall within a subjective remit. As Maeve Cook explains, 'ethical questions are by definition non-universalisable since they are concerned with the self-realisation of specific individuals and groups and are thus always bound to specific local contexts'.[27] Moral questions, on the other hand, are concerned with 'generalisable interests' and how to regulate the conflicts that may emerge on account of disputed norms. Moral questions and norms invoke the need for a process of discursive validation. As Habermas postulates, 'discursively justified norms bring to expression simultaneously both insight into what is equally in the interest of all and a general will that has absorbed into itself, without repression, the will of all'.[28] Thus, moral norms that emerge from moral questions, by their very nature, command the uncoerced assent of all concerned.

The appropriate forum for the adjudication of moral questions is a universal communication community of actors. As Habermas himself suggests, 'with moral questions, humanity or a presupposed republic of world citizens constitutes the reference system for justifying regulations that lie in the equal interests of all'.[29] Elsewhere he remarks that moral practical discourse represents for each of us the ideal extension of our 'community of communication' from within. However, in order to get to this ideal situation in which moral practical discourse is possible a degree of moral development is necessary.

KOHLBERG'S MODEL FOR MORAL DEVELOPMENT

Habermas sought to give credence to his arguments about the universality of the discourse ethics framework by drawing upon the insights of cognitive development psychology. In particular, he appealed to the work of Lawrence Kohlberg, who focused on the development of moral judgement.[30] Kohlberg's own work was an advancement of the work of developmental psychologist Jean Piaget who, in the first half of the twentieth century, established the view that children used a progressively more developed manner of moral judgement which complemented their intellectual and cognitive development.[31] A detailed exposition of his work is beyond the scope and intention of this chapter. Suffice to say that after Piaget, Kohlberg wanted to demonstrate the nature of the morality (or moral judgement) that people in general use and the way in which this morality 'matures' over several stages of development.

In conducting his 'moral research' Kohlberg set up a longitudinal study over fifteen years in which he studied 'the development of moral judgement and character, primarily, by following the same group of 75 boys at three-year intervals from early adolescence (at the beginning, the boys were aged 10–16) through young manhood (to age 22–28), supplemented by a series of studies of moral development in other cultures'.[32] In brief, at each experimental interval, his methodology included testing the boys with moral dilemmas and then asking them to put into their own words their interpretation of the moral judgements involved in each dilemma.[33] The intention here was to try and identify from a particular boy's interpretation of the judgement his position along a hierarchy of stages of moral reasoning. As part of his study a predefined hierarchy of stages which represented an underlying thought-organisation was established. Moral judgements for and against a moral dilemma differ at each stage, and each stage is supposed to constitute a hierarchy of moral-cognitive difficulty.

From his subsequent analysis of their discourse Kohlberg would determine what stage of moral reasoning a particular individual had reached. He surmised that his findings illustrated 'that forms of moral judgement clearly reflect forms of cognitive-logical capacity'.[34] In other words, moral judgement is primarily a reflection of the development stages in moral thought. Furthermore, in his examination of development in other cultures, which included a study of children in two villages, one Atayal (Malaysian Aboriginal) and one Taiwanese, Kohlberg claimed that he found similar 'aspects or categories of moral judgement and valuing'.[35] He suggested that 'there are marked individual and cultural differences in the definition, use and hierarchical ordering of these universal value concepts, but the major source of this variation, both within and between cultures, is development'.[36] Kohlberg further noted that:

> it means normatively that there is a sense in which we can characterise moral differences between groups and individuals as being more or less adequate morally. We are arguing then that even moderate or sociological relativism is misleading in its interpretations of the facts: not only is there a universal moral form, but the basic content principles of morality are universal.[37]

In Kohlberg's view, moral development in an individual, that is to say the growing capacity for moral judgement, is cross-cultural. More specifically, moral growth proceeds through six stages of moral development within three societal levels: the pre-conventional, conventional and post-conventional levels of morality. The different levels of morality and stages within them can be represented as follows.[38]

KOHLBERG'S STAGES OF MORAL DEVELOPMENT

Based on his two research publications, *The Philosophy of Moral Development* published in 1981, and *The Psychology of Moral Development*, published in 1984, Kohlberg has identified the six stages of moral development as follows:

Level 1: **Pre-conventional Morality** – at this level the actor believes that the rightness or wrongness of an action depends on what other people who are able to give punishment or rewards tell the actor to do.

Stage 1: **The Punishment and Obedience Orientation** – at this stage the physical consequences (fear of punishment) of action determine its rightness or wrongness. What is right is what others permit and what is wrong is what others punish; there is no conception of an underlying moral order.

Stage 2: **The Individualistic and Instrumental Orientation** – at this stage right action consists of that which is in the actor's immediate interest, that which will result in something good for the actor. Elements of fairness, of necessity and of equal sharing are present, but they are always interpreted in terms of self-interest. Reciprocity is a matter of 'you scratch my back and I'll scratch yours', not of loyalty, gratitude or justice.

Level 2: **Conventional Morality** – this level is called conventional because it refers to the level of morality on which most people operate most of the time. At this level the actor has shifted his or her perception of a moral arbitrator from an external authority figure to society at large. The attitude is one of conformity to personal expectations and social order. It is also an attitude of loyalty to society and of actively maintaining, supporting and justifying the social order.

Stage 3: **The Mutual Interpersonal Expectations, Relationships and Conformity** – at this stage the actor determines what is right action by living up to other people's expectations and by seeking peer approval. There is much conformity to stereotypical images of what is majority or 'natural' behaviour. Having good intentions and showing concern about others is a strong feature. Trust, loyalty, respect and gratitude are valued.

Stage 4: **The Law and Order Orientation** – an actor has respect for authority; the fixed rules and the maintenance of the social order. Loyalty to the system and adherence to its rules replaces the groups as a basis for determining right moral action.

Level 3: **Post-conventional Morality** – with appropriate experiences actors can reach this stage of morality and operate within it for at least some of the time. This level involves a shift by the actor from heteronomy to autonomy. That is to say that actors at this level use reflective judgement to reason through to their own sense of what makes an action right. Whatever an individual, group or society might say is right, the actor recognises the individual's responsibility to reason through his or her own beliefs and actions.

Stage 5: **The Social Contract and Individual Rights** – at this stage right action tends to be defined in terms of general individual rights, and standards that have been critically examined and agreed upon by the whole society. There is a clear awareness of the relativism of personal values and opinions and a corresponding emphasis upon procedural rules for reaching consensus. Rules that are imposed are unjust and can be challenged. Some values, such as life and liberty, are non-relative and must be upheld regardless of majority opinion.

Stage 6: **The Universal Ethical Principle Orientation** – at this stage the actor understands and acknowledges the principles of justice. These principles are abstract and ethical (the Golden Rule, the Categorical Imperative). They are universal principles of reciprocity of the equality of human rights, and of respect for the dignity of human beings, and are based on the perception that human beings have equal and inviolate worth. These principles are used to determine right and wrong moral action.

Kohlberg was not suggesting that there was a direct correlation between the age of an actor and the ability to function at a given stage. He did, however, propose that though pre-conventional moral reasoning is the dominant mode of thought in early and mid-childhood it is also found in many adolescents as well as among adult criminal offenders. Moral rules are embodied in an external authority capable of meting out rewards or punishment. Conventional morality develops in mid-adolescence and remains the norm for the majority of adults. Conformity in right action is derived from personal expectations and the social order. Post-conventional morality, on the other hand, according to the longitudinal study was rare even amongst intelligent adults.[39] The feasibility of attaining stage 6 remains a topic of vigorous debate, and some scholars question whether or not it even exists. Others argue that the whole idea of stages within the post-conventional level is misconceived because as the actor asserts autonomy and reflective judgement the researcher cannot claim the role of the expert who separates the stages naturally. Another way of approaching the issue is to view the post-conventional level as serving the function of being a regulative ideal which most humans can, and do, aspire to. It represents the point of politico-moral development at which the moral inclusion of the 'other' can be said to be well grounded in the principles of justice and reciprocity. It also represents the level of moral development that enables forgiveness between a victim and a perpetrator to take place.

This notion of reciprocity is also an important factor that emerges from Kohlberg's study. David Ingram contends that Kohlberg's study in effect enumerates three levels of reciprocity in which role-taking is a common feature and the ability to empathise with the other progresses with moral development.[40] The different stages represent successive modes of 'taking the role of others' in social situations. To this extent, these successive stages also represent and involve a process of 'internal cognitive re-organisation' within an actor: thus the changes in moral reasoning are 'qualitative' rather than 'quantitative'. As indeed Kohlberg notes, 'it is evident that natural moral development is grossly defined by a trend toward an increasingly internal orientation to norms'.[41] He further argues that the successive stages imply an invariant, or sequential, order which is defined by 'hierarchical integrations'. This is to say that 'higher stages include lower stages as components reintegrated at a higher level. Lower stages are in a sense available to, or comprehended by, persons at a higher stage. There is however a hierarchical order of preference for higher over lower stages'.[42] At higher stages actors become morally integrated with others and begin to acknowledge the moral criteria of universalisability.

GENDERED REVISIONS OF MORAL DEVELOPMENT

As we saw in Chapter 2, one of the main challenges that confronts moral knowledge is its ability to speak to the whole of human experience, which implies the need for gender sensitivity to women's experiences and concerns. This gendered critique at the level of epistemology challenges the masculine conceptions of human morality and problematises the Habermas and Kohlberg frameworks which aspire to genuine universality. Feminist criticisms have been levelled against the Kohlbergian framework of moral inclusivity and development. An extensive discussion is beyond the scope of this chapter, but to state the case briefly, a feminist critique can question whether the highest level of moral development consists exclusively of judgement based on 'abstract universal principles'. Carol Gilligan has criticised the parochial scope of Kohlberg's theory of moral development. She argued that Kohlberg's scope of morality is incomplete in that it mirrors the patterns of moral development in males but does not assess the possibility of a different developmental schema for females.[43] Gilligan sought to investigate whether there was a feminine way of addressing moral dilemmas. In particular, she wanted to examine whether women had a 'different voice' or a different way of moral reasoning from their male counterparts. Gilligan's research centred around the childhood, and subsequent adolescent, development in girls. Borrowing from Kohlberg, Gilligan asked the girls to provide interpretations of how they would resolve a moral dilemma, when presented with a hypothetical problem. Gilligan found that girls tended to make moral judgements of the problems in a different way from boys.[44] More specifically, girls tended to interpret situations in terms of relationships based on an obligation towards caring for the other. Gilligan describes 'a moral universe in which men, more often than women, conceive of morality as substantively constituted by obligations and rights and as procedurally constituted by the demands of fairness and impartiality'.[45] In this context, 'women, more often than men, see moral requirements as emerging from the particular needs of others in the context of particular relationships'.[46] Thus, whereas boys rely on an 'ethic of justice' or 'rights' (whereby moral judgement is predicated on 'abstract universal principles') girls invoke an 'ethic of care' based on relational notions of care. As far as this ethic of care is concerned, 'the exclusive focus on justice reasoning has obscured both its psychological reality and its normative significance'.[47]

Gilligan's research seeks to illustrate the way in which the Kohlberg construct has been blind to the developmental schema found in women. She shifts the focus of attention from abstract moral principles and examines instead what she claims is the observable world of social relationships. Through the process of caring for oneself as well as the other, the actor becomes cognisant of the multiple moral truths that can coexist as well as the contextually relative nature of moral judgement.[48] To underpin her framework, Gilligan identified a three-stage sequence of moral development which progresses from care of self to care of others, to the final stage where care of self is integrated with care of others. Thus, the pre-conventional stage emphasises the survival of the individual; the 'focus is on caring for the self in order to ensure survival'. The second conventional stage the actor begins to learn is that by sacrificing oneself for others one is judged as being 'good', whereas at the third pre-conventional stage 'care becomes the self-chosen principle of judgement that remains psychological in its concern with relationships and response but becomes universal in its condemnation of exploitation and hurt'.[49] In other words, the actor no longer sees a conflict between caring for oneself and caring for others. More importantly, avoiding hurting somebody else, or the adherence to non-violence, is perceived as a principle that has universal application.

For Gilligan, the ethic of care and the ethic of justice are different ways of organising the fundamental elements of moral judgement. According to Susan Hekman, 'Gilligan claims that individuals can see moral conflicts in terms of either justice or care but not both at once. Moral problems are thus not resolved by balancing justice and care but by taking one perspective rather than the other'.[50] Larissa Fast, Reina Neufeldt and Lisa Schirch, in their article 'Toward Ethically Grounded Conflict Interventions: Re-evaluating Challenges in the 21st Century', note that 'an ethic of care can provide important guideposts for conflict interventions'.[51] They observe that the ethic of care maintains that 'the common good is defined by and within communities'.[52] In other words, it emphasises that 'individuals are highly interconnected within communities and not autonomous selves'.[53]

Indeed, a major issue taken up by Gilligan's critics and defenders is precisely the issue of the 'hierarchy' between justice and care. One of Kohlberg's criticisms of Gilligan's construct was that in appealing to a justice/care perspective it confuses 'issues of justice' with those of the 'good life', thus subverting the boundaries of the moral domain. In other words, Kohlberg sought recourse in reaffirming moral boundaries in a traditional sense by suggesting that the moral values that Gilligan associates with women refer to 'personal' or private issues such as friendship and family relations. In his view, the morality of justice seeks to address that which is obligatory and that which is required of moral agents in terms of their duty in the universal public realm. Thus, Kohlberg notes that 'morality as justice best renders our view of morality as universal. It restricts morality to a central minimal core striving for universal agreement in the face of more relativist conceptions of the good'.[54] Elsewhere, Habermas has also argued that the kind of issues raised by Gilligan's ethic of care do not belong to the core domain of moral theory which, appropriately, has to deal with questions regarding the equal worth of every person in virtue of his or her humanity. This equal worth is demonstrated by the moral respect which is shown through acknowledging their needs, claims and points of view in our moral deliberations with them. The ethic of care in Habermas's view seeks to address what are effectively 'evaluative questions' concerned with forms of life or life goals. Thus, 'in modern societies in which moral questions of justice have been distinguished from evaluative questions of the good life, relations and obligations of care and responsibility are "personal" matters of self-realisation'.[55] From a different angle, feminist critics of Gilligan have argued that an appeal to the ethic of care can end up perpetuating their marginalisation. Essentialising women's moral development as being somehow 'different' gives credence to structures and institutions which exert dominance over women and confines them to their private sphere.[56]

Despite the gendered analysis into Kohlberg's framework there is no doubt that the notion of moral development is pertinent to understanding how human beings can either morally exclude or include others. In this sense, this framework has some insights that can be utilised to establish a philosophical framework for forgiveness.

MORAL DISCOURSE AND DEVELOPMENT: INSIGHTS INTO THE ETHICS OF FORGIVENESS

How do discourse ethics and moral development provide us with insights into forgiveness? The principle of discourse ethics establishes a basis upon which actors who might be affected by the consequences of a particular activity or practice have to be involved in determining the particular activity or practice. Forgiveness is an activity that cannot take place without the participation of all those who might be affected by it, including victims and perpetrators. If forgiveness is to be established as a moral norm then it must be, in principle, acceptable to everyone affected by it. Therefore, there is a natural confluence between the principle that discourse ethics seeks to establish and the ethics that are vital to ensuring an effective process of forgiveness. Thus, discourse ethics provides a philosophical procedure through which forgiveness can be promoted. Ultimately, this philosophical basis for promoting forgiveness provides the rationale as to why moral inclusivity between erstwhile disputants should be engendered.

The emphasis placed on bringing people together in a non-coercive framework to create better understanding through the inclusive validation of social and political norms is an essential aspect of the usefulness of moral discourse and moral development frameworks. Ethnic groups, as we saw in Chapter 3, faced with the oppression by a state coopted by a dominant ethnic group or groups, tend to revert to an insular construction of moral community. This construction is exclusionary of the other's moral community (be it another ethnic group, or the civil moral community constructed by a state). Any prospects for promoting forgiveness and reconciliation between such groups must first of all recognise this fact and then examine how the practical process of politico-moral development can be geared towards bringing about an incremental transition in the moral perceptions held by disputants. According to Benhabib, 'moral change and political transformation can only take place through learning to take the standpoint of the other into account'.[57] Forgiveness, which is central to sustaining peace, only becomes sustainable when parties have undergone a series of successive approximations, in the Kohlbergian sense, towards an attitude of moral inclusion and care towards the concrete other.

Moral judgement, required to effectuate forgiveness, is cross-cultural. Actors in the process of forgiving also have to achieve the highest levels of moral development in order to view their perpetrators as part of the universal moral community. Post-conventional morality, according to Kohlberg, also represents the level of moral development that enables forgiveness between a victim and a perpetrator to take place. Post-conflict processes that seek to forge forgiveness need to approach sub-national disputes as if they were moral conflicts over competing 'narratives' of identity and the entitlements that derive from that identity. Parties resort to violence when they see no other recourse to enable their moral claims to be fairly adjudicated, in the terminology of discourse ethics. In other words, sub-national conflict is the collapse of the inter-subjective, or inter-communal, moral consensus as to the form of political arrangement that should prevail. Parties have withdrawn their cooperation with the state and have resorted instead to violence and insurgency as their chosen avenue for making their views understood. In order to attempt to reverse this process it is clear that all groups concerned in the conflict will need to be given an outlet for political expression, in which they perceive that there is a genuine commitment towards establishing a framework for procedural justice. There is a need to progress through Kohlberg and Gilligan's stages of moral development in order to move away from moral self-centredness towards a concern for the other. This suggests that forgiveness, reconciliation and peacebuilding are ultimately gradual processes. When actors appeal to a pre-conventional world-view, in which their moral world-view is framed in terms of self-interest, they will resist adopting patterns of behaviour which are respectful of the principles of universal justice and care towards the concrete other. The task in attempting to promote forgiveness or reconciliation involves enabling the belligerents to get to a point at which the transition towards moral inclusion can begin.

PERCEPTIONS OF FORGIVENESS

Forgiveness and reconciliation are effectively processes of politico-moral development; they require the transformation of moral attitudes. They are on-going corrective processes which are non-linear and dynamic, manifested through periods of both moral progression and moral regression. When moral regression occurs and the moral exclusion of the other becomes more pronounced then parties resort to more coercive acts which present a challenge to processes of forgiveness, reconciliation and peacebuilding.

Brandon Hamber notes that 'in the past decade there has been an increasing focus on forgiveness and reconciliation in societies coming out of conflict'.[58] He goes on to observe that the concepts of forgiveness and reconciliation 'were previously the domain of philosophers and theologians but have become integrally linked to questions of political transition'.[59] Hamber questions whether trying to establish a notion of 'intergroup forgiveness' is helpful. Kadiangandu and Mullet have demonstrated that in the Democratic Republic of the Congo the notion of intergroup forgiveness makes sense and is relevant to some African communities.[60] They found that 'the wrongdoer must request forgiveness, preferably in public and for the whole community. The process should include special deference to the offended group and as a process should neither imply nor prohibit the expression of particular sentiments or emotions'.[61] Manzi and Gonzalez argue that intergroup forgiveness 'may be possible in some cases because even people who have no direct relation with the conflict (even those alive a generation after it) can assume responsibility for or feel guilt for their ingroup's misdeeds'.[62] Furthermore, 'they can feel motivated to compensate or repair the other group'. In a sense, intergroup forgiveness can be achieved under certain conditions, specifically the ability of victims and perpetrators to undergo politico-moral development.

The concepts of forgiveness and reconciliation are related to each other. Enright notes that in the case of interpersonal forgiveness a degree of moral development is required since ultimately forgiveness begins as a private act. Reconciliation is the act of healing that takes place following a process of forgiveness.[63] Drawing upon Jean Piaget's model of moral development, Enright argues that 'one may forgive and not reconcile, but one never truly reconciles without some form of forgiving taking place'.[64] An extensive discussion of reconciliation will be undertaken in the next chapter.

FORGIVENESS IN PRACTICE

There are three main challenges to demonstrating that forgiveness works. Firstly, it is a fact that forgiveness defies easy measurement, categorisation and documentation, and thus illustration. Secondly, forgiveness is not an event that can be witnessed but a process that takes place sometimes over years, decades and even generations.

Thirdly, forgiveness has both interpersonal and intergroup dimensions and it is difficult to demonstrate both of these aspects because of their intersubjective nature. Despite this caveat we can attempt to gain a practical understanding of efforts to promote forgiveness through an assessment of the efforts of the London-based international non-governmental organisation Moral Re-Armament (MRA). Moral Re-Armament was launched in 1938, at the East Ham Town Hall in London. The initiator of the MRA was Frank Buchman (1878–1961) at a time when Europe was in crisis.[65] Nazi Germany was engaged in a major military re-armament drive and had annexed Austria in March 1938. Western democracies were responding in kind with a re-armament drive of their own. Buchman believed that rather than prepare for war by stockpiling weapons humanity needed to 're-arm morally'.[66] He argued that as hostility accumulates between people fear is accentuated and the seeds of mutual domination and destruction are sown. In response to this Buchman held that the 'crisis' was 'fundamentally a moral one'. To precipitate moral recovery he maintained that this could start only when every individual admitted to his or her own faults instead of 'spotlighting' other people's. Essentially, he wanted to high-light the importance of forgiveness in healing rifts between people and nations as a way to promoting healing and reconciliation.

The activities of the MRA have spread worldwide. MRA representa-tives go to regions where conflict is rife and try to facilitate and encourage disputants to engage in dialogue and forgiveness, through which these disputants can acknowledge the other's humanity and history of victimisation and their fears. Parties can then use this in making conciliatory moves. The emphasis is, however, placed on a self-initiated and voluntary acknowledgement and recognition of the in-justices that one has done to his or her fellow human being. In effect, this involves the process of extending one's sense of moral community and fostering moral inclusion of the other. Thus, the interaction in this context is non-coercive and intersubjective. The MRA also holds assemblies which have as their objective the fostering of dialogue towards justice, forgiveness and reconciliation. Peter Everington, an MRA member, has noted that the MRA established a conference centre in Caux, Switzerland, in 1946, where activities focus on the human qualities needed to resolve conflict and to lay the foundation for enduring cooperation. Participants come forward of their own volition and openly say how they have endured injustice, or perpetrated in-justice, as a preface to forgiving their victimisers or those they have victimised.[67]

The MRA has maintained a long-term commitment to reconciliation in Cambodia which dates back to 1954. Michael Henderson, author of a book entitled *The Forgiveness Factor: Stories of Hope in a World of Conflict*, has followed the activities of the MRA, and notes 'throughout these years the facilities offered by the conference centre in Caux proved a useful neutral meeting ground where Cambodians of different factions could find a degree of trust with one another'.[68] Since 1990 Cambodian community leaders have met at Caux each year. Henderson reports on how a Khmer Rouge official voluntarily conveyed to fellow Cambodians how much he regretted 'the suffering imposed on their people under Pol Pot's regime and apologised for it'.[69] Later at the conference a Cambodian responded by saying that:

> national and regional reconciliation are possible provided we today accept to trust those men who apologised to us and to forgive them. If we refuse to do it in a place like Caux, we shall never be able to do it anywhere else.[70]

Though the efforts of one Khmer Rouge official are not representative of the intentions of the larger faction this nevertheless illustrates that reconciliation can acquire momentum through acknowledging past injustices and being prepared to build a new future. Commenting on the MRA efforts at Caux, in 1996, the then Secretary-General of the UN, Boutros Boutros-Ghali, observed that 'Caux shows us that reconciliation is always possible, that divided and warring people can eventually find common ground and a new beginning'.[71]

The MRA forgiveness forums and conferences are aimed at engendering understanding by encouraging the participants to move beyond their desire for vengeance and retaliation. But more importantly, they reveal moral presuppositions which the justice and care-oriented frameworks of ethical interaction allude to. In particular, their concern for non-violent strategies for resolving differences are emphasised. There is an attempt to foster caring concern for the harm which has historically befallen the other. In this way the parameters of the moral community are extended to the other. Thus, in one important sense MRA efforts, with their emphasis on forgiveness, point to the need for past opponents to develop caring relationships for the other's well-being. This corresponds to the standpoint espoused in Gilligan's formulation of the ethic of care, which 'requires us to perceive all rational beings as individuals with a concrete history, identity, and an emotional constitution'. MRA forgiveness forums also operate on the principle that the web of human relations is, in Benhabib's words, 'ties that bind and shape our moral identities'.

THE LIMITS OF FORGIVENESS

There are challenges to implementing a process of interpersonal or intergroup forgiveness. Hamber notes that 'to genuinely take responsibility for your group's past misdeeds, or to be able to forgive those who have harmed you, several obstacles need to be overcome and a range of variables considered'. In particular, if the victim forgives without perpetrators first apologising and accepting responsibility for the harm that they have committed then a forgiveness process is unlikely to succeed. Furthermore, if perpetrators refuse to be truthful and show genuine remorse then they will not prompt forgiveness from their victims. In addition, when efforts are made to institutionalise forgiveness and reconciliation processes, such as in the establishment of truth and reconciliation commissions, and victims feel compelled or pressurised to forgive or reconcile with their perpetrators then this only creates a process of false forgiveness and reconciliation. Further, there is a high threshold for 'attaining forgiveness given the anger many victims rightly feel following extreme suffering and injustice'.[72] However, an important caveat has to be made in the sense that to forgive is not to forget. Forgiveness, as we have been discussing throughout this chapter, requires both the victims and the perpetrators to undergo a process of moral development so that they can morally include the other and create conditions that will bring about understanding, which will provide the basis for healing and reconciliation.

CONCLUSION

Literature on the ethics of peacebuilding is still in a developmental stage. Efforts to understand the relevance of forgiveness to peacebuilding require further research as an integral component of building peace requires the forgiveness by victims of their perpetrators. The micro-level processes and mechanisms of peacebuilding need to be informed by the analysis of how to enable victims in what are increasingly violent sub-national conflicts to move from a condition in which they morally exclude their perpetrators as valid interlocutors to a situation in which they morally include and acknowledge the claims of the 'other'. As seen in Chapter 3, these foundations for an ethical approach to peacebuilding are not yet in place in the international system which practises a de facto bias towards nation-states. Chapter 3 demonstrated that in the prevailing institutional arrangements the Westphalian system already 'morally' excludes sub-national groups from articulating their ethical claims against nation-states in an internationally and legally sanctioned forum.

In order to create the conditions in which forgiveness and effective peacebuilding can take place the international community has to reconsider how to restructure the framework for interaction between subnational groups and nation-states. Specifically, we are at an important turning point in history in which humans, as a consequence of the geopolitical problems created by their self-made institutional structures, need to conceptualise and adopt new moral principles of interaction and implement new norms of political association and coexistence.

Without the parties' own consensual willingness to move towards mutual moral recognition sustainable peacebuilding cannot be consolidated. Expanding peacebuilding and forgiveness research to the topic of moral exclusion in this fashion is a way of opening up an avenue for analysis which has hitherto been marginalised and underdeveloped. The overall concern has to be how to establish peacebuilding processes that engender moral inclusion.

NOTES

1. Michael Henderson, *Forgiveness: Breaking the Chain of Hate* (London: Grosvenor, 2002).
2. Ervin Staub, 'Moral Exclusion and Extreme Destructiveness: Personal Goal Theory, Differential Evaluation, Moral Equilibration and Steps Along the Continuum of Destruction', paper presented at the American Psychological Association Meeting, New York, August 1987.
3. Susan Opotow, 'Moral Exclusion and Injustice: An Introduction', *Journal of Social Issues*, vol. 46, no. 1, 1990, p. 1 (1–20).
4. Ibid.
5. See the discussion of the notion of the 'social continuity of exclusion', in Vivienne Jabri, *Discourses on Violence* (Manchester: Manchester University Press, 1996).
6. Opotow, 'Moral Exclusion and Injustice', p. 4.
7. Ibid., p. 6.
8. Ibid., p. 6.
9. See R. Holt and B. Silverstein, 'On the Psychology of Enemy Images: Introduction and Overview', *Journal of Social Issues*, vol. 45, no. 1, 1989, pp. 1–11.
10. Kurt Spillmann and Kati Spillmann, 'On Enemy Images and Conflict Escalation', *International Social Science Journal*, no. 127, February 1991, p. 58 (57–76).
11. Ibid., pp. 57–8.
12. Ibid., pp. 57–8.
13. Donald Moon, 'Practical Discourses and Communicative Ethics', in Stephen White (ed.), *The Cambridge Companion to Habermas* (Cambridge: Cambridge University Press, 1995), p. 143 (143–66).

14. Jane Braaten, 'The Succession of Theories and the Recession of Practice', *Social Theory and Practice*, vol. 18, no. 1, Spring 1992, p. 98 (81–111).

15. Jürgen Habermas, *Moral Consciousness and Communicative Action*, trans. Christian Lenhardt and Shierry Weber Nicholson (Cambridge: Polity Press, 1990), p. 66.

16. Jürgen Habermas, *Between Facts and Norms: Contributions to a Discourse Theory of Law and Democracy*, trans. William Rehg (Cambridge: Polity Press, 1996), p. 107.

17. Ibid., p. 107.

18. Ibid., p. 108.

19. Ibid., pp. 108–9.

20. Ibid., p. 110. See also Harald Grimen, 'Consensus and Normative Validity', *Inquiry*, vol. 40, no. 1, March 1997, pp. 47–62, and Gunnar Skirbekk, 'The Discourse Principle and Those Affected', *Inquiry*, vol. 40, no. 5, March 1997, pp. 63–72.

21. Ursula Wolf, 'Moral Controversies and Moral Theory', *European Journal of Philosophy*, vol. 1, no. 2, 1993, p. 61 (58–68).

22. Douglas Rasmussen, 'Political Legitimacy and Discourse Ethics', in Tibor Machan and Douglas Rasmussen, *Liberty for the 21st Century: Contemporary Libertarian Thought* (Lanham, MD: Rowman & Littlefield, 1995), p. 354 (351–74).

23. Jürgen Habermas, *Justification and Application: Remarks on Discourse Ethics*, trans. Ciaran Cronin (Cambridge: Polity Press, 1993), p. 9 (emphasis added).

24. Seyla Benhabib, 'Afterword : Communicative Ethics and Contemporary Controversies in Practical Philosophy', in Seyla Benhabib and Fred Dallmayr (eds), *The Communicative Ethics Controversy* (Cambridge, MA: MIT Press, 1990), p. 354 (330–40).

25. Donald Moon, 'Constrained Discourse and Public Life', *Political Theory*, vol. 19, no. 2, May 1991, p. 202 (202–29).

26. Habermas, *Justification and Application*, p. 9.

27. Maeve Cooke, 'Habermas and Consensus', *European Journal of Philosophy*, vol. 1, no. 3, 1993, p. 252 (247–67).

28. Habermas, *Justification and Application*, p. 13.

29. Ibid.

30. For the main corpus of his work see Lawrence Kohlberg, *The Philosophy of Moral Development: Essays on Moral Development*, vol. 1 (San Francisco: Harper & Row, 1981) and *The Psychology of Moral Development: Essays on Moral Development*, vol. 2 (San Francisco: Harper & Row, 1984).

31. For his work, which was originally published in 1932, see Jean Piaget, *Moral Judgement of the Child*, trans. M. Gabain (New York: Free Press, 1965). For a discussion of his work see K. Helkama, 'Two Studies of Piaget's Theory of Moral Development', *European Journal of Social Psychology*, vol. 18, 1988, pp. 17–37.

32. Lawrence Kohlberg, 'From Is to Ought: How to Commit the Naturalistic

Study and Get Away with it in the Study of Moral Development', in Theodore Mischel (ed.), *Cognitive Development and Epistemology* (New York and London: Academic Press, 1971), p. 163 (151–235).

33. Ibid., pp. 181–3.
34. Ibid., pp. 184.
35. Ibid., pp. 166.
36. Ibid., pp. 176–7.
37. Ibid., pp. 176–7.
38. Ibid., pp. 164–70; see also Rudolph Schaffer, *Social Development* (Oxford: Blackwell, 1996), pp. 295–6, and Deni Elliot, 'Universal Values and Moral Development Theories', in Clifford Christians and Michael Traber (eds), *Communicative Ethics and Universal Values* (London: Sage 1997), pp. 75–6.
39. A. Colby, L. Kohlberg, J. Gibbs and M. Lieberman, 'A Longitudinal Study of Moral Judgement', *Monographs of the Society for Research in Child Development*, vols 1–2, no. 200, 1983.
40. David Ingram, 'The Limits and Possibilities of Communicative Ethics for Democratic Theory', *Political Theory*, vol. 21, no. 2, May 1993, p. 306 (294–321).
41. Kohlberg, *The Psychology of Moral Development*, n. 48, p. 90.
42. Kohlberg, 'From Is to Ought', p. 186.
43. A comprehensive treatise can be found in Carol Gilligan, *In a Different Voice: Psychological Theory and Women's Development* (Cambridge, MA: Harvard University Press, 1982); see also Carol Gilligan, 'Do the Social Sciences Have an Adequate Theory of Moral Development?', in Norma Haan (ed.), *Social Science as Moral Inquiry* (New York: Columbia University Press, 1983), pp. 35–51.
44. Gilligan, *In a Different Voice*, pp. 25–31.
45. Owen Flanagan and Kathryn Jackson, 'Justice, Care and Gender: The Kohlberg-Gilligan Debate Revisited', *Ethics*, vol. 97, April 1987, pp. 622–37.
46. Ibid., p. 623.
47. Ibid., p. 623.
48. Carol Gilligan, 'Moral Orientation and Moral Development', in Eva Kittay and Diana Meyers (eds), *Women and Moral Theory* (Totowa, NJ: Rowman & Littlefield, 1987), p. 19.
49. Gilligan, *In a Different Voice*, p. 74.
50. Susan Hekman, *Moral Voices, Moral Selves: Carol Gilligan and Feminist Moral Theory* (Cambridge: Polity Press, 1995), p. 9.
51. Larissa Fast, Reina Neufeldt and Lisa Schirch, 'Toward Ethically Grounded Conflict Interventions: Re-evaluating Challenges in the 21st Century', *International Negotiation*, vol. 7, 2002, p. 189 (185–207).
52. Ibid.
53. Ibid.
54. Lawrence Kohlberg with Charles Levine and Alexandra Hewer, 'Moral Stages: A Current Statement – Response to Critics, Appendix A', in

Lawrence Kohlberg, *The Psychology of Moral Development*, n. 130, p. 306.

55. For further discussion, see Seyla Benhabib, 'The Debate Over Women and Moral Theory Revisited', in Johanna Meehan (ed.), *Feminists Read Habermas: Gendering the Subject of Discourse* (London: Routledge, 1995), p. 186 (181–204).

56. Onora O'Neill, 'Justice, Gender, and International Boundaries', in R. Attfield, and B. Wilkins (eds), *International Justice and the Third World* (London: Routledge, 1992), p. 56.

57. Seyla Benhabib, 'In Defence of Universalism – Yet Again! A Response to Critics of Situating the Self', *New German Critique*, 1994, p. 189.

58. Brandon Hamber, 'Forgiveness and Reconciliation: Paradise Lost or Pragmatism?', *Peace and Conflict: Journal of Peace Psychology*, vol. 13, no. 1, 2007, p. 115 (115–25).

59. Ibid.

60. J. Kadiangandu and E. Mullet, 'Intergroup Forgiveness: A Congolese Perspective', *Peace and Conflict: Journal of Peace Psychology*, vol. 13, no. 1, 2007, pp. 37–49.

61. Hamber, 'Forgiveness and Reconciliation', p. 118.

62. J. Manzi and R. Gonzalez, 'Forgiveness and Reparation in Chile: The Role of Cognitive and Emotional Intergroup Antecedents', *Peace and Conflict: Journal of Peace Psychology*, vol. 13, no. 1, 2007, pp. 71–91; see quotation in Hamber, 'Forgiveness and Reconciliation', p. 118.

63. R. Enright and Human Development Study Group, 'Piaget on the Moral Development of Forgiveness: Identity or Reciprocity?', *Human Development*, vol. 37, no. 2, 1994, pp. 63–80; see also R. Enright, *Forgiveness is a Choice: A Step-by-Step Process for Resolving Anger and Restoring Hope* (Washington, DC: American Psychological Association, 2001).

64. Enright, *Forgiveness is a Choice*, p. 31.

65. Interview with Peter Everington, Moral Re-Armament (MRA), London, 2 April 1998.

66. Frank Buchman, *Remaking the World* (London: Blandford, 1961).

67. Interview with Everington.

68. Michael Henderson, *The Forgiveness Factor: Stories of Hope in a World of Conflict* (London: Grosvenor Books, 1996), p. 97.

69. Ibid., p. 98.

70. Ibid., pp. 98–9.

71. Ibid., pp. 98–9.

72. Hamber, 'Forgiveness and Reconciliation', p. 121.

CHAPTER 6

THE VALUE OF RECONCILIATION

INTRODUCTION

If and when the process of forgiveness is successfully undertaken then the parties involved are ready for genuine healing and reconciliation to begin. Effective reconciliation ultimately consolidates peacebuilding. However, as with forgiveness, reconciliation is a process, not an event, and to achieve effective reconciliation may require one, two or more generations. This chapter will begin by developing a conceptual understanding of reconciliation, which is a morally loaded term in its own right. The reconciliation process ultimately can only be conducted by the parties affected by a dispute. However, increasingly in the field of international and domestic politics truth and reconciliation commissions are being utilised to promote coexistence. This has particularly been the case in Africa. For example, South Africa and Sierra Leone established truth and reconciliation institutions to initiate meso-level reconciliation processes. By focusing on reconciliation, peacebuilding and transitional justice in Africa, this chapter will assess the merits and demerits of such institutions. It will also examine the valuable lessons that can be gained from indigenous approaches to micro-level reconciliation and peacebuilding, with examples drawn from Africa. These approaches possess ethical norms for resolving disputes between members of society and contain insights from which the world as a whole can benefit.[1] Ultimately, at the core of reconciliation processes is the institutionalisation of a process of transitional justice. Genuine peace is not sustainable without social, economic and political justice. This chapter will assess the interface between peacebuilding and transitional justice and develop a matrix for how to achieve peace with justice.

UNDERSTANDING RECONCILIATION

There is a degree of vagueness and lack of clarity that infuses debates on the meaning and purpose of reconciliation. In 2003, Brandon Hamber and Grainne Kelly 'carried out research motivated by the observation that reconciliation was ill-defined in Northern Ireland to the detriment of reconciliation practice'.[2] It is often viewed as a soft concept with religious origins. Ultimately, Hamber and Kelly found that 'reconciliation implied a deep and challenging process that required a level of community integration which some felt the communities with which they worked were not prepared or willing to grasp'.[3] In addition, 'the definition assumes that building peace requires attention to relationships. This means not only reconciling broken down relationships as the term confusingly implies, but building new relationships in some cases'.[4]

The most articulate framework of reconciliation is provided by Hizkias Assefa when he outlines and demarcates the essential aspects and components of reconciliation. Essentially for Assefa, a framework of reconciliation broadly includes:

1. an acknowledgement of the responsibility by the perpetrator;

2. the showing of genuine repentance or remorse by the perpetrator;

3. the payment where possible of compensation or the demonstration of a symbolic act of reparation by the perpetrator;

4. the request for forgiveness by the perpetrator;

5. the granting of mercy, where possible, by the victim;

6. an ongoing process of healing and reconciliation between the victims and perpetrators and/or their representatives.[5]

For Hamber and Kelly reconciliation 'is a voluntary act that cannot be imposed, and it involves five interwoven strands', comprising:

1. developing a shared vision of an interdependent and fair society;

2. acknowledging and dealing with the past;

3. building positive relationships;

4. significant cultural and attitudinal change;

5. substantial social, economic and political change (or equity).[6]

Reconciliation effectively seeks to overcome the hatred, suspicion and distrust of the past and to heal a society to the extent that coexistence becomes possible. In this sense, John-Paul Lederach argues that the process of reconciliation is deeply paradoxical.[7] He argues that:

> reconciliation can be seen as dealing with three specific paradoxes. First, in an overall sense, reconciliation promotes an encounter between the open expression of the painful past, on the one hand, and the search for the articulation of a long-term, interdependent future, on the other hand.[8]

Lederach further points out that the second paradox of reconciliation is based on the fact that it 'provides a place for truth and mercy to meet, where concerns for exposing what has happened and for letting go in favour of a renewed relationship are validated and embraced'.[9] The third paradox exists because 'reconciliation recognises the need to give time and place to both justice and peace, where redressing the wrong is held together with the envisioning of a common, connected future'.[10] These paradoxes can ultimately be reduced to the conundrum that 'reconciliation requires dealing with the past but at the same time participating in developing a shared vision for the future'.[11] Stuart Kaufman notes that 'resolving ethnic war requires reconciliation – changing hostile attitudes to more moderate ones, assuaging ethnic fears, and replacing the intragroup symbolic politics of ethnic chauvinism with a politics that rewards moderation'.[12] When seeking to unravel these paradoxes and in a quest to further our understanding of the different dimensions of reconciliation, we can sub-divide the process into three sub-components: social, political and economic reconciliation.[13]

SOCIAL, POLITICAL AND ECONOMIC RECONCILIATION

Social reconciliation refers to the importance of establishing dialogue, understanding, forgiveness and ultimately healing between actors in a social context. All societies have tension inherent in their structures and among their members. When this tension is inappropriately managed societies can fragment and even implode. The efforts required to bring about a restoration of societal harmony requires a process of social reconciliation.

Reconciliation has been viewed as an individual and inter-subjective process; however today it has moved into the political realm.[14] Following the political settlement of a conflict efforts are also made to put in place an institutional framework to advance reconciliation. However, the notion leaves open the question as to whether inter-group reconciliation is possible. One can point to populations, countries and governments that were once bitter enemies who currently enjoy improved relations.

Violent conflict or protracted authoritarian rule creates economic conditions in which there are huge disparities between the beneficiaries who gained from a previous historical circumstance, and the victims. Reconciliation cannot exclusively be consolidated by a social and political rapprochement between victims and perpetrators it also requires a deliberate policy of economic distribution of global, national or communal resources in order to assuage the grievances that were committed in the past. Hence economic reconciliation is an integral part of the healing process and generally takes several decades, generations or centuries to implement.

THE INTERFACE BETWEEN RECONCILIATION, PEACEBUILDING AND TRANSITIONAL JUSTICE

As discussed in Chapter 3, Africa as a region has borne a devastating burden of violent conflict. Several countries are emerging from conflict and the challenge of peacebuilding is immediately confronted by the demands for justice for the victims of human rights atrocities. Traditionally the pursuit of justice in international relations has been considered detrimental to achieving peace. One way to assess the linkage between reconciliation, peacebuilding and transitional justice is to consider peace and justice as mutually inclusive and complementary. The chapter will outline a peace with justice matrix. In terms of concrete case studies, this chapter will assess the creation of the International Criminal Court (ICC) as an attempt to administer justice for grave atrocities committed during conflict. It will suggest that the ICC makes a necessary first step in promoting justice but that ultimately more restorative forms of justice are necessary in order to bring about the socio-economic and political reconciliation that is necessary for peace and justice to coexist. The chapter will conclude by assessing indigenous African approaches for peacebuilding and explore whether they might provide the necessary framework for achieving peace with justice.

CONTEXTUALISING POSITIVE PEACEBUILDING IN AFRICA

The conflict and post-conflict societies of Africa are communities with highly traumatised populations. Among the key challenges for peace-building in this century will be the importance of promoting healing, reconciliation and justice for past atrocities within traumatised societies. The reconciliation process does not begin and end within a fixed timeframe. Healing and reconciliation are in fact processes that can take a lifetime. Given some of the atrocities that have been committed and the experiences that victims have gone through in Africa, it will take a long time for people to overcome the physical, emotional and mental anguish generated by conflict.

There are ongoing efforts to set up other commissions to establish an official and accurate record of the atrocities of the past and make recommendations to governments regarding reparations for victims, reforms of existing laws or institutional structures to prevent future abuses. Therefore, for the next few decades this issue of whether peace can be achieved without addressing the interests of justice will continue to be debated. The role that the law plays in enabling post-conflict societies to make their transition to democracy becomes crucial. Transi-tional justice refers to frameworks of the rule of law which enable a political transformation to take place within authoritarian or war-affected communities. The dilemma arises from the need to establish a balance between maintaining order on the one hand and facilitating a political transition on the other.[15]

The old adage goes that there can be no justice without peace. It is equally true, however, that there is no peace without justice. Pragmatists maintain that the best one can hope for is an uneasy compromise between what peace requires and what justice demands. This chapter will explore the nexus between peacebuilding and justice by assessing the challenges of establishing peace after conflict and the problem of promoting justice in situations which have been defined by the perpe-tuation of grievous human rights atrocities. By introducing this notion of positive peace with justice, then the false dichotomy between peace and justice dissolves. It becomes self-evident that positive peace can only be sustained with justice. Inversely, in order to attain justice for former victims positive peace is required.

This chapter will later look at the attempt to institutionalise this notion of ensuring justice when building peace by looking at the mandate of the International Criminal Court (ICC). The issue is that the ICC retains a logic of punitive justice, which can sometimes be at odds with promoting socially cohesive post-conflict communities. The ICC therefore falls short of the requirement to reconcile the requirements of peace with the demands of justice. Ultimately, it is necessary to adopt approaches to peacebuilding which place more of an emphasis on forgiveness and restorative justice rather than punitive justice. Restorative justice seeks to restore social harmony by encouraging the perpetrators of crimes to confess and show genuine remorse which provides victims with the basis for granting forgiveness and embracing reconciliation. This chapter therefore concludes with an assessment of whether some of the cultural and indigenous traditions for peacebuilding in Africa can fulfil this requirement of ensuring peace with justice, based on the restoration and healing of broken relationships.

COLONIAL INJUSTICE

The colonial systems of justice were superimposed on top of African systems of justice and governance and have been retained in most postcolonial state structures. Justice should not be meted through predetermined and inflexible prescriptions by applying the same model to every local population or country. It needs to be context-specific and relevant to the local communities' concepts of justice as well as sensitive to local social and cultural traditions. In northern Somalia (or Somaliland) the local population has made use of traditional leadership and governance structures to reconstruct a government and establish relatively peaceful conditions for its people, which is not currently the case in southern Somalia. Regrettably, the entity combining traditional and modern institutions of governance has not received recognition by the international community because there is no language or vocabulary to describe what Somaliland is other than the word 'nation-state'; this term, however, is unacceptable to most governments as it would implicitly legitimate secession and probably open the way to the break-up of many other states.

Therefore, to enable culture to begin to play a significant role in the reconstruction of Africa it will be necessary to establish education and training programmes for officials and civil society actors based on African cultural values, while bearing in mind that not all traditions are empowering, particularly on issues to do with gender equality. Progressive cultural principles promoting human dignity and the well-being of the individual and society can provide valuable insights into how Africa can be reconstructed by using its own indigenous value-systems which emphasise confronting corruption and promoting power sharing, inclusive governance and the equitable distribution of resources among all members of society.

THE CHALLENGE OF POST-CONFLICT PEACEBUILDING IN AFRICA

Countries in Africa that have made the transition from conflict include Angola, Mozambique, Sierra Leone, Liberia and the Southern part of the Sudan. South Africa made the transition from a minority-rule apartheid system to a pluralist liberal democracy; however the situation in the country is by no means stable and indeed the situation can only be described as one in which a fragile reconciliation exists. For these countries emerging from authoritarianism or conflict, social and economic justice in the form of the promotion of the well-being of large sections of their populations remains to be addressed if positive peace predicated on sustainable reconciliation processes is to be consolidated.

THE PEACE WITH JUSTICE MATRIX

The peace with justice matrix is a graphic representation of the nexus between peacebuilding and transitional justice.

Presence of Justice		
	Restorative Justice	Social Harmony and Reconciliation
	Punitive/Retributive Justice	
	Instability, Disorder Tension	
Absence of Justice		
	Negative Peace	Positive Peace

This matrix proposes a two-dimensional axis with peace on the horizontal and justice on the vertical. Along the horizontal axis from left to right, negative peace represents the condition of the absence of war, and positive peace indicates a situation in which social and economic justice has merged with political peacemaking and reconciliation. The vertical axis therefore represents the trend towards greater socio-economic and political justice.

This matrix suggests that there is a symbiotic relationship between peace and justice. In the absence of justice, a negative peace prevails. As justice increases so does the trend towards positive peace. The question arises as to what moral principles are necessary in order to meet the requirements of international transitional justice.[16] Transitional justice requires that those who are guilty of human rights abuses, war crimes and crimes against humanity need to be brought to account. Equally, victimised groups need to be able to build a future secure from threats or retaliation.

PUNITIVE AND RETRIBUTIVE JUSTICE VS RESTORATIVE JUSTICE

As a norm, punitive or retributive justice has been the main form of justice rendered often by state or intergovernmental instruments and mechanisms in order to control and shape anti-social behaviour as defined by the state or intergovernmental authority. This definition of justice often does not take into account the needs of victims for restitution, healing or reconciliation. Through these forms of justice, conflicts and their regulation or management become the property and sole preserve of the state or intergovernmental framework.

Restorative justice works on the principle of trying to, wherever possible, restore a relationship between the victim and the perpetrator so that they can continue to coexist in the same community.

The goal of this framework is for both sides to work together on the basis of consensus to achieve reconciliation. Within such a framework of reconciliation and restorative justice there are strong incentives for perpetrators to tell the truth, whereas in the framework of punitive or retributive justice there are incentives for hiding the truth. When perpetrators conceal the truth and do not face justice, it leaves the victims dissatisfied. Perpetrators become beneficiaries of the system of justice that fails to find the culpable party and this promotes a culture of impunity. Therefore, a process of restorative justice has a better chance of promoting positive peace as it does not encourage a framework which will permit impunity. If amnesty is provided for through a framework of restorative justice then immunity may have to be the price paid to enable victims and perpetrators to move forward and coexist.

Therefore, with regard to the above matrix the spectrum of justice proposes that punitive and retributive forms of justice can be contrasted with restorative forms of justice which promote more sustainable societies, and a general sense about the presence of justice. Restorative justice in this regard strives to ensure that the parties not only perceive but experience the efforts to promote social harmony by encouraging the perpetrators of crimes to confess and show genuine remorse which provides victims with the basis for granting forgiveness and embracing reconciliation.

From the matrix we can ultimately propose that in order for social harmony and reconciliation to prevail there needs to be a high degree of positive peace and a sense of justice having been done.

POST-CONFLICT JUSTICE: THE CASE OF THE INTERNATIONAL CRIMINAL COURT

A United Nations Conference adopted the Rome Statute of the International Criminal Court (ICC) in July 1998. The ICC has the jurisdiction to investigate the most serious violations of international human rights and humanitarian law, and bringing to justice individuals who commit the crime of aggression, war crimes, crimes against humanity and genocide. Based in the Hague, the ICC came into being when the Rome Statute was ratified on 1 July 2002. The ICC has jurisdiction over matters involving individual criminal responsibility.[17] It can identify the precise nature of the alleged crime as well as identify alleged suspects, potential witnesses and victims.

The ICC has some constraints, notably the fact that certain states which are not signatories to the Rome Statute can continue to commit human rights abuses. The ICC has jurisdiction over non-state parties or countries which have been referred by the UN Security Council to the Court. The ICC therefore provides a post-conflict legal framework to address grievous human rights atrocities. This framework, however, requires the cooperation of governments. As such it can play a role in contributing towards post-conflict transitional justice. Recently the United Nations Security Council decided to refer the situation prevailing in Darfur to the Prosecutor of the ICC. Through its Resolution 1593 the Council noted that 'the situation in Sudan continues to constitute a threat to international peace and security' and therefore 'acting under Chapter VII of the Charter of the United Nations' it decided to 'refer the situation in Darfur since 1 July 2002 to the Prosecutor of the International Criminal Court'.[18] In particular, it encouraged the ICC 'to support international cooperation with domestic efforts to promote the rule of law, protect human rights and combat impunity in Darfur'. Through this referral the UN was identifying a role for the ICC in promoting international peace and security. Specifically, it acknowledged that the ICC has an important role to play in promoting post-conflict peacebuilding. This view was reinforced by an association of non-governmental organisations under the label of the Darfur Consortium which has argued that the ICC has an important role to play in the peacebuilding process in the Sudan. If grievances of victims are not addressed this can in the long run impact upon the peace process.

Sanctions and legal judgements against perpetrators indicate to the victims and their communities that a culture of impunity will not be tolerated.

The ICC, however, is a criminal court and utilises a punitive and retributive model of justice. As such it has limitations when it comes to the promotion of healing and reconciliation as described earlier. Interestingly, the UN Security Council in its referral of the Darfur issue emphasised

> the need to promote healing and reconciliation, as well as the creation of institutions, involving all sectors of Sudanese society, such as truth and/or reconciliation commissions, *in order to complement judicial processes and thereby reinforce the efforts to restore long-lasting peace*, with the African Union and international support as necessary.[19]

The ICC has a role to play in terms of the transitional judicial process required to prosecute war crimes; however, it is not equipped to promote the healing and reconciliation of communities.

COURTS OR COMMISSIONS? THE DILEMMAS OF TRANSITIONAL JUSTICE AND RECONCILIATION

There are major constraints on obtaining the collaboration of governments when it comes to putting in place processes of transitional justice. The state or government might coopt such processes to suit its political agenda. There may be external pressure to put in place such processes. These constraints can also arise from the considerations of the immediate post-conflict situation. Perpetrators often do not hesitate to use the threat of continued war as a bargaining chip to receive amnesty and form part of the government. This situation happened in Sierra Leone when Foday Sankoh, the leader of the Revolutionary United Front (RUF), which had committed human rights atrocities including the amputation of the limbs of innocent civilians as young as two years old. The Lomé Peace Agreement, which brought the conflict to an end, made provisions for Mr Sankoh to be made vice-president. This act of amnesty would have compromised the commitment to preventing impunity, which is why the UN made an official reservation about aspects of the Sierra Leone peace agreement from the outset.

Following a decade-long war from 1991 to 2001 there was a need to address the violent crimes of the past.[20] A Special Court for Sierra Leone was established to prosecute those who were deemed to be most responsible for atrocities committed during the war. It was particularly designed for leaders who were alleged to have directed and organised the crimes committed during the war. Low-level soldiers would not be subject to the jurisdiction of the Court. Thirteen individuals were indicted to trials, including the former President of Liberia Charles Taylor, who today is in exile in Nigeria. The indictment against Foday Sankoh was withdrawn in December 2003 following his death. These individuals were charged with war crimes, crimes against humanity and other violations of humanitarian law. Some of these crimes included murder, rape, extermination, enslavement, looting and burning, sexual slavery, conscription of children into an armed force, forced marriage and attacks on humanitarian workers.

The Court made the provision that if the accused were found guilty they would be sentenced to prison but not to death. The trials of the Court are currently being concluded as of mid-2007, if additional indictees are not brought before the Court. The Court only deals with the leaders of armed movements and does not address the atrocities of lower-ranking individuals or groups. The Sierra Leonean Truth and Reconciliation Commission was created by the Lomé Peace Agreement on 7 July 1999 and then established by an Act of the Sierra Leonean Parliament on 10 February 2000. The mandate of the Commission was to create an impartial historical record of human rights abuses and violations of international humanitarian law related to the armed conflict in Sierra Leone. It had an ambitious mandate of seeking to address impunity, responding to the needs of victims and promoting healing and reconciliation. It also had a mandate of investigating, reporting the causes, nature and extent of human rights violations and establishing whether they were a direct result of the deliberate planning, policy and authorisation of any government, group or individual. Based on the model of the South African Truth and Reconciliation Commission established in 1995, the Sierra Leone Commission completed its statement-taking phase on 31 March 2003. An analysis of the statements indicated that they contained information on around 3,000 victims who had suffered more than 4,000 violations, of which 1,000 related to killings and 200 to rape. The Commission faced a problem when it sought to hold public hearings on the detainees held in the custody of the Court. As a result these detainees did not go through the TRC process.

The Commission subsequently issued its recommendations in October 2004. It identified the causes of the conflict and made several recommendations including legal, political and administrative reforms so as to prevent any repetition of the violations or abuses suffered. Its proposed measures were designed to facilitate the building of a new Sierra Leone based on the values of human dignity, tolerance and respect for the rights of all persons before the law. It also recommended the enshrining of human dignity, the banning of the death penalty and the repeal of all statutory and customary laws discriminating against women.

The Commission acknowledged the need for reparation and not retribution, for community and not victimisation, for reconstruction and not greed. It proposed a reparations programme and the establishment of a Special Fund for War Victims. It further recommended measures to deal with the needs of victims in the areas of community reparations, symbolic reparations, health, pensions, education, skills training and micro-credit. For victims of amputation and sexual violence, and the war wounded it proposed a programme to address their specific needs rather than giving cash handouts.

The Sierra Leone Commission worked to complement the Special Court. Most truth commissions have operated as an alternative to criminal transitional justice. The Commission was established as 'an alternative to criminal justice in order to establish accountability for the atrocities that had been committed during the conflict'.[21]

THE CASE FOR RECONCILIATION COMMISSIONS

There are ongoing efforts to establish other commissions in order to maintain an official and accurate record of the atrocities of the past and make recommendations to governments on reparations for victims, reforms of existing laws or institutional structures to prevent future abuses. Other cases of commissions in Africa include the Ghana National Reconciliation Commission, which is mandated to establish an accurate and complete historical record of abuses perpetrated against individuals during the periods of unconstitutional rule. Investigations began on 2 September 2002 and public hearings on 14 January 2003.

In Rwanda critics of the tribunal for Rwanda, based in Arusha, argue that it is taking too long to bring justice to victims. Others criticise the traditional form of justice known as *gacaca* and argue that the genocide was too complex to be addressed through this form of justice which does not entirely rehabilitate relationships, given the way it is currently operationalised by the government. There are those who advocate the establishment of a Rwandese Truth and Reconciliation Commission in order to establish an official record of the human rights violations that took place. This is not to be confused with the already existing National Unity and Reconciliation Commission (NURC) whose mandate is based on promoting national unity and reconciliation through education, research and advocacy. The former Speaker of the Rwandese

Parliament from 1997 to 2000, Joseph Sebarenzi, for example, has argued that the 'retributive justice' being utilised in Rwanda is not feasible because many people on both sides of the ethnic divide have been involved in genocide or mass killings and some of them were at the same time victims.[22]

THE CONTRIBUTION OF CULTURE TO PEACE WITH JUSTICE

There is also a case to be made for the consideration of alternative models of transitional justice in efforts to implement effective peacebuilding. Some cultural approaches to justice in Africa place an emphasis on healing and reconciliation. People derive their sense of meaning from their culture. What does it mean to be human? What is – or ought to be – the nature of human relations? These notions feed into the attitudes and values that we choose to embrace, which in turn determine how we interact with each other. Cultural attitudes and values therefore provide the foundation for the social norms by which people live. Through internalising and sharing these cultural attitudes and values with their fellow community members, and by handing them down to future generations, societies can – and do – reconstruct themselves on the basis of a particular cultural image.

In order to initiate the social reconstruction of war-affected communities, a key step would be to find a way for members of these communities to 're-inform' themselves with a cultural logic that emphasises sharing and equitable resource distribution. This, in effect, means emphasising the importance of reviving cultural attitudes and values that can foster a climate within which peace can flourish.

INDIGENOUS APPROACHES TO PEACEBUILDING: A MODEL FOR TRANSITIONAL JUSTICE?

Interestingly, we find that in Africa there are indigenous traditions for peacebuilding which can teach us a lot about healing and reconciliation.[23] The challenge today is for us to find ways of learning lessons from the local cultural approaches to peacebuilding. For example, in northern Somalia, traditional leadership institutions were used to bring together the clans and create a legislature and government drawing upon Somali tradition and combining these traditional structures with modern institutions of governance like the parliament. Today in northern Somalia there is a situation of relative peace and stability. Also, in Rwanda the government is currently making use of the traditional justice and reconciliation system known as *gacaca* to enable it to try and judge some of those who are accused of having been among the perpetrators of genocide in 1994. The interesting lesson to learn from this *gacaca* system is that it is largely organised on the basis of local community involvement. The local community is involved in encouraging the perpetrators to acknowledge what they have done and the victims are involved in determining what reparations need to be made so that the perpetrator can be integrated back into the community. In the post-conflict era, in Mozambique traditional healing and reconciliation practices were used to enable combatants, particularly child soldiers, to be re-integrated back into their communities. In Chad, Niger and Ghana, traditional institutions have been used in the past in order to address the low-intensity conflicts that affected these countries.

Among the countries of East, Central and Southern Africa we find a cultural world-view know as *ubuntu*. The idea behind this world-view is that a person is a person through other people. We are human because we live through others, we belong, we participate and we share. A person with *ubuntu* is open and available to others and does not feel threatened when others achieve because he or she recognises that they belong to a greater whole.[24] The lesson for peacebuilding from this tradition is that by adopting and internalising the principles of *ubuntu* we can contribute towards creating healthy relationships based on the recognition that within the web of humanity everyone is linked to everyone else. These principles of forgiveness and reconciliation which this tradition advocates provide us with strategies for peacebuilding. In his book *No Future without Forgiveness*, Archbishop Desmond Tutu suggests that these principles helped to guide the thoughts and actions of some of the victims and perpetrators who came before the South African Truth and Reconciliation Commission to confess and forgive.[25] There is indeed much that we should be learning from African indigenous approaches to peacebuilding.[26]

While traditional institutions provide us with many lessons which we can incorporate into ongoing peacebuilding processes, it is important for us also to recognise that some traditions have not always promoted gender equality and therefore we need to combine the best lessons that tradition has to offer with progressive modern norms and standards for the protection of human rights. In this way a combination of tradition and modernity can enable Africans to reconstruct their continent by drawing upon their cultural heritage.[27]

THE *UBUNTU* NEXUS BETWEEN PEACEBUILDING AND RESTORATIVE JUSTICE

As Chairman of the South African Truth and Reconciliation Commission, Tutu reflects in *No Future without Forgiveness* that he drew upon both his Christian values and his cultural values.[28] In particular, he highlights that he constantly referred to the notion of *ubuntu* when he was guiding and advising witnesses, victims and perpetrators during the Commission hearings.

Ubuntu is found in diverse forms in many societies throughout Africa. More specifically among the Bantu languages of East, Central and Southern Africa the concept of *ubuntu* is a cultural world-view that tries to capture the essence of what it means to be human. In southern Africa we find its clearest articulation among the Nguni group of languages. In terms of its definition, Tutu observes that

> *ubuntu* is very difficult to render into a Western language. It speaks to the very essence of being human. When you want to give high praise to someone we say, '*Yu, u nobuntu*'; he or she has *ubuntu*. This means that they are generous, hospitable, friendly, caring and compassionate. They share what they have.[29]

For Tutu, *ubuntu* 'also means that my humanity is caught up, is inextricably bound up, in theirs. We belong in a bundle of life. We say, "a person is a person through other people" (in Xhosa *Ubuntu ungamntu ngabanye abantu* and in Zulu *Umuntu ngumuntu ngabanye*). I am human because I belong, I participate, I share'.[30] In terms of character traits

> a person with *ubuntu* is open and available to others, affirming of others, does not feel threatened that others are able and good; for he or she has a proper self-assurance that comes with knowing that he or she belongs in a greater whole and is diminished when others are humiliated or diminished, when other are tortured or oppressed, or treated as if they were less than who they are.[31]

As a 'human being through other human beings', it follows that what we do to others feeds through the interwoven moral fabric of social, economic and political relationships to eventually impact upon us as well. Even the supporters of apartheid were in a sense victims of the brutalising system from which they benefited economically and politically: it distorted their view of their relationship with other human beings, which then impacted upon their own sense of security and freedom from fear. As Tutu observes: 'in the process of dehumanising another, in inflicting untold harm and suffering, the perpetrator was inexorably being dehumanised as well'.[32]

This notion of *ubuntu* sheds light on the importance of peacemaking through the principles of reciprocity, inclusivity and a sense of shared destiny between peoples. It provides a value system for giving and receiving forgiveness. It provides a rationale for sacrificing or letting go of the desire to take revenge for past wrongs. It provides an inspiration and suggests guidelines for societies and their governments on how to legislate and establish laws which will promote reconciliation. In short, it can 'culturally re-inform' our practical efforts to build peace and heal our traumatised communities. It is to be noted that the principles found in *ubuntu* are not unique; as indicated earlier, they can be found in diverse forms in other cultures and traditions. Nevertheless, an ongoing reflection and reappraisal of this notion of *ubuntu* can serve to re-emphasise the essential unity of humanity and gradually promote attitudes and values based on the sharing of resources and on coopera-tion and collaboration in the resolution of our common problems.

How, then, were the principles of *ubuntu* traditionally articulated and translated into practical peacemaking processes? *Ubuntu* societies main-tained conflict resolution and reconciliation mechanisms which also served as institutions for maintaining law and order within society. These mechanisms pre-dated colonialism and continue to exist and function today. *Ubuntu* societies place a high value on communal life, and maintaining positive relations within society is a collective task in which everyone is involved. A dispute between fellow members of a society is perceived not merely as a matter of curiosity with regards to the affairs of one's neighbour; in a very real sense an emerging conflict belongs to the whole community. According to the notion of *ubuntu*, each member of the community is linked to each of the disputants, be they victims or perpetrators. If everybody is willing to acknowledge this (that is, to accept the principles of *ubuntu*), then people may either feel a sense of having been wronged, or a sense of responsibility for the wrong that has been committed. Due to this linkage, a law-breaking individual thus transforms his or her group into a law-breaking group in the same way that a disputing individual transforms his or her group into a disputing group. It therefore follows that if an individual is wronged, he or she may depend on the group to remedy the wrong, because in a sense the group has also been wronged. We can witness these dynamics of group identity and their impact on conflict situations across the world.

Ubuntu societies developed mechanisms for resolving disputes and promoting reconciliation with a view to healing past wrongs and maintaining social cohesion and harmony. Consensus building was embraced as a cultural pillar with respect to the regulation and manage-ment of relationships between members of the community. Depending on the nature of the disagreement or dispute, the conflict resolution process could take place at the level of the family or the village, between members of an ethnic group or even between different ethnic nations situated in the same region.

In the context of the *ubuntu* societies found in southern Africa, particularly among the Xhosa, disputes would be resolved through an institution known as the *inkundla/lekgotla* which served as a group mediation and reconciliation forum.[33] This *inkundla/lekgotla* forum was communal in character in the sense that the entire society was involved at various levels in trying to find a solution to a problem which was viewed as threatening the social cohesion of the community. In principle the proceedings would be led by a Council of Elders and the Chief or, if the disputes were larger, by the King himself. The process of ascertaining wrongdoing and finding a resolution included family members related to the victims and perpetrators, even women and the young. The mechanism therefore allowed members of the public to share their views and to generally make their opinions known. The larger community could thus be involved in the process of conflict resolution. In particular, members of the society had the right to put questions to the victims, perpetrators and witnesses as well as to put suggestions to the Council of Elders on possible ways forward. The Council of Elders, in its capacity as an intermediary, had an investigative function and also played an advisory role to the Chief. By listening to the views of the members of the society, the Council of Elders could advise on solutions which would promote reconciliation between the aggrieved parties and thus maintain the overall objective of sustaining the unity and cohesion of the community.

The actual process involved five key stages:
- firstly, after a fact-finding process where the views of victims, perpetrators and witnesses were heard, the perpetrators – if considered to have done wrong – would be encouraged, both by the Council and by other community members in the *inkundla/lekgotla* forum, to *acknowledge responsibility or guilt*.
- secondly, perpetrators would be encouraged to *demonstrate genuine remorse or to repent*.
- thirdly, perpetrators would be encouraged to *ask for forgiveness* and victims in their turn would be encouraged to *show mercy*.
- fourthly, where possible and at the suggestion of the Council of Elders, perpetrators would be required to *pay an appropriate compensation or reparation* for the wrong done. (This was often more symbolic than a repayment in kind, with the primary function

of reinforcing the remorse of the perpetrators.) Amnesty could thus be granted, but not with impunity.

- the fifth stage would seek to consolidate the whole process by encouraging the parties to commit themselves to reconciliation. This process of reconciliation tended to include the victim and his or her family members and friends as well as the perpetrator and his or her family members and friends. Both groups would be encouraged to embrace coexistence and to work towards healing the relationship between them and thus contribute towards restoring harmony within the community, which was vital in ensuring the integrity and viability of the society. The act of reconciliation was vital in that it symbolised the willingness of the parties to move beyond the psychological bitterness that had prevailed in the minds of the parties during the conflict situation.

Frankly, this process was not always straightforward, and there would naturally be instances of resistance in following through the various stages of the peacemaking process. This was particularly so with respect to the perpetrators, who tended to prefer that past events were not relived and brought out into the open. In the same way, victims would not always find it easy to forgive. In some instances forgiveness could be withheld, in which case the process could be held up in an impasse, with consequences for the relations between members of the community. However, forgiveness, when granted, would generate such a degree of goodwill that the people involved, and the society as a whole, could then move forward even from the most difficult situations. The wisdom of this process lies in the recognition that it is not possible to build a healthy community at peace with itself unless past wrongs are acknowledged and brought out into the open so that the truth of what happened can be determined and social trust renewed through a process of forgiveness and reconciliation. A community in which there is no trust is ultimately not viable and gradually begins to tear itself apart. With reference to the notion of *I am because we are* and that of *a person being a person through other people*, the above process emphasises drawing upon these *ubuntu* values when faced with the difficult challenge of acknowledging responsibility and showing remorse, or of granting forgiveness.

As mentioned previously, this traditional peacemaking process covered offences across the board from family and marriage disputes, theft, damage to property, murder and wars. In the more difficult cases involving murder, *ubuntu* societies sought to avoid the death penalty because, based on the society's view of itself – as *people through other people* – the death penalty would only serve to cause injury to society as a whole. Though it would be more difficult to move beyond such cases, the emphasis would still be on restoring the broken relationships caused by the death of a member of the community.

The guiding principle of *ubuntu* is based on the notion that parties need to be reconciled in order to rebuild and maintain social trust and social cohesion, with a view to preventing a culture of vendetta or retribution from developing and escalating between individuals, families and society as a whole. We continue to observe how individuals and sections of society in the Republic of South Africa, epitomised by Mandela and Tutu, have drawn upon some aspects of their cultural values and attitudes to enable the country to move beyond its violent past. The South African Truth and Reconciliation Commission, which has as many critics as it has supporters, has also relied on the willingness of victims to recognise the humanity of the perpetrators, and there are documented cases of victims forgiving particular perpetrators. Tutu himself would always advise victims to forgive – if they felt themselves able to do so. His guiding principle was that without forgiveness there could be no future for the young South African Republic.

STRATEGIES FOR PROMOTING A JUST PEACE AS A BASIS FOR RECONCILIATION

Four key lessons are:

1. the importance of public participation in the peacemaking process;
2. the utility of supporting victims and encouraging perpetrators as they go through the difficult process of making peace;
3. the value of acknowledging guilt and remorse and the granting of forgiveness as a way to achieve reconciliation;
4. The importance of referring constantly to the essential unity and interdependence of humanity, as expressed through *ubuntu*, and living out the principles which this unity suggests, namely; empathy for others, the sharing of common resources and working with a spirit of cooperation in our efforts to resolve our common problems.

THE LIMITS OF TRUTH AND RECONCILIATION

All observers will have different benchmarks to determine whether truth and reconciliation processes have delivered a level of restorative justice that can enable peace to be consolidated and sustained over a long period of time. What is lacking is a significant appraisal of truth and reconciliation commissions coming from the victims themselves. There has been a substantial and growing body of literature developed by academics, peace practitioners and journalists. It is important to determine whether victims who have gone through such processes view them as being effective in addressing their grievances.

The challenge of making sure not to promote a culture of impunity was addressed in some of the illustrative cases discussed in this chapter. Through an elaborate process of acknowledging an offence and demonstrating genuine remorse perpetrators are not 'let off the hook', so to speak; rather they are given a chance to redeem themselves and rejoin society. Given the levels of suffering that have been incurred as a result of the conflicts around the world it would be more appropriate for future peacebuilding strategies to draw from these ethical insights and processes. The use of overtly retributive and punitive mechanisms which are based on legal structures borrowed from the colonial era or imposed by an externally driven 'donor' agenda are likely to cause more harm than good in the medium to long term. In this regard, Peter Penfold, a former British High Commissoner to Sierra Leone, has been critical of the Special Court, which he views as primarily having been driven by a donor agenda. The Special Court in Sierra Leone was established to try war criminals, but there was always the possibility that a retributive approach would ultimately cause more harm than good and be unable to dispense fairly justice to all those who may have been involved in war crimes during the conflict in the country.

A major limitation of some reconciliation processes is that perpetrators are often not apologetic for their acts because they believe that they were doing their jobs. They were following orders and doing their duty for their political leadership and more often than not they believe that they fulfilled what was right. Given the context of such political motives and effectively doing what the government or political leaders wanted, some perpetrators refuse to apologise for the pain and suffering caused by former policies and actions. This effectively undermines any possibility for achieving reconciliation. Therefore, reconciliation processes, particularly truth and reconciliation commissions, can stem from perpetrators effectively refusing to engage with what happened and thus they deny victims the ability to receive genuine acknowledgement of what they went through. Perpetrators and beneficiaries who were bystanders to the atrocities that were committed often declare that they did not know what was going on. Perversely, some perpetrators even feel betrayed because they were only following orders to keep their political masters in power.

CONCLUSION

This chapter has argued that reconciliation is a component of peace-building.[34] Reconciliation seeks to achieve social, political and economic justice. Peace and justice are mutually inclusive conditions necessary for the promotion of a harmonious and ethical society. It is therefore not a case of attempting to either achieve peace or promote justice, as some have argued. Rather, the challenge is to find a way of ensuring that negative peace, in sense of the absence of war, is transformed into positive peace. Positive peace is attained when efforts have been successful in promoting healing, reconciliation and coexistence on the basis of human rights and social, economic and political justice.[35] Positive peace therefore requires socio-economic and political justice. There is therefore also an ethical dimension to promoting positive peace. This chapter introduced the peace with justice matrix in order to demonstrate that both conditions are complementary and cannot be separated.

The chapter then discussed the establishment of the ICC. It noted that the ICC seeks to make an effort to administer justice for the victims of human rights atrocities, in the form of war crimes and crimes against humanity at a macro level. The chapter argued that the ICC as an institution cannot promote the healing that is necessary to attain positive peace. It argued that it is necessary to adopt approaches to peacebuilding which place more of an emphasis on forgiveness and restorative justice rather than punitive justice. Restorative justice seeks to restore social harmony by encouraging the perpetrators of crimes to confess and show genuine remorse, which provides victims with the basis for granting forgiveness and embracing reconciliation.

This chapter therefore looked at some of the micro-level cultural traditions for peacebuilding in Africa which place an emphasis on restoring and healing broken relationships. It also explored the interface between reconciliation, peacebuilding and transitional justice by proposing the notion that the best way to approach this issue is to consider peace and justice as mutually inclusive and complementary. The matrix proposes a two-dimensional axis with peace on the horizontal and justice on the vertical. Negative peace represents the condition of the absence of war, and positive peace indicates a situation in which social and economic justice has merged with political peacemaking and reconciliation.

Ultimately, the question has to be addressed as to whether international war crimes tribunals and the ICC can work in isolation as instruments of peacebuilding and reconciliation in post-conflict situations. International criminal tribunals, which utilise punitive or retributive frameworks of justice at a macro and meso level, are limited when it comes to promoting reconciliation, which requires more restorative forms of justice.

Traditionally the pursuit of justice in international relations has been considered detrimental to achieving peace. But this issue is resolved if we consider the need to promote *positive* peace which implies the actualisation of restorative justice. The conflict and post-conflict societies of Africa are communities with highly traumatised populations. Among the key challenges for peacebuilding in this century will be the importance of promoting healing and reconciliation within traumatised societies. The reconciliation process does not begin and end within a fixed time frame; healing and reconciliation are in fact processes that take a lifetime. As illustrated by the *ubuntu* tradition of reconciling communities, as a consequence of some of the atrocities that have been committed and the experiences that victims have gone through, it will take a long time for people to overcome the physical, emotional and mental anguish generated by conflict. The social and economic project is by no means complete and indeed the situation can only be described as one in which a fragile reconciliation exists. The economic well-being of large sections of the population remains to be addressed if a more sustainable meso- and micro-level moral reconciliation process is to be consolidated.

NOTES

1. Barney Pityana, 'The Renewal of African Moral Values', in M. Makgoba (ed.), *African Renaissance: The New Struggle* (Johannesburg: Mafube Publishing), pp. 137–48.
2. Brandon Hamber and Grainne Kelly, 'Reconciliation: Time to Grasp the Nettle?', *Scope: Social Affairs Magazine*, February 2007, p. 14.
3. Ibid.
4. Ibid.
5. Hizkias Assefa, 'Reconciliation', in L. Reychler and T. Paffenholz (eds), *Peacebuilding: A Field Guide* (Boulder, CO: Lynne Rienner, 2001); see also Hizkias Assefa, 'Coexistence and Reconciliation in the Northern Region of Ghana', in Mohammed Abu-Nimer (ed.), *Reconciliation, Justice and Coexistence: Theory and Practice* (Lanham, MD: Lexington, 2001).
6. Hamber and Kelly, 'Reconciliation: Time to Grasp the Nettle?', p. 14.
7. John-Paul Lederach, *Building Peace: Sustainable Reconciliation in Divided Societies* (Stockholm: IDEA, 2003).
8. Ibid., p. 20.
9. Ibid., p. 20.
10. Ibid., p. 20.

11. Hamber and Kelly, 'Reconciliation: Time to Grasp the Nettle?', p. 14.
12. Stuart Kaufman, 'Escaping the Symbolic Politics Trap: Reconciliation Initiatives and Conflict Resolution in Ethnic Wars', *Journal of Peace Research*, vol. 43, no. 2, 2006, pp. 201–18.
13. Yacov Bar-Siman-Tov (ed.), *From Conflict Resolution to Reconciliation* (Oxford: Oxford University Press, 2004), pp. 11–38.
14. Brandon Hamber, 'Forgiveness and Reconciliation: Paradise Lost or Pragmatism?', *Peace and Conflict: Journal of Peace Psychology*, vol. 13, no. 1, p. 118.
15. N. Kritz (ed.), *Transitional Justice: How Emerging Democracies Reckon with Former Regimes* (Washington, DC: United States Institute of Peace Press, 1995) and A. J. McAdams, *Transitional Justice and the Rule of Law in Democracies* (Notre Dame: Notre Dame University Press, 1997).
16. D. Shurman and A. McCall Smith, *Justice and the Prosecution of Old Crimes: Balancing Legal, Psychological, and Moral Concerns* (Washington, DC: American Psychological Association, 2000).
17. C. Butegwa, 'The International Criminal Court: A Ray of Hope for the Women of Darfur?', *Pambazuka News*, no. 241, 2006.
18. United Nations Security Council, *Resolution 1593 (2005)* (New York: United Nations, 2005).
19. Ibid., p. 1.
20. Tim Murithi and Helen Scanlon, *African Perspectives on the UN Peacebuilding Commission* (Cape Town: Centre for Conflict Resolution, 2006), p. 22.
21. Sierra Leone Truth and Reconciliation Commission, *Report of the Commission*, October 2004.
22. J. Sebarenzi, 'Rwanda: The Fundamental Obstacles to Reconciliation', *GSC Quarterly*, no. 3, Winter 2002.
23. I. William Zartman, *Traditional Cures for Modern Conflicts: African Conflict Medicine* (Boulder, CO: Lynne Rienner, 2000).
24. Desmond Tutu, *No Future Without Forgiveness* (London: Rider, 1999).
25. See Rama Mani, *Beyond Retribution: Seeking Justice in the Shadows of War* (Cambridge: Polity Press, 2002); Charles Villa-Vicencio and Wilhelm Verwoerd (eds), *Looking Back, Reaching Forward: Reflections on the Truth and Reconciliation Commission of South Africa* (Cape Town: University of Cape Town, 2000) and Lyn Graybill, 'South Africa's Truth and Reconciliation Commission: Ethical and Theological Perspectives', *Ethics and International Affairs*, vol. 12, 1998, pp. 43–62.
26. Timothy Murithi and Dennis Pain (eds), *African Principles of Conflict Resolution and Reconciliation*, Conference Report (Addis Ababa: Shebelle Publishing Ltd, 1999).
27. See Ngugi wa Thiong'o, *Moving the Centre: The Struggle for Cultural Freedoms* (Nairobi: East African Publishers, 1993) and Mohamed Salih, *African Democracies and African Politics* (London: Pluto, 2001).
28. Tutu, *No Future Without Forgiveness*, p. 34.

29. Ibid., pp. 34–5.
30. Ibid., pp. 34–5.
31. Ibid., pp. 34–5.
32. Ibid., pp. 34–5.
33. N. Masina, 'Xhosa Practices of Ubuntu for South Africa', in W. Zartman (ed.), *Traditional Cures for Modern Conflicts: African Conflict Medicine* (London: Lynne Rienner, 2000).
34. Hamber and Kelly, 'Reconciliation: Time to Grasp the Nettle?', p. 14.
35. C. Lerche, 'Peacebuilding through Reconciliation', *The International Journal of Peace Studies*, vol. 5, available at http://www.gmu.edu/academic/ijps/vol5_2/lerche.htm

CHAPTER 7

TOWARDS AN AGENDA FOR ETHICAL PEACEBUILDING

INTRODUCTION

This chapter will argue that the persistence of violent conflict means that humanity is not effectively implementing and sustaining peacebuilding and non-violent approaches to resolving their disputes. The chapter will propose that more work needs to be done to promote a better under-standing of why non-violent approaches for building peace are much better in the long run than any apparent short-term gains made through violence. This will include promoting an international macro-level political dispensation in which ethical norms will play a greater role in defining the nature of the behaviour of states with regard to each other, and also the nature of the relationship between governments and their citizens. The idea that all world citizens have a moral duty to promote multi-level peacebuilding provides a basis for a global ethic of negotiation, mediation, forgiveness and reconciliation. This will require a concerted effort at the micro-level to advance the teaching, training and research of peacebuilding strategies and techniques to children, teenagers and adults alike. Only by adopting a sustained and committed agenda for ethical peacebuilding can humanity make the transition towards genuine peaceful change and revitalise the hopes and aspira-tions for a more harmonious future for humanity.

THE PERSISTENCE OF VIOLENT CONFLICT

Some of the most devastating contemporary conflicts have been defined by sub-national actors resorting to violence as a means by which to counter the predatory power of governments. This is evident in the cases of the Liberation Tigers of Tamil Eelam who are poised against the

160

Government of Sri Lanka; the SLA and JEM who are confronting the Government of Sudan in Darfur; and the still unresolved disputes in Kashmir involving India and Pakistan as well as the perennial disputes between Israel and the Palestinians in the occupied territories. In the era of the so-called 'war on terror', governments are now inclined to describe these insurgents within their territories as terrorists, thus using the increasingly dominant narrative and rhetoric of the war on terror to justify their strong-arm and repressive use of the means of coercion at their disposal to quell such uprisings. Yet in the eyes of these sub-national ethnic polities many of these governments are not legitimate expressions of their political will. Thus, solutions to such conflicts will involve the politico-moral development of the nation-state, perhaps even to the point where it legislates itself out of existence. However, given the dominant appeal to realpolitik this is not a likely outcome or scenario in many of the conflicts that plague the world today.

SUB-NATIONAL DISPUTES AS MORAL CONFLICTS

The marginalisation of ethnic polities by other dominant ethnic groups which have usurped the governing instruments means that they are unable to articulate their political will without recourse to violence. As discussed in Chapter 3, this creates a volatile situation in which the actions of the 'usurped' state in effect de-legitimate it in the eyes of the sub-national group. Rupeshinge has observed that 'the state itself has often been party to conflict or has been partisan or has escalated the conflict by imposing authoritarian stratagems'.[1] The state with its monopoly over the instruments of violence is in a strong position to reinforce its coercive regime and to undermine the ability of ethnic groups to participate equally in the formation of their political life. This serves as a strong force of mobilisation against the state. If such a situation emerges the ensuing conflict is effectively a dispute that is bound to undermine the stability of the institution of the state. Rupeshinge further notes that:

> contrary to theories which define the state, particularly in the Third World formation, as an arbitrator or a neutral actor, it is important to bear in mind that the state is neither an arbitrator nor neutral: it is itself a focal point of competition, an actor in the conflict.[2]

Locked, as the international system still is, in a discourse that privileges the primacy of the state, then the international community plays into the hands of the ethnic 'usurpers' of the state.[3]

Peacebuilding on the international stage requires a normative shift. It requires the creation of norms which will enable sub-national actors to be included in a morally legitimate political process as an alternative way forward for the system of states. Traditional conceptual frameworks view the objective of conflict resolution in terms of restoring the 'fictional' state to a pre-given image of its former self. This is illustrated by persistent efforts to restore the Somali state between 1991 and 2007. The collapse of states, discussed in Chapter 3, suggests that fictional, mainly post-colonial states, and their inability to foster and sustain political coexistence, may be part of the problem. To a large extent efforts to come to terms with sub-national conflicts in which states are participating belligerents, and hence promote sustainable peacebuilding, have traditionally framed the problem in terms of breakaway groups seeking to undermine the structure of the state. As we have seen, according to the moral-legal principles of the United Nations Charter states are often viewed as being concrete and immutable. Thus, conventional readings of these problems begin from the a priori assumption that the 'nation-state' is indivisible and therefore subsequent efforts to resolve the sub-national dispute tend to focus on how to 'put' the state back together again. However, if we begin the analysis of most of these sub-national/state conflicts with the assumption that the imposition of the state upon human collectivities – predominantly in Africa, Asia, Latin America and Eastern Europe – was an attempt to forge a viable institution for political governance then we are more likely to be able to acknowledge the limitations and pitfalls of this experiment. Only then will we be able to entertain new efforts at forging other forms of political association, and put in place ethical processes for building peace. From a moral standpoint the solutions are not pre-given and it may be that the majority of ethnic groups will embrace a statist framework as the best way forward for their particular context. Equally, other groups will prefer to attempt to constitute post-nationalist frameworks which are less centralised and more sensitive to the claims of sub-national groups.

Given the fact that moral communities, be they nation-states or ethnic groups, privilege their own 'normative order and world-view' above those of other polities, there is an important sense in which sub-national disputes can be viewed as moral conflicts. The term moral conflicts in this regard, to adopt the definition proposed by Barnett Pearce and Stephen Littlejohn, designates 'situations in which the social worlds or moral orders of the participants are incommensurate'.[4] That is to say that between sub-national groups and the state there are fundamental moral differences in their world-views; on legitimate governance, for instance. Each moral community considers its own position to be normatively right and that of the opposing moral community to be dangerous. Thus, enemy images contribute towards the creation of these moral conflicts. The refusal of one party to grant another the ethical recognition that it demands through its claims constitutes a fundamental moral disagreement which can escalate and lead to violence and destruction. When moral approval is withdrawn from the state and shifted onto an ethnic polity, in some cases, 'the different sub-groups of an ethnic category begin to perceive themselves as members of a political community of destiny and to fight for control of the state'.[5] In other cases, as Tamara Dragadze has observed,

> self-determination movements, whose aim is to acquire the power to govern without reference to the central power from which they want to secede, seek to defy the latter's counterclaims either by virtue of their separate identity or by stating that, even if some form of commonality were recognised, the central power has from now on lost that moral right to govern them.[6]

The intransigence by a moral community's opponent or oppressor precipitates the separatist forces which lead to a moral conflict. It becomes increasingly clear that we need to begin to understand human collectivities in terms of the way in which the 'internalisation' of identity, through their moral world-view, confronts us with a situation in which disputes are essentially of an ethical nature. Only then are we in a better position to determine and effectuate the interaction needed to establish the transformation, through interaction and exchange, of their exclusionary moral order.

Moral conflicts in effect demand a different type of transformative ethical dialogue. By extension, sub-national groups in conflict with nation-states also demand a different type of transformative ethical dialogue. Pearce and Littlejohn note that 'moral conflicts are difficult to manage and, if mishandled, produce particularly costly and painful patterns of social relations'.[7] Essentially such conflicts require mechanisms which are ultimately geared towards fostering moral inclusion. For Opotow, moral inclusion 'refers to relationships in which the parties are approximately equal, the potential for reciprocity exists, and both parties are entitled to fair processes and some share of community resources'.[8] In terms of sub-national groups and the Westphalian system it is clear that they do not yet have moral-legal equality with nation-states. In a paradoxical sense, if they did this would undermine the Westphalian system. Nevertheless, when it comes to ensuring sustainable peace this book is making the case that sub-national groups do need to be granted a degree of moral equality. Otherwise, sub-national groups will continue to be denied the opportunity to articulate their views on the 'justness' of the processes and structural changes that are necessary to ensure sustainable peacebuilding. Sub-national groups do not receive 'fair' access to the resources and institutions of the international system. Thus, for peacebuilding to be effective in addressing sub-national conflicts, a certain amount of reflection must be made on the politico-legal and institutional frameworks for peacemaking and reconciliation that exist in the international system.

Lewis Coser observed that 'all political structures tend to provide channels for expression of claims and grievances of the underlying population'.[9] He further notes that:

> yet it can be taken as axiomatic that these channels, having been designed to register power balances of the past, tend to be insufficient when it comes to accommodating claims of new groupings not previously considered as political actors worthy of having their voices heard and their contributions counted.[10]

Sub-national groups are in effect the 'new groupings' that were previously not 'considered as political actors worthy of having their voices heard' and as such they have brought to light the insufficiency of the international system's 'political structures' when it comes to providing them with the appropriate 'channels for expression' and articulating their claims. Amy Gutman suggests that 'just procedural mechanisms for peacefully resolving disagreements are a condition of basic human well-being'.[11] Sub-national conflicts are on one level moral conflicts and as such they can only ultimately be effectively addressed by opening up forums of dialogue that were previously closed. To ensure effective multi-level peacebuilding it is therefore necessary to ensure that human polities have access to processes and institutions which will enable them to admit the moral validity claims onto the political agenda.

VIOLENCE AS COMMUNICATION: TOWARDS A SUB-NATIONAL CONFLICTOLOGY

As alluded to previously, sub-national conflicts can be more appropriately viewed as moral conflicts. They represent a contestation between communal and state interest as well as competition over claims to moral order, truth and reality. This disputation that emerges between different world-views. Conceptualising sub-national conflicts as moral conflicts alludes to the tension that has emerged between the philosophical beliefs from which groups derive and affirm their freedoms to which they believe they have a legitimate and moral claim. Thus, sub-national conflict is an attempt by disputants to make their voice heard, albeit a very destructive one. Hence violence can be viewed in these situations as a form of communication.

In a world of increasing complexity a divergence of interests will always define the human condition. Politics is precisely about how these diverging interests are negotiated by human communities. Hence, conflict, in a generic sense, is at the heart of politics. The process of communication and negotiation can proceed along harmful and destructive lines or it can be channelled through harmless and more constructive avenues. In the former case, war is an extreme form of harmful communication in which human collectivities seek to dominate or destroy other human polities. When a state of war prevails then all the political processes through which these polities can communicate, resolve or address their concerns in a less harmful way has self-evidently collapsed. Parties no longer appeal to less harmful forms of communication to express their will; rather they resort to harmful ways to ensure that their interests prevail.

At the heart of the 'conflictology' of (or the study of sub-national conflicts) sub-national disputes is the need to understand the dynamics of the transition from harmful to harmless ways of addressing a divergence of interests. It may be more appropriate to consider conflicts as not being resolved, but converted into different forms of expression. What is essential is to bring about the conversion of these conflicts from a manifestly destructive state to a manifestly non-destructive state. This is to a significant, but not exclusive, extent dependent upon the medium, mechanisms and institutions through which human polities can express their will and be heard. Violence is usually justified by reason and the only way to reduce the violence is for people to become aware and be allowed to express the reasons that they harbour for their acts. If institutions prevent a party from having its concerns articulated then the possibility of the conflict being converted to one in which harmful expression is minimised recedes. In effect the institution that is supposedly responsible for enabling the will of human polities to be heard is in effect perpetuating a form of harm and moral exclusion, as discussed in Chapter 5.

In the case of sub-national conflict, if there is to be a concerted effort to minimise the manifestation of physical violence or war, then all parties concerned must be able to give assent to the institutions through which their claims will be heard. Thus, as discussed in Chapter 5, a Habermasian moral logic as articulated in the formulation of a principle of discourse ethics necessarily needs to prevail in the process of negotiation to resolve disputes. It is important to note, however, that the mere existence of such moral institutions does not guarantee that the conflicts will be solved; rather what it does guarantee is that the institutions themselves will not be the factor preventing the conflict from being resolved (by perpetuating a logic of structural marginalisation or even domination). Peacebuilding will always ultimately depend on the willingness of the parties to enter into a spirit of reconciliation. Disputants cannot be forced to free themselves from acts of violence which continue to constrain them in a mutually reinforcing cycle of domination.

The transition towards the implementation of ethical institutions of conflict resolution and peacebuilding which are just will be a lengthy one given the nature of the current geopolitical imperatives on the so-called war on terror. However, if we acknowledge that sub-national disputes are analogous to moral conflicts this evokes the need to understand what moral conflict resolution entails. As Kevin Gibson proposes, 'mediators need philosophers'.[12] Establishing a more explicit synthesis between moral philosophy and peacebuilding will encourage peacemakers, policy-makers and researchers to examine their own ethical assumptions.

ESTABLISHING INTERNATIONAL INSTITUTIONS TO PROMOTE ETHICAL PEACEBUILDING

It is necessary to promote an international political dispensation in which ethical norms will play a greater role in defining the nature of the behaviour of states with regard to each other, and also the nature of the relationship between governments and their citizens. As Chapter 3 demonstrated, there is a residual appeal to many of the doctrines which defined the Cold War world. At the top of this list is an appeal reference to nation-states as the dominant form of political community. International and regional organisations seem to be largely reacting to the sporadic outbreak of sub-national conflicts rather than actively pursuing a coherent and well-thought-out policy to address them. Conflict has led to the collapse of states, such as Somalia, and the international decision-makers seem to be appealing for the restoration of the state in the image of its former self, rather than exploring new forms of political community which will enable sustainable peace to prevail. This betrays an adherence to a statist world-view and overlooks the possibility that even if the original state were restored it may not have the support of its populace to remain a viable going concern in the longrun.

The UN and regional organisations do not provide permanent and official forums where all warring parties, including the various sub-national factions, can freely articulate their claims and obtain a just and ethical resolution to their grievances. The use of ad hoc intergovernmental initiatives, such as special representatives and peace envoys, is increasingly prominent. For example, currently the UN has deployed former Swedish Foreign Minister Jan Eliasson to try and assist in resolving the conflict in the Darfur region of Sudan, which has led to the death of close to 300,000 people and the displacement of two million people in neighbouring Chad and the Central African Republic (CAR). Similarly, the African Union has its own envoy in the form of the former Secretary-General of the Organization of African Unity, Salim Ahmed Salim, as the Special Envoy of the African Union to the Inter-Sudanese talks on the conflict in Darfur. But there is no permanent international forum where the sub-national factions, which include the Sudan Liberation Army (SLA) and the Justice and Equality Movement (JEM), can engage the Government of Sudan in a legitimate and ethical procedural process. Therefore, what remains absent despite all these important efforts taking place is an effective and satisfactory official mechanism which can morally acknowledge and respond to the transformed nature of conflicts. Rasmussen notes that 'conflict is handled by disparate measures, rather than by a fully articulated system. Since there is no system to call them to order, such measures flourish'.[13] Specifically with regard to sub-national conflict William Zartman observes that 'not only is the international response weak, its very weakness causes an increasingly stronger challenge in a vicious circle of action and inaction'.[14] This weak international response has been attributed to the fact that the leadership in the most powerful countries, which dominate the international system, has decreased the amount of political energy that it devotes to containing, managing and settling ethnic disputes in all corners of the world, which tended to be part of the strategic imperative of the Cold War. This is particularly the case with conflicts which fall outside the remit of their immediate economic and political interests, such as Rwanda, Tajikistan and Western Sahara. An ethical imperative in international and sub-national conflict resolution is yet to be formally articulated and constituted because of the legacy of the anterior realist order which was reluctant to explicitly adopt moral positions on political issues. Today, the dominant narrative of the 'war on terror' has further suppressed any attempt to emphasise such an ethical imperative in international and sub-national conflict resolution. Sub-national groups that have legitimate grievances can not be easily stigmatised as 'terrorist' groups with all the political and economic consequences that such an appellation brings.

CAN THE UN PEACEBUILDING COMMISSION PROMOTE ETHICAL PEACEBUILDING?

Clearly, the international system needs a mechanism that will enable the increasing sub-national conflicts to be addressed in an ethical way. Regrettably, the UN, for the sixty years of its existence, has had more conflict resolution failures than successes – particularly during the Cold War – and has not lived up to its ambitious mandate of maintaining international peace and security. As discussed in Chapter 4, the first post-Cold War effort to reform the UN in order to address effectively the issue of building peace was undertaken by the former UN Secretary-General Boutros Boutros-Ghali. In his landmark report *An Agenda for Peace*, published in 1992, Boutros-Ghali set out an international strategy for conflict prevention, peacemaking, peacekeeping and post-conflict reconstruction peacebuilding.[15] Macro-level peacebuilding has therefore been part of the lexicon of building war-affected communities for more than a decade. The United Nations has maintained an engagement with conflict situations around the world and is currently implicated in peacebuilding efforts in countries such as Colombia, Kosovo, Tajikistan, South Sudan and the Central African Republic.

As the world continued to undergo geopolitical change the relevance of the UN to the transformed global context became an issue. Significant international political divisions were created as a result of the illegal 2003 US-led invasion of Iraq. Launched without UN authorisation, the Iraq invasion created deep structural fault lines within the Security Council, which paralysed the Council and threatened to tear it apart. Sensing a turning point in the relations within the UN, Secretary-General Kofi Annan read a speech to the General Assembly in which he noted that 'the events of 2003 exposed deep divisions among members of the UN on fundamental questions of policy and principle'.[16] Annan further noted that 'we have come to a fork in the road. This may be a moment no less decisive than 1945 itself, when the United Nations was founded'.[17] To try and bring a semblance of order to the disunited nations Annan established a High-Level Panel on Threats, Challenges and Change on 3 November 2003. The idea behind the creation of the High-Level Panel was to ensure that the UN remains capable of fulfilling its primary purpose as enshrined in Article 1 of its Charter, which is 'to maintain international peace and security, and to that end: to take effective collective measures for the prevention and removal of threats to the peace, and for the suppression of acts of aggression or other breaches of the peace'.[18] Several member states of the UN viewed the US invasion of Iraq, together with its so-called 'coalition of the coerced', as an 'act of aggression' and a 'breach of the peace'.[19] They maintained the belief that it was therefore in direct contravention to the Charter, purpose and principles of the UN. If a member state could act in such a way what did this mean in practice about the future relevance of the UN? Annan was justified in being concerned about the viability of the UN and its ability to uphold its stated principles and to try to salvage the disunity among its nations. He was also justified in his concern that the UN was not living up to its commitment to save succeeding generations from the scourge of war, which led to some of the recommendations on how to improve peacebuilding.

At the end of 2004, the High-Level Panel submitted a report to the Secretary-General entitled *A More Secure World: Our Shared Responsibility*.[20] The report focused on an assessment of present and future security threats so that collective strategies could be developed to address them. The High-Level Panel examined six key areas including: civil wars and large-scale violence and genocide; interstate conflict threats and the use of force; socio-economic issues, including poverty and HIV/AIDS, environmental degradation; weapons of mass destruction; terrorism and transnational organised crime. On the specific issue of the resolution of civil wars and inter-state conflict the Panel made recommendations with reference to the challenges of peacebuilding.

One of the recommendations that the High-Level Panel came up with was the creation of a Peacebuilding Commission, a Peacebuilding Support Office and a Peacebuilding Fund. The Panel felt that the current UN peacebuilding efforts were not sufficiently coherent. There was therefore a clear and compelling need to pull together all the different parts of the United Nations that work on post-conflict reconstruction. The Panel report noted that 'deploying peace enforcement and peacekeeping forces may be essential in terminating conflicts, but they are not sufficient for long-term recovery'. The report further argued that 'serious attention is needed to focus on the longer-term process of peacebuilding in all its multiple dimensions' and went on to state that it was vital to invest adequately in peacebuilding and development to ensure that a country does not relapse into conflict.[21]

The Secretary-General took on board this suggestion and in March 2005 issued his report *In Larger Freedom: Towards Development, Security and Human Rights for All.*[22] This report recommended that the UN member states should agree to establish a Peacebuilding Commission to fill the institutional gap that exists with regard to assisting countries to make the transition from war to lasting peace. Annan noted that the UN's record in implementing and monitoring peace agreements has been tainted by some devastating failures, for example in Angola in 1993, Rwanda in 1994 and challenges in Bosnia in 1995 and East Timor in 1999. Approximately half of all countries that emerge from war lapse back into violence within five years. Therefore an integral part of addressing the 'scourge of war' has to be to establish an institutional framework to ensure that peace agreements are implemented and post-conflict peacebuilding is consolidated.

It was after Annan's report that debates about the creation of the UN Peacebuilding Commission increased. This culminated in September 2005 with the UN World Summit and the 60th session of the General Assembly at which the recommendations of the report were reviewed. The General Assembly adopted an Outcome Document[23] at the close of the meeting which the Secretary-General described as 'a once-in-a-generation opportunity'[24] to forge a global consensus on development, security, human rights and United Nations renewal. The Outcome Document, however, was a compromise between the competing interests of member states. It was a watered-down document which dodged key issues like nuclear disarmament and Security Council reform. On UN Security Council reform in particular, the meeting pledged to issue yet *another* report in December 2005.

THE FUNCTIONS OF THE UN PEACEBUILDING COMMISSION

The Outcome Document in paragraph 97 recognised 'the need for a coordinated, coherent and integrated approach to post-conflict peacebuilding and reconciliation'. The Document also identified the importance of 'achieving sustainable peace and recognising the need for a dedicated institutional mechanism to address the special need of countries emerging from conflict towards recovery'. On this basis the General Assembly decided 'to establish a Peacebuilding Commission as an intergovernmental advisory body'.[25] The established Peacebuilding Commission, backed by a Peace Support Office and 'a multi-year standing Peacebuilding Fund', marks a new level of strategic commitment to enhance and sustain peace after conflict.

As noted previously, the Peacebuilding Commission 'brings together all relevant actors to advise on and propose integrated strategies for post-conflict Peacebuilding and recovery'.[26] The core work of the Peacebuilding Commission is its country-specific activities. It strives to ensure that the international community supports national authorities, but the focus is on country-based realities. The Peacebuilding Commission has committed itself to ensuring that national priorities are supported by the necessary mobilisation of resources. Predictable and reliable funding will need to be identified for the short-term early recovery activities as well as financial investment for development over the medium- to longer-term period of recovery. The Peacebuilding Fund is tasked with ensuring the provision of these resources.

The Peacebuilding Commission has been endowed with a monitoring and review function. It meets at regular intervals to review progress towards medium-term recovery goals, particularly with regard to developing public institutions and laying the foundations for economic recovery. Its role will be to alert the international community if progress is not being made so as to avoid a relapse into violent conflict. In this way the Peacebuilding Commission, through effective post-conflict peacebuilding and reconstruction, also, in theory, has a preventive role in terms of curtailing the recuurence of violence.[27] During the debates leading up to the creation of the Peacebuilding Commission various countries did not want to provide the Commission with a conflict prevention or preventive diplomacy role.[28] This was due to fears of an infringement on their sovereignty. The Peacebuilding Commission will therefore focus more on post-conflict peacebuilding than conflict prevention.

More concretely, the Peacebuilding Commission has an Organisational Committee for every country which includes representatives from that country; countries in the region engaged in the post-conflict process; and other countries involved in relief efforts and/or political dialogue, as well as relevant regional and sub-regional organisations; the major financial, troop and civilian police contributors involved in the recovery effort; the senior United Nations representative in the field and other relevant United Nations representatives; and regional and international financial institutions, as may be relevant.[29]

In order to support this work, the Peacebuilding Commission is assisted by a Peacebuilding Support Office staffed by qualified experts in the field of peacebuilding. The Peacebuilding Support Office prepares the substantive inputs for meetings of the Peacebuilding Commission through analysis and information gathering. The office also contributes to the planning process for peacebuilding operations by working with the relevant lead departments in the UN, international community and civil society. The office conducts an analysis of best practices and develops policy guidance as appropriate.

The establishment of the Peacebuilding Commission is a recognition of the necessity to address global security challenges through global responses. In the same Outcome Document in 2005 the UN institutionalised the norm of the 'responsibility to protect' which now needs to become mainstreamed in international politics.[30] However, military interventions should be consistent with the purpose and principles of the UN Charter and in particular they should comply with the provisions of Article 51, which authorises the use of force only in cases of legitimate self-defence. Challenges such as the humanitarian catastrophe in the Darfur region of the Sudan have proved to be particularly resistant to UN action, due to the interests of powerful countries behind the scenes, notably China's oil interests. Local solutions to peacebuilding are preferable because actors would have a better understanding of the region they are working in. In the absence of robust local peace operations there is still a need to strengthen the role of the UN in keeping global peace and promoting economic development and democratic consolidation. The UN also has to play a role in consolidating post-conflict reconstruction through the effective monitoring and policing of the illicit trade of natural resources and small arms as well as curtailing the activities of mercenaries in war-affected regions. It also has to continue to play an important role in assisting with refugees and internally displaced persons.

The Peacebuilding Commission will have utility for a significant number of countries around the world. The US will be able to make use of it for rebuilding Iraq and Afghanistan, Europe for rebuilding the still troubled Balkans, France for its post-conflict interventions in Côte d'Ivoire and Haiti, Russia when it so chooses for Chechnya and so on. Post-conflict reconstruction requires the building of infrastructure which is vital for development. All of these issues will be assisted by an effective Peacebuilding Commission.

The Organizational Committee of Peacebuilding Commission comprises thirty-one members and its decision-making process will be based on consensus. The UN Security Council is represented by seven members, including the five permanent members, while the UN Economic and Social Council (ECOSOC) is represented by seven members. Membership also includes the main financial and peacekeeping contributors to the UN.[31]

The successful creation and operationalisation of the Peacebuilding Commission has significant implications. This is an unprecedented framework which if it succeeds in its objectives can reduce and ultimately stop the loss of human life due to the recurrence of conflict. The world is plagued with a number of post-conflict situations which urgently need to be addressed. If the Peacebuilding Commission is politicised then the opportunity for it to function in the short to medium term will be severely hampered. If given the necessary backing, that is, appropriately funded, a pragmatic Peacebuilding Commission can go a long way 'to improve our success rate in building peace in war-torn countries'.[32] The challenge as with all other institutional building will be to convert the rhetoric into reality. The partnership between the Peacebuilding Commission and other intergovernmental organisations needs to be established.

The Peacebuilding Commission was inaugurated in June 2006; after two years in existence, it still has to demonstrate whether it can effectuate a paradigm shift in terms of building peace. The year was dedicated to establishing the Commission's modalities for operation. Issues such as whether civil society groups could be included in the activities of the Commission were subjected to lengthy debates. The Commission considered the cases of Burundi and Sierra Leone during its first session. It travelled to both countries to elicit the views of citizens and government officials. The Peacebuilding Fund was operationalised to assist these countries in their efforts to consolidate peace. However, other than issuing statements and pronouncements on the importance of continuing with their peacebuilding agendas, the Commission has not yet succeeded in effectuating a paradigm shift in the necessities and complexities of building peace. Yet it is too early to pass definitive judgement on the Peacebuilding Commission since it has only been functional for two years. It remains a positive innovation mainly because it establishes and projects moral authority on the issue of peacebuilding across the world. However, this moral authority will be squandered if the Commission continues to seem distant and displaced from the concrete challenges of building peace on the ground.

AN ETHICAL AGENDA FOR PEACEBUILDING AND POST-NATIONAL DEMOCRATIC GOVERNANCE

Peacebuilding cannot be consolidated solely by effective negotiation, mediation, forgiveness and reconciliation. Post-conflict solutions need to reassure sub-national groups that their cultural and socio-economic survival will be secured in the post-conflict settlement. This will involve devising ethical constitutional frameworks which enable all communal groups to maintain their culture while respecting the different traditions of other communities, which will require inclusive forums for negotiation based on a respect for the moral principle of consent, as discussed in Chapter 5. All parties must agree on a set of procedural norms as to how these negotiations are to proceed. Institutions for post-conflict democratic governance must ensure the equal participation of all sections of the society. This will involve reworking the notion of national sovereignty so that it is no longer defined in terms of geographical boundaries but by the will of the people who are affected by this sovereign jurisdiction. In most instances some degree of sovereignty will have to be conceded to the sub-national polities. Ultimately, post-national forms of governance will have to be established by bringing about the discursive transformation of the prevailing nationalist construct. As Gerard Delanty observes, 'rather than presupposing cultural consensus, post-national identity is based on the acceptance of dissent and cultural difference'.[33] It is important to note that the formation of a post-national democratic order hinges upon the ability of those affected to identify with the democratic values which underpin it. In order to consolidate peace it is important to recognise that there are divided political allegiances in war-affected countries. To counteract the powerful instinct which underpins communal solidarity and drives one group to impose its vision of nationhood on the other, a post-national identity has to be constructed; this would encourage everyone to open their exclusionary nationalist identity discourses to reflection and self-criticism. Post-nationalist identity becomes embodied and protected by a constitutional framework. Loyalty begins to be thought of in terms of loyalty to the all-inclusive structures of democracy. In the case of Northern Ireland, the previously competing claims of the Catholics and Protestants in the Province seem to have been reconciled in the re-activation of the Northern Ireland Assembly in 2007. Following a long and arduous peace process that was given new impetus by the signing of the Good Friday Agreement on 10 April 1998, mediated by the former US Senator George Mitchell, today the Province stands on the precipice of consolidating peace. The Good Friday Agreement established the parameters through which the people of Northern Ireland would decide the future of the region based on the principle of consent and the inclusive and equal participation of all parties and communities. The Northern Ireland Assembly is elected through an electoral system of proportional representation. A controlling Executive Committee has been constituted by representatives from parties that achieved a certain percentage of the voting population. In response to the aspirations of the nationalists, a Northern and Southern Ireland body has been established. Similarly, to assuage the concerns of unionists a British–Irish Council has been established.

In effect, the new constitutional arrangement in Northern Ireland represents the reworking of the political identity of the British and Irish nation-states. A degree of sovereignty has been devolved to the sub-national entity in the form of the Northern Ireland Assembly. Innovatively, sovereignty over the Province is now effectively shared between Britain and Ireland. If this peacebuilding process prevails, it will represent the emergence and consolidation of the belief among the parties affected that they can depend on the reconstituted entity of Northern Ireland to safeguard and respect the plurality of their socio-cultural traditions.[34] This process was based on the principles of consent and moral inclusion. Habermas observes that 'a commitment to the principle of the constitutional state and democracy . . . can only become a reality in different states (which are on the way towards becoming post-national societies), when these principles strike root in the various political cultures in different ways'.[35] For Habermas, constitutional patriotism is based on an adherence to democratic and constitutional norms and not with the traditional territorial and formalistic represen-tation of a nation-state. Moreover, these norms can only be validated discursively by all those who will be affected by them. In this sense, the recent developments in Northern Ireland are, and will remain, infor-mative to the extent that they provide a useful example of the practical implementation of conflict resolution and the initiation of peacebuilding in the context of a sub-national conflict.

REGIONAL ORGANISATIONS AND THE CONSOLIDATION OF PEACEBUILDING AND GOVERNANCE

Building peace and transcending sub-national conflicts cannot be left entirely to the volition of nation-states. The conditions at the macro level have to be conducive to promoting peacebuilding in the meso and micro levels. By appealing to international law, states still curtail the legal recognition of national minorities as coherent political units. In many situations there is the suspicion that granting autonomy, however defined, may only be a staging post in a sub-national drive towards secession. In Europe, the Organization for Security and Cooperation in Europe (OSCE) and the Council of Europe have made significant inroads into elaborating a European standard of sub-national minority rights. Achieving an appropriate balance between sovereign state rights and national minority rights remains the main challenge confronting these bodies. As Jennifer Jackson Preece observes,

> the compromise that was eventually adopted recognised individual rather than collective rights, [this] made the content of minority provisions largely reflect the post-1945 human rights status quo and explicitly acknowledged that such provi-sions were constrained by the traditional statist tenets of international relations such as state sovereignty, territorial integrity, non-intervention.[36]

However, states' rights have not prevented the 'recognition of two new norms regulating state conduct towards minorities and the emergence of recommendations in favour of minority autonomy and self-govern-ment'.[37] The progressive aspects of the recommended norms regulating state conduct towards sub-national groups are an encouraging sign that there is potential for substantial developments as far as the international and regional guarantee of minority or sub-national government is concerned. The European regional organisations have developed their positions on this issue substantially more than their Asian, African and American counterparts. The Association of South-East Asian Nations (ASEAN) has endeavoured to play a key role as a regional security organisation by remaining reluctant to interfere with domestic conflicts. According to Muthiah Alagappa, 'the de facto role of the Association in intrastate conflicts is limited to preventing external interference, and providing diplomatic support to members in international fora'.[38] In addition, 'ASEAN has refrained from intervention or intermediation in domestic conflicts even when there was a distinct possibility that the conflict would deteriorate into civil war with negative consequences for regional stability and the survival of the Association'.[39] Likewise, the African Union still maintains a sacrosanct view of sovereignty, thus limiting its functionality as a guarantor of sub-national self-determination. However, the AU Constitutive Act, signed in Lomé, Togo, in July 2000, has adopted a more interventionist stance when sub-national groups are under threat from member states of the continental body, particularly when there is the potential for war crimes, crimes against humanity and genocide. The Organization of American States (OAS) passed a Resolution in 1991 requiring it to react to violations of the democratic process in its member countries. With reference to this Organization, Tom Farer notes that 'although external action is not often decisive, the credible threat of externally imposed economic or military sanctions can give an incipient democracy breathing space or can facilitate its restoration after a coup'.[40] To what extent this guarantee of democracy extends to promoting and sustaining sub-national autonomy in the Americas still remains to be seen.

There is a strong likelihood that violent campaigns for secession within various other states may arise.[41] The international community can offset such a trend by creating norms which enable sub-national groups to feel secure in their current political systems and guarantee their sub-national self-government. The seeds for such an institutional evolution are already embedded in the UN Declaration on the Rights of Persons Belonging to National or Ethnic, Religious, and Linguistic Minorities, which was proclaimed by the General Assembly in 1992. This Declaration laid out provisions advocating the rights of minorities

to participate in relevant national and regional decisions, to establish and maintain associations, and to have contact both within and across international frontiers. Moreover, the 1992 formulation reinforced a certain collective element by again acknowledging that these rights could be exercised individually as well as in community with other members of the group.[42]

MORAL CITIZENS BUILDING PEACE: EDUCATING FOR ETHICAL PEACEBUILDING

The echo effect of ineffective peacebuilding in all regions of the planet suggests that the idea that all world citizens have a moral duty to promote peacebuilding provides a basis for a global ethic of negotiation, mediation, forgiveness and reconciliation. This will require a concerted effort to advance the teaching, training and research of peacebuilding strategies and techniques to children, teenagers and adults alike.[43] Fast, Neufeldt and Schirch observe that 'a widely researched and accepted ethical framework in conflict intervention to help achieve best practice does not currently exist'.[44] Therefore, it is necessary to advance a research and policy development agenda with specific reference to ethical peacebuilding. This requires a concerted effort to ensure that curricula are informed by the tenets and principles of peacebuilding.

CONCLUSION

Throughout human history, and in the world today, conflict is predicated on systematically distorted communication, manipulation, deception and unequal access to information. Efforts to resolve disputes need to focus on establishing equality in the procedural institutions for airing grievances, if the intention is to allow the claims of disputants to be heard. It remains to be seen whether the newly established UN Peacebuilding Commission will be able to fulfil this function. Meso-level peacebuilding can only be consolidated by forging a post-national constitutional framework of democratic governance. The recent developments in sub-national governance in Northern Ireland herald an innovative way of bringing about the practical implementation of the post-national constitutional state. International and regional organisations have a responsibility for creating and enforcing norms to establish and protect sub-national groups and ensure their cultural, political and economic autonomy. Thus, the ethical nation-state must engender a renewed sense of legitimacy, stability and responsibility driven by the moral principle of inclusivity and respect for the need by sub-national groups to govern themselves. Democratic peace can only be legitimately sustained when there is effective moral communication between the governing and the governed. Ultimately, peacebuilding should be viewed as a moral initiative based on discernible moral principles. This book offers a suggestion of what these principles should aspire to, and in so doing it seeks to open up for debate a realm of research and analysis which has hitherto been consigned to the margins of the field of international relations. Future research has an obligation to more effectively assess and articulate the limitations and legacies which have to be overcome and the goals that have to be achieved in terms of building peace. Only by adopting a sustained and committed agenda for ethical peacebuilding can humanity make the transition towards genuine peaceful change and revitalise the hopes and aspirations for a more harmonious future for humanity.

NOTES

1. Kumar Rupeshinge, 'Internal Conflicts and Their Resolution: The Case of Uganda', in Kumar Rupeshinge (ed.), *Conflict Resolution in Uganda* (Oslo: International Peace Research Institute, 1989), p. 4 (pp. 1–23).
2. Ibid., p. 3.
3. Stephen Stedman, 'Conflict and Conflict Resolution in Africa', in Francis Deng and I. William Zartman (eds), *Conflict Resolution in Africa* (Washington, DC: The Brookings Institution, 1991), p. 376.
4. Barnett Pearce and Stephen Littlejohn, *Moral Conflict: When Social Worlds Collide* (London: Sage, 1997), p. x.
5. Andreas Wimmer, 'Explaining Xenophobia and Racism: A Critical Review of Current Research Approaches', *Ethnic and Racial Studies*, vol. 20, no. 1, January 1997, p. 32 (17–41).
6. Tamara Dragadze, 'Self-determination and the Politics of Exclusion', *Ethnic and Racial Studies*, vol. 19, no. 2, April 1996, p. 347 (340–51).
7. Pearce and Littlejohn, *Moral Conflict: When Social Worlds Collide*, p. 6.
8. Susan Opotow, 'Moral Exclusion and Injustice: An Introduction', *Journal of Social Issues*, vol. 46, no. 1, 1990, p. 2.
9. Lewis Coser, *Continuities in the Study of Social Conflict* (New York: Free Press, 1967), p. 96.
10. Ibid.
11. Amy Gutman, 'The Challenge of Multiculturalism in Political Ethics', *Philosophy & Public Affairs*, Vol. 22, No.3, 1993, p. 178 (171–206).
12. Kevin Gibson, 'The Ethical Basis of Mediation: Why Mediators Need Philosophers', *Mediation Quarterly*, vol. 7, no. 1, Fall 1989, pp. 41–50.
13. Lewis Rasmussen, 'Peacemaking in the Twenty-first Century: New Rules, New Roles, New Actors', in William Zartman and Lewis Rasmussen (eds), *Peacemaking in International Conflict: Methods and Techniques* (Washington, DC: United States Institute for Peace, 1997), p. 38 (23–50).
14. William Zartman, 'Introduction: Toward the Resolution of International Conflict', in Zartman and Rasmussen (eds), *Peacemaking in International Conflict*, p. 6.
15. Boutros Boutros-Ghali, *An Agenda for Peace : Preventive Diplomacy, Peacemaking and Peacekeeping* (New York: United Nations, 1992).
16. Kofi Annan, Speech to the UN General Assembly, 23 September 2003.

17. Ibid.
18. United Nations, *Charter of the United Nations*, 24 October 1945, Chapter I, Article 1.
19. Ibid.
20. High-Level Panel on Threats, Challenges and Change, *A More Secure World: Our Shared Responsibility* (New York: United Nations, 2004).
21. Ibid. See also a discussion on the potential of countries relapsing into conflict in Anthony Pereira, 'The Neglected Tragedy: The Return to War in Angola, 1992–3', *Journal of Modern African Studies*, vol. 32, no. 1, 1994, pp. 1–25.
22. Kofi Annan, *In Larger Freedom : Towards Development, Security and Human Rights for All*, UN document A/59/2005, 21 March 2005.
23. United Nations General Assembly, *Outcome Document*, 14 September 2005.
24. Centre for Conflict Resolution, *A More Secure Continent: African Perspectives on the High-Level Panel Report* (Cape Town: Centre for Conflict Resolution, April 2005).
25. UN, *Outcome Document*, paragraph 97.
26. Ibid.
27. Catherine Guicherd, 'Picking up the Pieces: What to Expect from the Peacebuilding Commission', *Friedrich Ebert Stiftung: Briefing Papers*, Report of conference organised by the Friedrich Ebert Foundation (FES) in cooperation with the German Federal Ministry of Economic Cooperation and Development (BMZ), 6 December 2005, p. 3.
28. African Union, *The Common African Position on the Proposed Reform of the United Nations: The Ezulwini Consensus*, Seventh Extraordinary Session of the Executive Council, Ext/EC.CL/2 (VII), Addis Ababa: African Union, 7–8 March 2005.
29. UN, *Outcome Document*, paragraph 100.
30. International Commission on Intervention and State Sovereignty, *The Responsibility to Protect* (Ottawa: International Development Research Centre, 2001); Francis Deng et al., *Sovereignty as Responsibility: Conflict Management in Africa* (Washington, DC: The Brookings Institution, 1996); and Thomas Weiss and Don Hubert, *The Responsibility to Protect: Research, Bibliography and Background* (Ottawa: International Development Research Centre, 2001).
31. Jurgen Stetten and Jochen Steinhilber, 'UN Peacebuilding Commission', *Friedrich Ebert Stiftung: Dialogue on Globalisation* (New York: FES, 11 January 2006), p. 2.
32. Kofi Annan, UN Secretary-General Address to the World Summit, 14 September 2005.
33. Gerard Delanty, 'Habermas and Post-National Identity: Theoretical Perspectives on the Conflict in Northern Ireland', *Irish Political Studies*, vol. 11, 1996, p. 21 (20–32).
34. David Bloomfield, *Peacemaking Strategies in Northern Ireland: Building Complementarity in Conflict Management Theory* (London: Macmillan, 1997).

35. Jurgen Habermas, 'The Limits of Neo-Historicism', in Peter Dews (ed.), *Autonomy and Solidarity: Interviews with Jurgen Habermas* (London: Verso, 1992), p. 241.

36. Jennifer Jackson Preece, 'National Minorities Rights vs. State Sovereignty in Europe: Changing Norms in International Relations?', *Nations and Nationalism*, vol. 3, no. 3, 1997, p. 354 (354–64).

37. Ibid.

38. Muthiah Alagappa, 'Regionalism and the Quest for Security: ASEAN and the Cambodian Conflict', *Journal of International Affairs*, vol. 46, no. 2, Winter 1993, p. 448 (439–67).

39. Ibid.

40. Tom Farer (ed.), *Beyond Sovereignty: Collectively Defending Democracy in the Americas* (Baltimore: Johns Hopkins University Press, 1996), pp. 4–5.

41. Marc Weller, 'The International Response to the Dissolution of the Socialist Federal Republic of Yugoslavia', *American Journal of International Law*, vol. 86, no. 3, July 1992, p. 606 (569–607).

42. Preece, 'National Minorities Rights vs. State Sovereignty in Europe', p. 354.

43. European Centre for Conflict Prevention, *People Building Peace: 35 Inspiring Stories from Around the World* (Utrecht: European Centre for Conflict Prevention, 1999).

44. Larissa Fast, Reina Neufeldt and Lisa Schirch, 'Toward Ethically Grounded Conflict Interventions: Re-evaluating Challenges in the 21st Century', *International Negotiation*, vol. 7, 2002, p. 186.

CHAPTER 8

CONCLUSION

This book has demonstrated that there is a moral dimension to peace-building. The proliferation of sub-national disputes suggests that the processes, institutions and mechanisms need to be redesigned if necessary to promote positive peace, predicated on social harmony, forgiveness and reconciliation. International institutions need to move beyond their statist bias and adopt a more morally inclusive predisposition towards sub-national polities. The moral analysis of peacebuilding developed in this book is explicitly concerned with re-establishing the link between ethics and politics, which has historically been undermined by the practical and ideological constraints of the Cold War and the so-called 'war on terror'. To this end, this book will make a useful contribution to the repertoire of moral knowledge available to researchers, practitioners and policy-makers involved in addressing disputes in the global arena. This book also contributes towards opening up an avenue of research which has largely remained at the margins of the field of international relations and politics.

The objective of this book was to integrate an ethical dialect into the language of peacebuilding. It also sought to make explicit the moral nature of the politics of peacebuilding. To achieve this, Chapter 2 of this book was predicated on unmasking the implicit moral presuppositions of the realist school of thought and how it has impacted upon conflict resolution and peacebuilding. This chapter questioned the efficacy of traditional power political mechanisms for international dispute settlement given their statist bias and their over-reliance on coercive strategies to achieve agreement between disputants. Chapter 3 argued that the mechanisms which are designated with the task of dealing with sub-national conflict should promote moral development between disputants. By referring to and developing the tradition of critical international relations theory this book sought to demonstrate that power political mechanisms for settling disputes are ineffective in the long run.

In the specific case of sub-national conflicts such mechanisms continue to perpetuate structural domination and moral exclusion by reinforcing an asymmetrical power relationship between sub-national and state polities.

In terms of the discussions developed in the individual chapters this book sought to advance international relations knowledge on several important fronts. At the conceptual and normative level Chapter 2 developed an argument for the importance of adopting a moral epistemology of peacebuilding. This chapter was predicated on an innovative synthesis between moral philosophy and peace research. Building upon the work developed by the Frankfurt School of critical theory, Chapter 2 endeavoured to make the claim that all knowledge is ipso facto normative. Therefore, in terms of the growth of knowledge we therefore need to be more oriented towards understanding how the violence, injustice and inequality inherent in our social and political institutions can be reduced.

Chapter 3 examined how the phenomenon of sub-national conflict and it ability to precipitate the collapse of state has rendered it a truly global problem which needs to be addressed through a new ethic of international political responsibility. Chapter 4 provided a historical and empirical analysis of negotiation and mediation processes as integral to the peacebuilding process. This chapter examined the work of the League of Nations in forging peace in the ethnically stratified regions of Upper Silesia, the Åland Islands and the Saar region. It illustrated how the League sought to operationalise an ethical framework for the pacific settlement of disputes. Chapter 4 also briefly looked at the work of the United Nations in the Cold War and its challenges in the post-Cold War world. The efforts of the Quakers demonstrated that there is a long and established moral tradition of peacebuilding in non-official circles.

Chapter 5 explored the nature of forgiveness and demonstrated that it was an integral component of peacebuilding. This Chapter drew from the moral philosophy of Jürgen Habermas and the moral development framework of Lawrence Kohlberg. It articulated the notion of discourse ethics and deployed it to illustrate that forgiveness is a process predicated on the moral development and gradual moral inclusion of others by individuals and communities. The efforts of the non-governmental organisation the Moral Re-Armament group to convene forgiveness forums were assessed. Chapter 6 assessed the issue of reconciliation and demonstrated that it has social, political and economic dimensions. The importance of understanding the nexus between peace and justice was discussed, with the articulation of a 'peace with justice' matrix. The philosophical orientation of the International Criminal Court towards retributive justice was assessed and contrasted with notions of restorative justice. Also assessed was the effort of the Special Court for Sierra Leone, which has adopted a retributive justice model to address atrocities after conflict. The retributive aspects of the Court were contrasted with the restorative justice model espoused by the truth and reconciliation commissions in South Africa and Sierra Leone. Ultimately, reconciliation was described as a key component of the peacebuilding process.

Chapter 7 consolidated and built upon the foundational and analytical themes developed in earlier chapters. It further made the point that as far as sub-national disputes are concerned, what is required is the creation of new moral norms and mechanisms for peacebuilding. It also discussed the role of international institutions in consolidating peacebuilding by examining the establishment, functions and initiatives of the UN Peacebuilding Commission established in June 2006. Chapter 7 also briefly discussed the role of regional organisations like the Organization for Security and Cooperation in Europe, the African Union, the Association of South East Asian States and the Organization of American States in promoting norms to build peace. This chapter also emphasised the link which exists between peacebuilding and the process of post-conflict democratisation. It emphasised the importance of forging post-national communities as a basis for building and consolidating peace. By examining the recent democratisation efforts in Northern Ireland this chapter argued that the post-conflict peacebuilding process should continue to appeal to the moral norms of inclusion and tolerance so that democratic regimes do not become focal points for dissension and the potential re-ignition of violent sub-national conflict.

Ultimately, there is a significant utility in articulating and examining the moral dimension of peacebuilding for four reasons:

1. Firstly, it highlights the need for a new mindset as far as processes, institutions and mechanisms for addressing sub-national conflict are concerned;
2. Secondly, it demonstrates the unity which necessarily exists between the theory and practice of peacebuilding, and in so doing it illustrates the need for critical reflection in the way we think about and adopt practices for resolving violent conflict;
3. Thirdly, it demonstrates that ethics have been, and still are, integral to international political processes, specifically the building of peace, and in this regard, the role of the researcher, practitioner, and policy-maker is not only to understand the

condition that affects world politics, at a given point in time, but also to examine ways through which we can reduce violence, injustice and inequality to enhance the prospects for genuine human freedom;

4. Fourthly, it points out that peacebuilding is a lengthy and slow process which can take generations to effectuate. The overall objective of this process is fundamentally to bring about the political and moral development of disputants to a point where they can morally include their erstwhile opponents as a basis for consolidating peace.

It is essential to point out that the importance of ensuring an ethical approach to peacebuilding is not something that is currently articulated and embraced by the mainstream of international relations practitioners. However, it is an approach that the international community can aspire to. It is thus vital to adopt an agenda for ethical peacebuilding. Like the impetus behind this book, what we need to do is equip ourselves with the necessary conceptual instruments and tools of understanding through which we can transform our political communities and foster global conditions in which humanity can identify the causes and reduce the debilitating effects of violent sub-national conflict. The creation of norms that move away from privileging the nation-state as the only significant actor in international relations is a necessary prerequisite for minimising the destructive effects of sub-national conflict which is primarily driven by the contesting claims for control of the state. Local, regional and global transformations are dramatically changing the monopoly of power once enjoyed by the state at the height of the Westphalian order. To the counter-argument which suggests that nation-states would never agree to give up their power, it is worthwhile to note that it was the formation of norms around the notion of sovereignty that led to their emergence. It is also worthwhile to consider the pooling of sovereignty that is underway among the member states of the European Union and the attempts to establish a continent-wide system of supra-national authority that is articulated in the Constitutive Act which has been signed by fifty-three member states of the African Union. The Westphalian system was created as a result of the debilitating effects of war which necessitated the formation of norms promoting and protecting territorial sovereignty. Once again the international community is faced with a defining moment in time in which a reconsideration of the existing system is in order and long overdue. A concerted political effort will be required to make such a normative shift. It is evident that the powerful actors within the state system can enforce the maintenance of existing norms as long as they suit their self-interests. But the increasing problem of the collapse of weaker states, when subjected to centrifugal sub-national conflicts, has regional as well as global consequences in the form of war crimes, crimes against humanity, genocide, ethnic cleansing, refugee flows, internally displaced persons, illicit trade in natural resources and illegal trade in armaments and narcotic substances, all of which have transnational effects.

Ultimately, we need to understand that with the internationalisation of ethnic conflicts it is no longer feasible to view the problem of peacebuilding as someone else's concern. The heterogeneity that exists in all nation-states implicates all citizens of the world in the process of peacebuilding. The 'domesticisation' of international politics is consummated when citizens in diverse and remote corners of the world continue to express an identification with the suffering and destruction of the societies of the 'other'. Though political power remains in the hands of a dominant global elite still steeped in the language and practices of realpolitik, there is a sense in which the moral argument for some kind of effective strategy for peacebuilding is gaining momentum. Such a progressive force in international politics can only help to focus the minds of politicians, practitioners and researchers as to the opportunities offered by this moment of crisis to establish, forge and consolidate the ethics of peacebuilding.

INDEX

187